The Making of
Economic Society

Colloquy on the Anatomy of Economic Man

Present at the colloquy (left to right): Adam Smith, Thomas Malthus, David Ricardo, Jeremy Bentham, John Stuart Mill, Francois Marie Charles Fourier, Claude Henri Saint-Simon, Auguste Comte, Karl Marx, and Pierre Joseph Proudhon.

Carrying on the Anatomical Studies

Left to right: Thorstein Veblen, Joseph Schumpeter, John Maynard Keynes, and Alfred Marshall.

PRENTICE HALL SERIES IN ECONOMICS

ELEVENTH EDITION

The Making of Economic Society

Robert L. Heilbroner and William Milberg

Prentice
Hall

Upper Saddle River, New Jersey 07458

Library of Congress Cataloging-in-Publication Data

Heilbroner, Robert L.
    The making of economic society / Robert Heilbroner and William Milberg.—11th ed.
      p. cm.
    Includes indexes.
    ISBN 0-13-091050-3
    1. Economic history.   I. Milberg, William S., 1957.   II. Title.
HC51.H44   2001
330.9—dc21   2001021124
                                              CIP

Executive Editor: Rod Banister
Managing Editor: Gladys Soto
Editor-in-Chief: P. J. Boardman
Assistant Editor: Marie McHale
Media Project Manager: Bill Minick
Marketing Manager: Joshua McClary
Marketing Assistant: Christopher Bath
Production Manager: Gail Steier de Acevedo
Production Coordinator: Kelly Warsak
Permissions Coordinator: Suzanne Grappi
Associate Director, Manufacturing: Vincent Scelta
Manufacturing Buyer: Natacha St. Hill Moore
Cover Designer: Bruce Kenselaar
Composition: BookMasters, Inc.
Full-Service Project Management: BookMasters, Inc.
Printer/Binder: Hamilton Printing Company
Cover Printer: Phoenix Color Corp.

10
ISBN 0-13-091050-3

for Shirley and Hedy

Brief Contents

Contents

Introduction:
A Word from the Authors

It is almost 40 years since *The Making of Economic Society* first appeared, making the present edition nearly as old as I was when I wrote it. Is it the same book as it was then? Yes and no. Yes, because an unchanged purpose of these pages is to make the mysterious part of our world called "economic society" comprehensible—and more than that, interesting to you. But the word "make," however, has another meaning. Here it refers to what is happening under our feet, or behind our back, as the economic society, with whose past we are now familiar, becomes a force shaping the economic world in which we will be living tomorrow.

Thus, although the first part of our book has as its purpose explaining how the economy came to be what it is, the second part seeks to help us anticipate what that world may look like 10 or 20 years from now. Of course no one can predict tomorrow's economic future with perfect accuracy, or we would all become millionaires by buying the stocks that will be worth more tomorrow than today. But foresight, however, is not the same as prediction. It does not attempt to read the future in detail, but to make us aware of mighty developments—the changing impact of modern technology and the appearance of a vast global system—that helps us ready ourselves for the forces shaping the economic world to come. Even in so general a task, one cannot hope to anticipate the newspapers headlines in 2010 much less 2020, but we can prepare ourselves for problems that will not become part of our economic lives for another 5, 10, and 20 years down the pike.

This leads to a last word in my introduction. In the first several editions of this book, I wrote both halves of the book myself. This was because the problems and promises of the second part were still closely related to what I had covered in the first—the future seemed more an extension of the present than a journey into strange territory.

But then things began to change. Jet planes filled the skies and computers sat on every desk. A hitherto unknown number with 12 zeros, called a trillion, became necessary to express economic magnitudes. Thus, as the editions went on, it became increasingly clear that the problems and possibilities of the future could no longer be dealt with largely as extensions of the present.

Robert Heilbroner

As the reader will soon discover in first section of the book, Robert Heilbroner and I are mainly interested in bringing to life the massive processes that have gradually created the world in which we live. In the second section, we look for the forces that are shaping the world into which we are now moving. Here we become familiar with the new world force of globalization—a word already on many people's lips, whose implications are, however, far from clear. Trying to describe this force more clearly, and to explore its consequences more fully will be a main theme of the final pages of this edition of *The Making of Economic Society*. By that time, perhaps, the reader will see how the contemporary phase of global capitalism is different from earlier phases of international economic expansion.

For our purposes, globalization is not just the increased international interconnectedness of national economies. It is also characterized by an increase in the scope and depth of the use of markets to try to solve the economics problem of production and distribution. The market solution to the economic problem has today been adopted more widely and extensively than ever before in world history. This unprecedented appeal to market forces has important implications for the creation and distribution of wealth, for the way companies organize the process of work, and for the role of government in determining economic and social outcomes. Marketization has not pervaded all aspects of economic society (in fact the expanded role of transnational corporations indicates that although international trade is more important, the internal workings of large companies—those distinctly nonmarket institutions of work, production, investment, and profit—will be as important as markets in determining what jobs are available where, and at what pay). But the expansion of markets—from the growth of stock markets in Asia and Latin America, to the privatization of telecommunications in Eastern Europe and southern Africa, to the explosion of e-commerce accessible globally—sets the tone for the great debates in today's economic society. Many of these debates concern the scope of government; that is, its policies of taxing, spending, and regulation. And different countries will resolve these debates differently. One of the key themes of the last part of this edition of *The Making of Economic Society* is that capitalism takes very different forms in different places. Thus in this volume we are not interested in the fate of modern capitalism, but of the varieties of capitalism that, although connected, seek their own solutions to the economic problem.

There are a number of new features in this eleventh edition of *The Making of Economic Society* including two new chapters. Also, in past editions, we ended each chapter with a list of key concepts and some questions that tested student understanding of the material in the chapter. In this edition, we retain the key concepts and questions, but close each chapter with a discussion of the broader economic, philosophical, ethical, and historical implications of the material in the chapter. We have titled these sections "Thinking Back, Looking Ahead." The ideas are intentionally more speculative and provocative than what is found in the body of the chapters themselves. We hope the reader has as much fun discussing these sections as we did in writing them.

Finally, we would like to express our thanks to Susan Eisner of Ramapo College, Jay P. Corrin of Boston University, Danny Taylor of New Mexico State University, and Gunnar Valgeirsson of California State University–Fresno, for their useful comments on the previous edition.

William Milberg

CHAPTER

The Economic Problem

N ow that we have decided on our course of exploration, it would be convenient if we could immediately begin to examine our economic past. But not quite yet. Before we can retrace economic history, we need to know what economic history *is,* and that, in turn, requires us to take a moment to clarify what we mean by *economics* and by the economic problem itself.

The answer is not a complicated one. In its broadest sense, economics is the study of a process we find in all human societies—*the process of providing for the material well-being of society.* In its simplest terms, economics is the study of how humankind secures its daily bread.

This hardly seems like a particularly exciting subject for historical scrutiny. Indeed, when we look back over the pageant of what is usually called "history," the humble matter of bread hardly strikes the eye at all. Power and glory, faith and fanaticism, ideas and ideologies are the aspects of the human chronicle that crowd the pages of history books. If the simple quest for bread is a moving force in human destiny, it is well concealed behind what one philosopher has called "that history of international crime and mass murder which has been advertised as the history of mankind."[1]

Yet, if mankind does not live by bread alone, it is obvious that it cannot live without bread. Like every other living thing, the human being must eat—the imperious first rule of continued existence. This first prerequisite is less to be taken for granted than at first appears, for the human organism is not in itself a highly efficient mechanism for survival. From each 100 calories of food it consumes, it can deliver only about 20 calories of mechanical energy. On a decent diet, human beings can produce just about one horsepower-hour of work daily, and with that they must replenish their exhausted bodies. With what is left over, they are free to build a civilization.

As a result, in many countries, the sheer continuity of human existence is far from assured. In the vast continents of Asia and Africa, in the Near East, even in some countries of South America, brute survival is the problem that stares humanity in the face. Millions of human beings have died of starvation or malnutrition in our present era, as countless hundreds of millions have died over the long past. Whole nations are acutely aware of what it means to face hunger as a condition of ordinary life; it has been said, for example, that a peasant in Bangladesh, from the day he or she is born to the day he or she dies, may never know what it is to have a full stomach. In many of the so-called underdeveloped nations, the life span of the average person is less than half of ours. Not so many years ago, an Indian demographer made the chilling calculation that of 100 Asian and 100 American infants, more Americans would be alive at age 65 than Asians

---

[1]Karl Popper, *The Open Society and Its Enemies,* 3rd ed. (London: Routledge, 1957), II, p. 270.

at age 5! The statistics, not of life but of premature death throughout most of the world, are overwhelming and crushing.

THE INDIVIDUAL AND SOCIETY

Thus we can see that economic history must begin with the crucial problem of survival and on how humankind has solved that problem. For most Americans, this may make economics seem very remote. Few of us are conscious of anything resembling a life-or-death struggle for existence. That it might be possible for us to experience severe want, that we might ever know in our own bodies the pangs of hunger experienced by an Indian villager or a Bolivian peon, is a thought nearly impossible for most of us to entertain seriously.[2]

Short of a catastrophic war, it is highly unlikely that most of us ever will know the full meaning of the struggle for existence. Nonetheless, even in our prosperous and secure society, there remains, however unnoticed, an aspect of life's precariousness, a reminder of the underlying problem of survival. *This is our helplessness as economic individuals.*

For it is a curious fact that as we leave the most primitive peoples of the world, we find the economic insecurity of the individual many times multiplied. The solitary Eskimo, Bushman, Indonesian, or Nigerian peasant, left to his or her own devices, will survive a considerable time. Living close to the soil or to his or her animal prey, such an individual can sustain his own—more rarely, her own—life, at least for a while, single-handedly. Communities numbering only a few hundred can live indefinitely. Indeed, a considerable percentage of the human race today lives in precisely such fashion—in small, virtually self-contained peasant communities that provide for their own survival with a minimum of contact with the outside world. This portion of humankind may suffer great poverty, but it also knows a certain economic independence. If it did not, it would have been wiped out centuries ago.[3]

When we turn to the New Yorker or the Chicagoan, on the other hand, we are struck by exactly the opposite condition—by a prevailing ease of material life coupled with an extreme dependence on others. We can no longer envisage the solitary individual or the small community surviving unaided in the great metropolitan areas where most Americans live, unless they loot warehouses or stores for food and necessities. The overwhelming majority of Americans have never grown food, caught game, raised meat, ground grain into flour, or even fashioned flour into bread. Faced with the challenge of clothing themselves or building their own homes, they would be hopelessly untrained and unprepared. Even to make minor repairs in the machines that surround them, they must call on other members of the community whose business it is to fix cars or repair plumbing, for example. Paradoxically, perhaps, the richer the nation, the more apparent is this inability of its average inhabitant to survive unaided and alone.

---

[2]Although the sight of homeless people huddled on the sidewalks of our major cities tells us that even rich countries can harbor poverty.

[3]Anthropological investigation shows that small-scale, traditional societies may also enjoy a kind of affluence, in that they voluntarily spend many hours at leisure rather than in hunting or gathering. See Marshall Sahlins, *Stone Age Economics* (New York: Aldine, 1972).

Division of Labor

There is, of course, an answer to the paradox. We survive in rich nations because the tasks we cannot do ourselves are done for us by an army of others on whom we can call for help. If we cannot grow food, we can buy it; if we cannot provide for our needs ourselves, we can hire the services of someone who can. This enormous *division of labor* enhances our capacity a thousandfold, because it enables us to benefit from other people's skills as well as our own. In our next chapter, it will play a central role.

Along with this invaluable gain, however, comes a certain risk. It is a sobering thought, for example, that we depend on the services of only about 200,000 people, out of a national labor force of 130 million, to provide us with that basic commodity, coal. A much smaller number—roughly 60,000—makes up our total airline pilot crew. An even smaller number of workers are responsible for running the locomotives that haul all the nation's rail freight. Failure of any one of these groups to perform its functions would cripple us. As we know, when from time to time we face a bad strike, our entire economic machine may falter because a strategic few—even garbage collectors—cease to perform their accustomed tasks.

Thus, along with the abundance of material existence as we know it goes a hidden vulnerability: Our abundance is assured only insofar as the organized cooperation of many regiments, even small armies, of people is to be counted upon. Indeed, our continuing existence as a rich nation hinges on the tacit precondition that the mechanism of social organization will continue to function effectively. *We are rich, not as individuals, but as members of a rich society, and our easy assumption of material sufficiency is actually only as reliable as the bonds that forge us into a social whole.*

Economics and Scarcity

Strangely enough, then, we find that humankind, not nature, is the source of most of our economic problems, at least above the level of subsistence. To be sure, the economic problem itself—that is, the need to struggle for existence—derives ultimately from nature. If goods were as free as air, economics—at least in one sense of the word—would cease to exist as a social preoccupation.

However, if the stringency of nature sets the stage for the economic problem, it does not impose the only strictures against which people must struggle. For scarcity, as a felt condition, is not solely the fault of nature. If Americans today, for instance, were content to live at the level of Mexican peasants, all our material wants could be fully satisfied with but an hour or two of daily labor. We would experience little or no scarcity, and our economic problems would virtually disappear. Instead, we find in the United States—and indeed, in all industrial societies—that as the ability to increase nature's yield has risen, so has the reach of human wants. In fact, in societies such as ours, where relative social status is importantly connected with the possession of material goods, we often find that "scarcity" as a psychological experience becomes *more* pronounced as we grow wealthier: Our desires to possess the fruits of nature race out ahead of our mounting ability to produce goods.

Thus, the "wants" that nature must satisfy are by no means fixed. However, for that matter, nature's yield itself is not a constant. It varies over a wide range, depending on the social application of human energy and skill. Scarcity is, therefore, not attributable to nature alone but to "human nature" as well; and economics is ultimately concerned not merely with the stinginess of the physical environment, but equally with the appetite of the human being and the productive capability of the community.

The Tasks of Economic Society

Hence we must begin a systematic economic analysis by singling out the functions that social organization must perform to bring human nature into social harness. And when we turn our attention to this fundamental problem, we can quickly see that it involves the solution of two related and yet separate elemental tasks. A society must

production
1. organize a system to assure the *production* of enough goods and services for its own survival, and

distribution
2. arrange the *distribution* of the fruits of its production so that more production can take place.

These two tasks of economic continuity are, at first look, very simple, but it is a deceptive simplicity. Much of economic history is concerned with the manner in which various societies have sought to cope with these elementary problems. What strikes us in surveying their attempts is that most of them were partial failures. (They could not have been *total* failures, or society would not have survived.) Therefore, we had better look more carefully into the two main economic tasks to see what hidden difficulties they may conceal.

PRODUCTION AND DISTRIBUTION

Mobilizing Effort

What obstacles does a society encounter in organizing a system to produce the goods and services it needs?

production
Because nature in the raw rarely gives us exactly what we need in the quantities we seek the production problem is usually one of applying engineering or technical skills to the resources at hand, of avoiding waste and utilizing social effort as efficaciously as possible.

This is indeed an important task for any society, and a great deal of formal economic thought, as the word itself suggests, is devoted to economizing, yet this is not the core of the production problem. Long before a society can concern itself about using its energies "economically," it must first marshal the energies to carry out the productive process itself. That is, *the basic problem of production is to devise social institutions that will mobilize human energy for productive purposes.*

This basic requirement is not always so easily accomplished. For example, in the United States in 1933, the energies of nearly one-quarter of our workforce were somehow prevented from engaging in the production process. Although millions of unemployed men and women were eager to work, although empty factories were available for them to work in, despite the existence of pressing wants, a terrible and mystifying breakdown called a depression, resulted in the disappearance of a third of the previous annual output of goods and services.

We are by no means the only nation that has, on occasion, failed to find work for large numbers of willing workers. In the very poorest nations, where production is most desperately needed, we frequently find that mass unemployment is a chronic condition.

The streets of many Asian cities are thronged with people who cannot find work, but this, too, is not a condition imposed by the scarcity of nature. There is, after all, an endless amount of work to be done, if only in cleaning filthy streets or patching up the homes of the poor, building roads, or digging ditches. What is lacking is a social mechanism to mobilize human energy for production purposes. This is the case just as much when the unemployed are only a small fraction of the workforce as when they constitute a veritable army.

These examples point out to us that the production problem is not solely a physical and technical struggle with nature. On these aspects of the problem will depend the ease with which a nation can forge ahead and the level of well-being it can reach with a given effort. But the original mobilization of productive effort itself is a challenge to its *social organization,* and on the success or failure of that social organization will depend the volume of the human effort that can be directed to nature.

Allocating Effort

Putting men and women to work is only the first step in the solution of the production problem. They must not only be put to work, they must be put to work to produce goods and services that society needs. Thus, *in addition to assuring a large enough quantity of social effort, the economic institutions of society must also assure a viable allocation of that social effort.*

In a nation such as India or Bolivia, where the great majority of the population is born in peasant villages and matures to be peasant cultivators, the solution to this problem offers little to tax our understanding. The basic needs of society—food and fiber—are precisely the goods that its peasant population "naturally" produces. In an industrial society, however, the proper allocation of effort becomes an enormously complicated task. People in the United States demand much more than bread and cotton. They need such things as automobiles, yet no one "naturally" produces an automobile. On the contrary, in order to produce one, an extraordinary spectrum of special tasks must be performed. Some people must make steel; others must make rubber. Still others must coordinate the assembly process itself. This is but a tiny sampling of the far from natural tasks that must be performed if an automobile is to be produced.

As with the mobilization of its total production effort, society does not always succeed in the proper allocation of its effort. It may, for instance, turn out too many cars or too few. Of greater importance, it may devote its energies to the production of luxuries while large numbers of its people are starving. It may even court disaster by an inability to channel its productive effort into areas of critical importance.

Such allocative failures may affect the production problem quite as seriously as a failure to mobilize an adequate quantity of effort, because a viable society must produce not only goods, but the *right* goods, and the allocative question alerts us to a still broader conclusion. It shows us that the act of production, in and of itself, does not fully answer the requirements for survival. Having produced enough of the right goods, society must now *distribute* those goods so that the production process can go on.

Distributing Output

Once again, in the case of the peasant family that feeds itself from its own crop, this requirement of adequate distribution may seem simple enough, but when we go beyond the most small-scale, traditional society, the problem is not always so readily solved. In many of the poorest nations, urban workers have often been unable to work effectively because of their meager compensation. Worse yet, they have often languished on the job while granaries bulged with grain and the well-to-do complained of the hopeless laziness of the masses. On the other side of the picture, the distribution mechanism may fail because the rewards it hands out do not succeed in persuading people to perform their tasks. Shortly after the Russian Revolution in 1917, some factories were organized into communes in which managers and janitors pooled their pay, and from which all drew equal allotments. The result was a rash of absenteeism among the previously better-paid workers and a threatened breakdown in industrial production. Not until the old unequal wage payments were reinstituted did production resume its former course.

As was the case with failures in the production process, distributive failures need not entail a total economic collapse. Societies can exist—and most do exist—with badly distorted productive and distributive efforts. Only rarely, as in the instance just noted, does maldistribution interfere with the ultimate ability of a society to staff its production posts. More frequently, an inadequate solution to the distribution problem reveals itself in social and political unrest, or even in revolution.

Yet this, too, is an aspect of the total economic problem. If society is to ensure its steady material replenishment, it must parcel out its production in a fashion that will maintain not only the capacity but also the willingness to go on working. And so, once again, we find the focus of economic inquiry directed to the study of human institutions. For a viable economic society, we can now see, must not only overcome the stringencies of nature, but also contain and control the intransigence of human nature.

THREE SOLUTIONS TO THE ECONOMIC PROBLEM

Thus, to the economist, society presents itself in what is to the rest of us an unaccustomed aspect. Underneath the problems of poverty or pollution or inflation, he or she sees a process at work that must be understood before we can turn our attention to the issues of the day, no matter how pressing. That process is society's basic mechanism for accomplishing the complicated tasks of production and distribution necessary for its own continuity.

But the economist sees something else as well, something that at first seems quite astonishing. Looking over the diversity of contemporary societies, and back over the sweep of all history, he or she sees that humankind has succeeded in solving the production and distribution problems in but three ways. That is, within the enormous diversity of the actual social institutions that guide and shape the economic process, the economist divines but three overarching *types* of systems that separately or in combination enable humankind to solve its economic challenge. These great systemic types can be called economies run by *tradition*, economies run by *command*, and economies run by the *market*. Let us briefly see what is characteristic of each.

Tradition

Perhaps the oldest and, until a very few years ago, by far the most generally prevalent way of solving the economic challenge has been that of tradition. Tradition is a mode of social organization in which both production and distribution are based on procedures devised in the distant past, ratified by a long process of historic trial and error, and maintained by the powerful forces of custom and belief. Perhaps at its root, it is based on the universal need of the young to follow in the footsteps of their elders—a profound source of social continuity.

Societies based on tradition solve their economic problems very manageably. First, they typically deal with the production problem—the problem of assuring that the needful tasks will be done—by assigning the jobs of fathers to their sons. Thus, a hereditary chain ensures that skills will be passed along and jobs will be staffed from generation to generation. In ancient Egypt, wrote Adam Smith, the first great economist, "every man was bound by a principle of religion to follow the occupation of his father and was supposed to commit the most horrible sacrilege if he changed it for another."[4] It was not merely in antiquity that tradition preserved a productive orderliness within society. In our own Western culture, until the fifteenth or sixteenth century, the hereditary allocation of tasks was also the main stabilizing force within society. Although there was some movement from country to town and from occupation to occupation, birth usually determined one's role in life. One was born to the soil or to a trade; and on the soil or within the trade, one followed in the footsteps of one's family.

In this way tradition has been the stabilizing and impelling force behind a great repetitive cycle of society, ensuring that society's work would be done each day very much as it had been done in the past. Even today, among the less industrialized nations of the world, tradition continues to play this immense organizing role. In India, for example, until very recently, one was born to a caste that had its own occupation. "Better thine own work is, though done with fault," preached the Bhagavad-Gita, the great philosophic moral poem of India, "than doing others' work, even excellently."

Tradition not only provides a solution to the production problem of society, but it also regulates the distribution problem. Take, for example, the Bushmen of the Kalahari Desert in South Africa, who depend for their livelihood on their hunting prowess. Elizabeth Marshall Thomas, a sensitive observer of these peoples, reports on the manner in which tradition solves the problem of distributing their kill by applying the "rules" of kinship:

> The gemsbok has vanished. . . . Gai owned two hind legs and a front leg. Tsetchwe had meat from the back, Ukwane had the other front leg, his wife had one of the feet and the stomach, the young boys had lengths of intestine. Twikwe had received the head and Dasina the udder.
>
> It seems very unequal when you watch Bushmen divide the kill, yet it is their system, and in the end no person eats more than the other. That day Ukwane gave Gai still another piece because Gai was his relation, Gai gave meat to Dasina because she was his wife's mother. . . . No one, of course, contested Gai's large share, because he had been the hunter and by their law that much belonged to him. No one doubted that he would share his large amount with others, and they were not wrong, of course; he did.[5]

The manner in which tradition can divide a social product may be, as the illustration shows, very subtle and ingenious. It may also be very crude and, by our standards,

---

[4]Adam Smith, *The Wealth of Nations* (New York: Modern Library, 1937), p. 62.
[5]Elizabeth Marshall Thomas, *The Harmless People* (New York: Knopf, 1959), pp. 49–50.

harsh. Tradition has regularly allocated to women in nonindustrial societies the most meager portion of the social product. But however much the end product of tradition may accord with, or depart from, our accustomed moral views, we must see that it is an effective *method* of dividing society's production.

The Cost of Tradition

Traditional solutions to the economic problems of production and distribution are most commonly encountered in primitive agrarian or nonindustrial societies where, in addition to serving an economic function, the unquestioning acceptance of the past provides the necessary perseverance and endurance to comfort harsh destinies. Yet even in our own society, tradition continues to play a part in solving the economic problem. It plays its smallest role in determining the distribution of our own social output, although the persistence of such traditional payments as tips to waiters, allowances to minors, or bonuses based on length of service are all vestiges of older ways of distributing goods, as are differentials between men's and women's pay for equal work.

More important is the continued reliance on tradition, even in the United States, as a means of solving the production problem—that is, in allocating the performance of tasks. Much of the actual process of selecting employment in our society is heavily influenced by tradition. We are all familiar with families in which sons follow their fathers into a profession or a business. On a somewhat broader scale, tradition also dissuades us from certain employments. Children of American middle-class families, for example, do not usually seek factory work, although factory jobs may pay better than office jobs, because blue-collar employment is not in the middle-class tradition.

Thus, even in our society, clearly not a "traditional" one, custom provides an important mechanism for solving the economic problem. Now, however, we must note one very important consequence of the mechanism of tradition. *Its solution to the problems of production and distribution is a static one.* A society that follows the path of tradition in its regulation of economic affairs does so at the expense of large-scale, rapid social and economic change.

Thus, the economy of a Bedouin tribe or a Burmese village is in many respects unchanged today from what it was a hundred or even a thousand years ago. The bulk of the peoples living in tradition-bound societies repeat, in the daily patterns of their economic life, much of the routine that characterized them in the distant past. Such societies may rise and fall, wax and wane, but external events—war, climate, political adventures and misadventures—are mainly responsible for their changing fortunes. Internal, self-generated economic change is but a small factor in the history of most tradition-bound states. *Tradition solves the economic problem, but it does so at the cost of economic progress.*

Command

A second manner of solving the problem of economic continuity also displays an ancient lineage. This is the method of imposed authority, of economic command. It is a solution based not so much on the perpetuation of a viable system by the changeless reproduction of its ways as on the organization of a system according to the orders of an economic commander-in-chief.

Not infrequently we find this authoritarian method of economic control superimposed upon a traditional social base. Thus, the pharaohs of Egypt exerted their economic dictates above the timeless cycle of traditional agricultural practice on which the Egyptian economy was based. By their orders, the supreme rulers of Egypt brought into being the enormous economic effort that built the pyramids, the temples, the roads. Herodotus, the Greek historian, tells us how the pharaoh Cheops organized the task.

> [He] ordered all Egyptians to work for himself. Some, accordingly, were appointed to draw stones from the quarries in the Arabian mountains down to the Nile, others he ordered to receive the stones when transported in vessels across the river. . . . And they worked to the number of a hundred thousand men at a time, each party during three months. The time during which the people were thus harassed by toil lasted ten years on the road which they constructed, and along which they drew the stones; a work, in my opinion, not much less than the Pyramid.[6]

The mode of authoritarian economic organization was by no means confined to ancient Egypt. We encounter it in the despotisms of medieval and classical China that produced, among other things, the colossal Great Wall, or in the slave labor by which many of the great public works of ancient Rome were built, or, for that matter, in any slave economy, including that of the pre–Civil War United States. Only a few years ago we would have discovered it in the dictates of the Soviet economic authorities. In less drastic form, we find it also in our own society; for example, in the form of taxes—that is, in the preemption of part of our income by the public authorities for public purposes.

Economic command, like tradition, offers solutions to the twin problems of production and distribution. In times of crisis, such as war or famine, it may be the only way in which a society can organize its workers or distribute its goods effectively. Even in the United States, we commonly declare martial law when an area has been devastated by a great natural disaster. On such occasions we may press people into service, requisition homes, impose curbs on the use of private property such as cars, or even limit the amount of goods a family may consume.

Quite aside from its obvious utility in meeting emergencies, command has a further usefulness in solving the economic problem. Unlike tradition, the exercise of command has no inherent effect of slowing down economic change. Indeed, the exercise of authority is the most powerful instrument society has for *enforcing economic change*. Authority in communist China or Russia, for example, effected radical alterations in their systems of production and distribution. Again, even in our own society, it is sometimes necessary for economic authority to intervene in the normal flow of economic life to speed up or bring about change. The government may, for instance, utilize its tax receipts to lay down a network of roads that will bring a backwater community into the flux of active economic life. It may undertake an irrigation system that will dramatically change the economic life of a vast region. It may deliberately alter the distribution of income among social classes.

The Impact of Command

To be sure, economic command that is exercised within the framework of a democratic political process is very different from that exercised by a dictatorship: There is an immense social distance between a tax system controlled by Congress and outright expropriation or labor impressment by a supreme and unchallengeable ruler. Yet

---

[6]*History,* trans. Cary, Book II, p. 124, Freeport, NY: Books for Libraries Press, 1972.

though the means may be much milder, the mechanism is the same. In both cases, command diverts economic effort toward goals chosen by a higher authority. In both cases, it interferes with the existing order of production and distribution to create a new order ordained from "above."

This does not in itself serve to commend or condemn the exercise of command. The new order imposed by the authorities may offend or please our sense of social justice, just as it may improve or lessen the economic efficiency of society. Clearly, command can be an instrument of a democratic as well as of a totalitarian will. There is no implicit moral judgment to be passed on this second of the great mechanisms of economic control. Rather, it is important to note that no society—certainly no modern society—is without its elements of command, just as none is devoid of the influence of tradition. *If tradition is the great brake on social and economic change, economic command can be the great spur to change.* As mechanisms for assuring the successful solution to the economic problem, both serve their purposes, both have their uses and their drawbacks. Between them, tradition and command have accounted for most of the long history of humankind's economic efforts to cope with its environment and with itself. The fact that human society has survived is testimony to their effectiveness.

The Market

There is, however, a third solution to the economic problem, a third way of maintaining socially viable patterns of production and distribution. This is the *market organization of society*—an organization that, in truly remarkable fashion, allows society to ensure its own provisioning with a minimum of resource to either tradition or command.

Because we live in a market-run society, we are apt to take for granted the puzzling—indeed, almost paradoxical—nature of the market solution to the economic problem. But assume for a moment that we could act as economic advisers to a society that had not yet decided on its mode of economic organization. Suppose, for instance, that we were called on to act as consultants to a nation emerging from a history of tradition-bound organization.

We could imagine the leaders of such a nation saying, "We have always known a highly tradition-bound way of life. Our men hunt and our women gather fruits as they were taught by the force of example and the instruction of their elders. We know, too, something of what can be done by economic command. We are prepared, if necessary, to sign an edict making it compulsory for many of our men to work on community projects for our collective development. Tell us, is there any other way we can organize our society so that it will function successfully—or better yet, *more* successfully?"

Suppose we answered, "Well, there is another way. One can organize a society along the lines of a market economy."

"I see," say the leaders. "What would we then tell people to do? How would we assign them to their various tasks?"

"That's the very point," we answer. "In a market economy, no one is assigned to any task. In fact, the main idea of a market society is that each person is allowed to decide for himself or herself what to do."

There is consternation among the leaders. "You mean there is no assignment of some men to farming and others to mining? No manner of designating some women for gathering and others for weaving? You leave this to people to decide for themselves?

But what happens if they do not decide correctly? What happens if no one volunteers to go into the mines, or if no one offers himself as a bus driver?"

"You must rest assured," we tell the leaders, "none of that will happen. In a market society, all the jobs will be filled because it will be to people's advantage to fill them."

Our respondents accept this with uncertain expressions. "Now look," one of them finally says, "let us suppose that we take your advice and allow our people to do as they please. Let's talk about something specific, like cloth production. Just how do we fix the right level of cloth output in this 'market society' of yours?"

"But you don't," we reply.

"We don't! Then how do we know there will be enough cloth produced?" *too little*

"There will be," we tell him. "The market will see to that."

"Then how do we know there won't be *too much* cloth produced?" he asks *too much* triumphantly.

"Ah, but the market will see to that too!"

"But what is this market that will do these wonderful things? Who runs it?"

"Oh, nobody runs the market," we answer. "It runs itself. In fact, there really isn't any such *thing* as 'the market.' It's just a word we use to describe the way people behave."

"But I thought people behaved the way they wanted to!"

"And so they do," we say. "But never fear. They will want to behave the way you want them to behave."

"I am afraid," says the chief of the delegation, "that we are wasting our time. We thought you had in mind a serious proposal. What you suggest is inconceivable. Good day."

Could we seriously suggest to such an emergent nation that it entrust itself to a market solution of the economic problem? That will be a problem to which we shall return. But the perplexity that the market idea would rouse in the mind of someone unacquainted with it may serve to increase our own wonderment at this most sophisticated and interesting of all economic mechanisms. How does the market system assure us that our mines will find miners, our factories workers? How does it take care of cloth production? How does it happen that in a market-run nation each person can indeed do as he or she wishes and, withal, fulfill needs that society as a whole presents?

Economics and the Market System

Economics, as we commonly conceive it and as we shall study it in much of this book, is primarily concerned with these very problems. Societies that rely primarily on tradition to solve their economic problems are of less interest to the professional economist than to the cultural anthropologist or the sociologist. Societies that solve their economic problems primarily by the exercise of command present interesting economic questions, but here the study of economics is necessarily subservient to the study of politics and the exercise of power.

It is a society organized by the market process that is especially interesting to the economist. Many (although not all) of the problems we encounter in the United States today have to do with the workings or misworkings of the market system, and precisely *because* our contemporary problems often arise from the operations of the market, we study economics itself. Unlike the case of tradition and command, in which we quickly grasp the nature of the production and distribution mechanisms of society, when we turn to a market society we are lost without a knowledge of economics. For in a market society, it is not at all clear that even the simplest problems of production and distribution will be solved by the free interplay of individuals; nor is it clear how and to what extent the market mechanism is to be blamed for society's ill—after all, we can find poverty and misallocation and pollution in nonmarket economies too!

In subsequent parts of this book, we shall analyze these puzzling questions in more detail, but the task of our initial exploration must now be clear. As our imaginary interview with the leaders of an emergent nation suggests, the market solution appears very strange to someone brought up in the ways of tradition or command. Hence the question arises: How did the market solution itself come into being? Was it imposed, full-blown, on our society at some earlier date? Or did it arise spontaneously and without forethought? This is the focusing question of economic history to which we now turn, as we retrace the evolution of our own market system out of the tradition- and authority-dominated societies of the past.

Key Concepts and Key Words

Provisioning
wants
Scarcity

1. Economics is the study of how humankind ensures its material sufficiency, that is, how societies arrange for their *material provisioning.*

2. Economic problems arise because the wants of most societies exceed the gifts of nature, giving rise to the general condition of *scarcity.*

3. Scarcity, in turn (whether it arises from nature's stinginess or people's appetites), imposes two severe tasks on society:

Production
   - It must mobilize its energies for *production*—producing not only enough goods, but the right goods; and

Distribution
   - It must resolve the problem of *distribution,* arranging a satisfactory solution to the problem of Who Gets What?

Division of labor

4. These problems exist in all societies, but they are especially difficult to solve in advanced societies in which there exists a far-reaching *division of labor.* People in wealthy societies are far more socially interdependent than people in simple societies.

5. Over the course of history, there have evolved three types of solutions to the two great economic problems. These are *tradition, command,* and the *market* system.

Tradition

6. Tradition solves the problems of production and distribution by enforcing a continuity of status and rewards through social institutions such as the kinship system. *Typically, the economic solution imposed by tradition is a static one,* in which little change occurs over long periods of time.

Command

7. Command solves the economic problem by imposing allocations of effort or reward by a *governing authority.* Command can be a means for achieving rapid and far-reaching economic *change.* It can take an extreme totalitarian or a mild democratic form.

Market

8. The market system is a complex mode of organizing society in which order and efficiency emerge "spontaneously" from a seemingly uncontrolled society. We shall investigate the market system in great detail in the chapters to come.

Questions

1. If we could produce all the food we needed in our own backyards, and if technology were so advanced that we could all make anything we wanted in our basements, would an "economic problem" exist?

2. Suppose that everyone was completely versatile—able to do everyone else's work just as well as his or her own. Would a division of labor still be useful in society? Why?

3. Modern economic society is sometimes described as depending on "bureaucrats" who allow their lives to be directed by the large corporations or government agencies for which they work. Assuming that this description has some truth, would you think that modern society should be described as one of tradition, command, or the market?

4. In what way do your own plans for the future coincide with or depart from the occupations of your parents? Do you think that the so-called generational split is observable in all modern societies?

5. Economics is often called the science of scarcity. How can this label be applied to a society of considerable affluence such as our own?

6. What elements of tradition and command do you think are indispensable in a modern industrial society? Do you think that modern society could exist without any dependence on tradition or without any exercise of command?

7. Much of production and distribution involves the creation or the handling of *things*. Why are production and distribution *social* problems rather than engineering or physical problems?

8. Do you consider humankind's wants to be insatiable? Does this imply that scarcity must always exist?

9. Take some of the main problems that disturb us in the United States today: neglect, poverty, inflation, pollution, racial discrimination. To what extent do you find such problems in societies run by tradition? by command? What is your feeling about the responsibility the market system bears for these problems in the United States?

Thinking Back, Looking Ahead

ECONOMICS VIEWED FROM ABOVE

Most textbooks end their chapters with a section devoted to reviews of the central ideas and important words the chapter has put forward. Thus in the last edition of our book, we put forward as the first key concept: Economics is the study of how humankind ensures its material sufficiency, that is, how societies arrange for their *material provisioning*.

There is only one trouble with this absolutely true statement: It is not likely to make you *think about* what you have just learned, so here is another way to consider the statement.

Let us suppose that as members of a giant spaceship, we visit a new planet and discover that its abundant grass-like covering is delicious as well as nutritious. In fact, each day's food supplies are easily gathered by only half the crew. No wonder we have named our planet Bountiful.

Unfortunately, our captain is not well liked because he has staked off a particularly succulent alley for officers only. In addition, there is a heated discussion between the male and female crew members about when to go back home.

One day on the communication screen we read that each crew member must answer and sign the following questionnaire:

Are there any economic problems on Bountiful? Any political ones? Social ones? Your immediate reply is important.

Now comes the question for you to consider. Is the captain's act economic or political? Is the heated discussion about when to return home a social or a political dispute? Suppose that the female members refused to gather food unless the spaceship returned much sooner than the male members wanted. Is this a political or a social dispute? Could it have economic consequences?

The question for you to consider is: What makes a problem economic, political, or social? There is no one right answer to this seemingly simple question, but that is the way to begin really thinking about economics.

Here are our answers:

RH: "They are political questions with economic consequences."

WM: "Wrong! They are social questions with political consequences."

What do you think? Is it possible that both are right? How would you define these three key words?

CHAPTER 2

The Premarket Economy

"**N**obody ever saw a dog make a fair and deliberate exchange of one bone for another with another dog," wrote Adam Smith in *The Wealth of Nations*. "Nobody ever saw one animal by its gestures and natural cries signify to another, this is mine, that yours; I am willing to give this for that."[1]

Smith was writing about "a certain propensity in human nature . . . ; the propensity to truck, barter, and exchange one thing for another." That such a propensity exists as a universal characteristic of humankind is perhaps less likely than Smith believed, but he was certainly not mistaken in putting the act of exchange at the very center of his scheme of economic life. There can be no doubt that buying and selling lie at the very heart of a market society such as he was describing, and so, as we now begin to study the rise of the market society, what could be more natural than to commence by tracing the pedigree of markets themselves?

It comes as something of a surprise, perhaps, to discover how very ancient is that pedigree. Communities have traded with one another at least as far back as the last Ice Age. We have evidence that the mammoth hunters of the Russian steppes obtained Mediterranean shells in trade, as did also the Cro-Magnon hunters of the central valleys of France. In fact, on the moors of Pomerania in northeastern Germany, archeologists came across an oaken box, replete with the remains of its original leather shoulder strap, in which were a dagger, a sickle head, and a needle—all of Bronze Age manufacture. According to the conjectures of experts, this was very likely the sample kit of a prototype of the traveling salesman, an itinerant representative who collected orders for the specialized production of his community.[2]

As we proceed from the dawn of civilization to its first organized societies, the evidences of trade and of markets increase rapidly. As Miriam Beard has written:

> Millennia before Homer sang, or the wolf suckled Romulus and Remus, the bustling damkars (traders) of Uruk and Nippur . . . were buckling down to business. Atidum the merchant, in need of enlarged office facilities, was agreeing to rent a suitable location from Ribatum, Priestess of Shamash, for one and one-sixth shekels of silver per year—so much down and the rest in easy installments. Abu-wakar, the rich shipper, was delighted that his daughter had become Priestess of Shamash and could open a real estate office near the temple. Ilabras was writing to Ibi: "May Shamash and Marduk keep thee! As thou knowest, I had issued a note for a female slave. Now the time to pay is come."[3]

---

[1]Adam Smith, *The Wealth of Nations* (New York: Modern Library, 1937), p. 13.
[2]*Cambridge Economic History of Europe* 2nd Edition, M. M. Postan and H. J. Habakkuk, general editors (Cambridge, England: Cambridge University Press, 1966), II, p. 4.
[3]Miriam Beard, *A History of the Business Man* (New York: Macmillan, 1938), p. 12.

Therefore, at first glance it seems we can discover evidences of market society deep in the past. These disconcerting notes of modernity, however, must be interpreted with caution. If markets, buying and selling, even highly organized trading bodies, were well-nigh ubiquitous features of ancient society, they must not be confused with the presence of a market society. Trade existed as an important adjunct to society from earliest times, but the fundamental impetus to production, or the basic allocation of resources among different uses, or the distribution of goods among social classes was largely divorced from the marketing process. That is, the *markets of antiquity were not the means by which those societies solved their basic economic problems.* They were subsidiary to the great processes of production and distribution rather than integral to them; they were "above" the critical economic machinery rather than within it. As we shall see, between the deceptively contemporary air of many markets of the distant past and the reality of our contemporary market economy lies an immense distance over which society would take centuries to travel.

THE ECONOMIC ORGANIZATION OF ANTIQUITY

We must ourselves traverse that distance if we are to understand how contemporary market society came into being and, indeed, if we are to understand what it is. Only by immersing ourselves in the societies of the past, only by seeing how they did, in fact, solve their economic problems, can we begin to understand clearly what is involved in the evolution of the market society that is our own environment.

Needless to say, it would make an enormous difference which of the many premarket societies of the past we visited as general observers. To trace economic history from the monolithic temple-states of Sumer and Akkad in the third millennium B.C. to the "modernity" of classical Greece or Rome that date from roughly the fifth and fourth centuries B.C. in to the years of the Christian era is to undertake a cultural journey of immense distance. Yet, traveling only as economic historians, we will find that it makes much less difference in which of the societies of antiquity we light. Because as we examine these societies, we can see that, underlying their profound dissimilarities of art or political rule or religious belief, there are equally profound similarities of economic structure, similarities we call to mind less frequently because they are in the "background" of history and rarely adorn its more exciting pages. But these identifying characteristics of economic organization are the ones that now interest us as we turn our gaze to the past. What is it that we see?

Agricultural Foundation of Ancient Societies

The first and perhaps the most striking impression is the overwhelmingly agricultural aspect of all these economies.

In a sense, of course, all human communities, no matter how industrialized, live off the soil: All that differentiates an "industrial" society from an "agricultural" one is the number of the nonagricultural population that its food growers can support. Thus, an American farmer working large acreage with abundant equipment can feed nearly a hundred nonfarmers, while an Asian peasant, tilling his tiny plot with little more than a stick-plow, may be hard pressed, after he has paid his landlord, to sustain his own family.

Over all of antiquity, the capacity of the agricultural population to sustain a non-farming population was very limited. Exact statistics are unavailable, but we can project backward to the situation that prevailed in all these ancient nations by looking at the underdeveloped regions of the world today, where the levels of technique and the productivity of agriculture bear a close—too close—resemblance to those of antiquity. Thus in India, in Egypt, in the Philippines, Indonesia, Brazil, Colombia, and Mexico, we find that it takes two farm families to support one nonfarm family. In tropical Africa, a survey made some years ago told us that "the productivity of African agriculture is so low that it takes anywhere from two to ten people—men, women, and children—to raise enough food to supply their own needs and those of *one* additional—non–food-growing—adult."[4] Those sad findings of almost 50 years ago are still largely true.

Antiquity was not *that* badly off; indeed, at times it produced impressive agricultural outputs, but neither was it remotely comparable to American farm productivity, with its enormous capacity to support a nonagricultural population. All ancient societies were basically rural economies. This did not preclude, as we shall see, a very brilliant and wealthy urban society or a far-flung network of international trade. Yet the typical economic personage of antiquity was neither trader nor urban dweller but rather a tiller of the soil, and it was in rural communities that the economies of antiquity were ultimately anchored.

This must not lead us to assume that economic life was therefore comparable to that of a modern agricultural country like Denmark or New Zealand. Contemporary farmers, like businesspeople, are very much bound up in the web of transactions characteristic of a market society. They sell their output on one market; they buy their supplies on another. The accumulation of money, and not of wheat or corn, is the object of their efforts. Books of profit and loss regularly tell them if they are doing well or not. The latest news of agricultural technology is studied and is put into effect if it is profitable.

None of this properly describes the "farmer" of ancient Egypt, of antique Greece or Rome, or of the great Eastern civilizations. With few exceptions, the tiller of the soil was a peasant, and a peasant is a social creature very different from a farmer. He is not on the alert for new technologies, but, on the contrary, clings with stubborn persistence—and often with great skill—to his well-known ways. He must do so, because a small error might mean starvation. He does not buy the majority of his supplies, but fashions them himself; similarly, he does not produce for a "market," but principally for his own family. Finally, he is often not even free to consume his own crop but typically must hand over a portion—a tenth, a third, half, or even more—to the owner of his land.

For in the general case, the peasant of antiquity did not own his land. We hear of the independent citizen-farmers of classical Greece and republic Rome, but these were exceptions to the general rule in which peasants were but tenants of a great lord. Even in Greece and Rome, the independent peasantry tended to become swallowed up as the tenants of huge commercial estates. The Roman historian Pliny mentions one such enormous estate or *latifundium* (literally, "broad farm") with a quarter of a million head of livestock and a population of 4,117 slaves.

Hence the peasant, who was the bone and muscle of the economies of antiquity, was himself a prime example of the nonmarket aspect of these economies. Although some cultivators freely sold a portion of their own crop in the city marketplaces, the great majority of agricultural producers scarcely entered the market at all. For many of these

---

[4]George H. T. Kimble, *Tropical Africa* (New York: Twentieth Century Fund, 1960), I, p. 572. (Italics added.)

producers—especially those who were slaves—this was, accordingly, an almost cashless world, where a few coppers a year, carefully hoarded and spent only for emergencies, constituted the only link with a world of market transactions.[5]

Thus, whereas the peasant's legal and social status varied widely in different areas and eras of antiquity, in a broad view the tenor of his economic life was singularly constant. Of the web of transactions, the drive for profits of the modern farmer, he knew little or nothing. Generally poor, tax ridden, and oppressed, prey to nature's caprices and to the exploitations of war and peace, bound to the soil by law and custom, the peasant of antiquity—like the peasant of today who continues to provide the agricultural underpinnings to some countries of the East and South—was dominated by the economic rule of tradition. His main stimulus for change was command—or, rather, obedience. Labor, patience, and the incredible endurance of the human being were his contributions to civilization.

Economic Life of the Cities

The basic agricultural cast of ancient society and its typical exclusion of the peasant cultivator from an active market existence make all the more striking another common aspect of economic organization in antiquity. This is the diversity, vitality, and ebullience of the economic life of the cities.

Whether we turn to ancient Egypt, classical Greece, or Rome, we cannot help but be struck by this contrast between the relatively static countryside and the active city. In Greece, for example, a whole panoply of goods passed across the docks of the Piraeus: grain from Italy, metal from Crete and even Britain, books from Egypt, perfume from still more distant origins. In the fourth century B.C. Isocrates, in the *Panegyricus,* boasts: "The articles which it is difficult to get, one here, one there, from the rest of the world; all these it is easy to buy in Athens." So, too, Rome developed a thriving foreign and domestic commerce. By the time of Augustus, four centuries later, 6,000 loads of ox-towed barges were required to feed the city annually,[6] while in the city forum a crowd of speculators converged as on "an immense stock exchange."[7]

Therefore, something that at least superficially approximated our own society was visible in many of the larger urban centers of antiquity, and yet we must not be beguiled into concluding that this was a market society similar to our own. In at least two respects, the differences were profound.

The first of these was the essentially restricted character and scope of the market function of the city. Unlike the modern city, which is not only a receiver of goods shipped in from the hinterlands but also an important exporter of goods and services back to the countryside, the cities of antiquity tended to assume an economically parasitic role vis-à-vis the rest of the economy. Much of the trade that entered the great urban centers of Egypt, Greece, and Rome (over and above the necessary provisioning of the city masses) was in the nature of luxury goods for its upper classes, rather than raw materials to be worked and then sent out to a goods-consuming economy. The cities were the vessels of civilization, but as centers of economic activity, they were separated by a wide

---

[5]This is not, let us note, only an ancient condition. Traveling in Morocco, John Gunther reported of the local peasant-serfs, "formerly they got no wages—what would they need money for—but this is changing now." *Changing now—in 1953!* From John Gunther, *Inside Africa* (New York: Harper, 1955), p. 104.
[6]*Cambridge Economic History of Europe,* II, p. 14.
[7]W. C. Cunningham, *An Essay on Western Civilization* (New York: 1913), p. 164.

gulf from the country, making them enclaves of economic life rather than nourishing components of integrated rural–urban economies.

Slavery

Even more important was a second difference between the ancient city economies and a contemporary market society: their reliance on *slave labor.*

Slavery on a massive scale was a fundamental pillar of nearly every ancient economic society. In Greece, for instance, the deceptively modern air of the Piraeus masks the fact that much of the purchasing power of the Greek merchant was provided by the labor of 20,000 slaves who toiled under sickening conditions in the silver mines of Laurentium. At the height of "democratic" Athens in the fourth century B.C., it is estimated that at least one-third of its population were slaves. In Rome of 30 B.C., some 1,500,000 slaves—on the latifundia, in the galleys, the mines, the "factories," the shops—provided a major impetus in keeping the economic machinery in motion.[8] Seneca even tells us that a proposal that they wear special dress was voted down lest, recognizing their own number, they might know their strength.

Slaves were not, of course, the only source of labor. Groups of free artisans and workmen, often banded together in *collegia* or fraternal bodies, also serviced the Roman city, as did similar free workmen in Greece and elsewhere. In many cities, especially latter-day Rome, a mass of unemployed (but not enslaved) laborers provided a source of casual work. Yet, without the motive power of the slave, it is doubtful if the brilliant city economies of the past could have been sustained. This brings us to the central point: The flourishing market economy of the city rested atop an economic structure run by tradition and command. Nothing like the free exercise and interplay of self-interest guided the basic economic effort of antiquity. If an astonishingly modern urban market structure greets our eye, we must not forget that its merchants are standing on the shoulders of innumerable peasants and slaves.

The Social Surplus

The presence of great agglomerations of urban wealth amid a far poorer rural setting alerts us to another characteristic of ancient economic society: the special relationship between its wealth and its underlying economic organization.

In any society, the existence of wealth implies that a *surplus* has been wrung from nature, that society has not only solved its economic production problem but has achieved a margin of effort above whatever is required for its own existence. Perhaps what first astonishes us when we regard the civilizations of the ancient world is the size of surplus that could be got from a basically poor peasant population. The temples of the ancient Assyrian kings, the extraordinary treasures of the Aztecs, the pyramids and pleasure craft of the pharaohs of Egypt, the Acropolis of Athens, and the magnificent roads and architecture of Rome all testify to the ability of an essentially agricultural civilization to achieve a massive surplus, pry considerable amounts of labor loose from the land, support it at whatever low level necessary, and put it to work building for posterity.

But the stupendous achievements of the past testify as well to something else. The surplus productive potential that society manages to achieve, whether by technology or

---

[8]K. J. Beloch, *Die Bevölkerung der Griechisch-Römischen Welt* (Rome: "L'Erma" di Bretschneider, 1968), p. 478.

by adroit social organization, can be applied in many directions. It can be directed to agricultural improvements, such as irrigation ditches or dams, where it will increase the bounty of the harvest still further. Applied to the tools and equipment of the city workman, it will raise his ability to produce. Or the surplus may be used to support a nonworking religious order, or a class of courtiers and idle nobility. If it were not for its amazing capacity to produce a surplus, the United States could never support its armed forces—any more than the former Soviet Union could have, if *its* economy had not given rise to more output than it required for sheer self-perpetuation.

accumulation of wealth

 Thus, the social form taken by the accumulation of wealth reveals a great deal about any society. "To whom does the surplus accrue?" is a question that invariably sheds important light on the structure of power within that society.

Wealth and Power

To whom did the wealth of antiquity accrue? At first glimpse, it seems impossible to answer in a phrase. Emperors, nobles, religious orders, merchant traders—all enjoyed the wealth of antiquity at one time or another. But at a second look, an interesting and significant generalization becomes possible: Most wealth did not go to those who played a strictly *economic* role. Although there are records of clever slaves in Egypt and Rome who became wealthy, and although rich merchants and bankers are visible throughout the annals of antiquity, theirs was not the primary route to wealth. Rather, *in ancient civilization, wealth was generally the reward for political, military, or religious power or status, and not for economic activity.*

There was a reason for this. Societies tend to reward most highly the activities they value most highly, and in the long and turbulent centuries of antiquity, political leadership, religious tutelage, and military prowess were unquestionably more necessary for social survival than trading expertise. In fact, in many of these societies, economic activity itself was disdained as essentially ignoble. As Aristotle wrote in his *Politics,* "in the best-governed polis . . . the citizens may not lead either the life of craftsmen or of traders, for such a life is devoid of nobility and hostile to perfection of character." It was a theme on which Cicero would later expand in his essay *De Officiis* (Book I), written in the first century A.D.:

> The toil of a hired worker, who is paid only for his toil and not for artistic skill, is unworthy of a free man and is sordid in character. For in his case, money is the price of slavery. Sordid too is the calling of those who buy wholesale in order to sell retail, since they would gain no profits without a great deal of lying. . . . Trade on a small retail scale is sordid, but if it is on a large wholesale scale including the import of many wares from everywhere and their distribution to many people without any misrepresentation, it is not to be too greatly censured. . . .

Especially, added the great lawyer, "if those who carry on such trade finally retire to country estates, after being surfeited or at least satisfied with their gains."

Over and above the lesser social function of the merchant compared with the general, the consul, or the priest, this disdain of wealth obtained from "ignoble" economic activity reflected an economic fact of great importance: Society had not yet integrated the production of wealth with the production of goods. Wealth was still a surplus to be seized by conquest, squeezed from the underlying agricultural and slave populations;

not yet the result of a system of continuously increasing production in which some part of an expanding total social output might accrue to many classes of society.

And so it would be for many centuries. Until the smallest as well as the largest activities of society received their price tag, until purchases and sales, bids and offers penetrated down to the lowest orders of society, the accumulation of wealth remained more a matter of political, military, or religious power than of economics. To sum it up: *In premarket societies, wealth tended to follow power; not until the market society would power tend to follow wealth.*

"Economics" and Social Justice in Antiquity

Before we move on to view the economic system of antiquity in transition and evolution, we must ask one more question: What did contemporary economists think of it?

The answer we find is an interesting one: There were no contemporary "economists." Historians, philosophers, political theorists, and writers on manners and morals abounded during the long span of history we here call "antiquity," but economists, as such, did not exist. The reason is not far to seek. The economics of society—that is, the mode by which society organized itself to meet the basic tasks of economic survival—was hardly such as to provoke the curiosity of a thoughtful man. There was little or no "veil" of money to pierce, little or no complexity of contractual relationship in the marketplace to unravel, little or no economic rhythm of society to interpret. As the harvest flourished, as the justice or injustice of the tax-gathering system varied, as the fortunes of war and politics changed, so went the lot of the peasant proprietor, the slave, the petty craftsman, and the trader. As relative military strength rose or fell, as individual merchants fared luckily or otherwise, as the arts prospered or declined, so went the pulse of trade. If there was such a thing as economic "growth," it was invisible—too small or irregular to interest an observer. As prowess in war or politics permitted, or as local monopolies or marriage dictated, so fared the individual acquisitor of wealth. In all of this, there was little to try the analytic powers of economic-minded observers.

If there was a problem of economics—aside from the eternal problems of poor harvests, fortunes of war, and so on—it was inextricably mingled with the problem of social justice. As far back as the early Assyrian tablets, we have records of reformers who sought to alleviate taxes on the peasantry, and throughout the Bible—indeed, down through the Middle Ages—a strain of primitive communism, of egalitarian sharing, runs through the background of religious thought. In the Book of Leviticus, for example, there is mentioned the interesting custom of the *jubilee,* a limit of 50 years on leases, after which each landowner was to "return to each man unto his possession."[9] But despite the fact that religion was concerned with riches and poverty, and thus with the distributive problem of economics, the span of antiquity saw little or no systematic inquiry into the *social system* that produced riches or poverty. If riches were an affront, this was due to the personal failings of greedy people; if social justice were to be obtained, it must be achieved by personal redistribution, by alms and charity. The idea of

---

[9]That is, lands that had been forfeited in debt and so on, were to be restored to their original owners. The wrath of the later prophets such as Amos indicates that the injunction must have been observed largely in the breach.

an "economic" study of society, as contrasted with a political or moral one, was conspicuous largely by its absence.

There was, however, one exception we should note. Aristotle, the great pupil of Plato, turned his powerful scrutiny to economic affairs, and with him the systematic study of economics, as such, truly begins. Not that Aristotle was a radical social reformer. Much is summed up in his famous sentence. "From the hour of their birth, some are marked out for subjection, others for rule."[10] But the student of the history of economic thought turns first to Aristotle for questions whose treatment he or she can subsequently trace down through the present time: questions such as, "What is value?" "What is the basis of exchange?" "What is interest?"

We will not linger here over Aristotle's formulations of these ideas, but one point we might note, because it accords with what we have already seen of the attitude of antiquity to economic activity itself. When Aristotle examined the economic process, he differentiated it into two branches—not production and distribution, as we have done, but *use* and *gain*. More specifically, he differentiated between *oeconomia*—whence "economics"—and *chrematistiké,* from which we have no precise derivative term. By *oeconomia,* the Greek philosopher meant the art of household management, the administration of one's patrimony, the careful husbanding of resources. *Chrematistiké,* on the other hand, implied the use of nature's resources or of human skill for aquisitive purposes; *Chrematistiké* was trade for trade's sake, economic activity that had as its motive and end not use, but profit. Aristotle approved of *oeconomia* but not of *chrematistiké,* and within the scope of the essentially limited market structure of antiquity, where the city trader all too frequently exploited the country peasant, it is not hard to see why. The much more difficult problem of whether a market society, in which *everyone* strives for gain, might warrant approval or disapproval never appears in Aristotle's writings, because it never appeared in ancient history. The market society, with its genuinely perplexing questions of economic order and economic morality, had yet to come into being. Until it did, the philosophy needed to rationalize that order was understandably lacking.

ECONOMIC SOCIETY IN THE MIDDLE AGES

Our overview of economic organization has thus far scanned only the great civilizations of antiquity. Now we must turn in somewhat closer focus to the society far nearer in time and, what is more important, immediately precedent to ours in terms of social evolution. This is the vast expanse of history we call the Middle Ages, an expanse that stretches over and describes the Western world, from Sweden to the Mediterranean, "beginning" with the fall of Rome in the fifth century and "ending" with the Renaissance a thousand years later.

Modern scholarship emphasizes more and more the diversity that characterizes that enormous span of time and space, a diversity not alone of social appearance from century to century but also of contrast from locality to locality within any given period. It is one thing to speak of "life" in the Middle Ages when one has in mind a tenth-century peasant community in Normandy where, it is estimated, the average inhabitant probably never saw more than two or three hundred persons in his lifetime or commanded a

---

[10]Aristotle, *Politics,* Book I, translated by T. Saunders, Oxford: Clarendon Press, 1995.

vocabulary of more than six hundred words[11]; it is another when we mean the worldly city of Florence in the fourteenth century, about which Boccaccio wrote so engagingly.

Even more relevant for our purposes is the need to think of the Middle Ages in terms of economic variety and change. The early years of feudal economic life are very different from the middle or later years, particularly insofar as general well-being is concerned. The commencement of feudalism coincided with a period of terrible retrenchment, deprivation, and depopulation. During the fifth century, the population of Rome actually fell from 1,500,000 to 300,000. But by the twelfth century, towns had again expanded (after 600 years!) to the limits of their old Roman walls and even spilled out beyond; and by the beginning of the fourteenth century, a very considerable prosperity reigned in many parts of Europe.[12] Then came a series of catastrophes: a ghastly 2-year famine in 1315; thereafter, in 1348, the Black Death, which carried off between one-third and two-thirds of the urban population; a century-long devastating struggle between England and France and among the petty principalities of Germany and Italy. All these misfortunes pulled down the level of economic existence to dreadful depths. Neither stasis nor smooth linear progress, but enormous and irregular secular tides mark the long history of feudalism, and they caution us against a simplistic conception of its development.

Our purpose, however, is not to trace these tides, but rather to form a generalized picture of the *economic structure* that, beneath the swings of fortune, marks the feudal era as a unique way station of Western economic history. Here we can begin by noting the all-important development that underlay the genesis of that economic structure: *This was the breakdown of large-scale political organization.*

The Fall of Rome

For as Rome "fell" and as successive raids and invasions from north, east, and south tore apart the European countryside, the great administrative framework of law and order was replaced by a patchwork quilt of small-scale political entities. Even in the ninth century, when Charlemagne's Holy Roman Empire assumed such impressive dimensions on the map, beneath the veneer of a unified "state" there was, in fact, political chaos: Neither a single language, nor a coordinated central government, nor a unified system of law, coinage, or currency, nor, most important, any consciousness of "national" allegiance bound the statelets of Charlemagne's day into more than temporary cohesion.

We note this striking difference between antiquity and the Middle Ages to stress the tremendous economic consequences that came with political dissolution. As safety and security gave way to local autarky and anarchy, long voyages of commodities became extremely hazardous, and the once-vigorous life of the great cities impossible. As a common coin and a common law disappeared, merchants in Gaul could no longer do business with merchants in Italy, and the accustomed network of economic connections was severed or fell into disuse. As disease and invasion depopulated the countryside, people turned of necessity to the most defensive forms of economic organization, to forms aimed at sheer survival through self-sufficiency. A new need arose, a need to

---

[11]George G. Coulton, *Medieval Village, Manor and Monastery* (New York: Harper, Torchbooks, 1960), p. 15.
[12]There is some evidence that in England around the year 1500 real wages for common laborers achieved a level that they would not surpass for at least three centuries (*Economica,* November 1956, pp. 296–314.)

compress the viable organization of society into the smallest possible compass. For centuries, this insularity of economic life, this extreme self-reliance, would be the economic hallmark of the Middle Ages, and its overall mode of social and political order would be called *feudalism*.

Manorial Organization of Society

Feudalism brought with it a new basic unit of economic organization: the *manorial estate.*

What was such an estate like? Typically, it was a large tract of land, often including many thousands of acres, which was "owned" by a feudal lord, spiritual or temporal.[13] The word "owned" is properly in quotation marks, because the manor was not first and foremost a piece of economic property. Rather, it was a social and political entity in which the lord of the manor was not only landlord, but protector, judge, police chief, and administrator as well. Although himself bound into a great hierarchy in which each lord was some other lord's servant (even the pope was the servant of God), the feudal noble was, within the confines of his own manor, quite literally "lord of the land." He was also undisputed owner and master of many of the people who lived on the land, for the serfs of a manor, although not slaves, were in many respects as much the property of the lord as were his (or their) houses, flocks, or crops.

At the focal point of the estate was the lord's homestead, a great manor house, usually armed against attack from marauders, walled off from the surrounding countryside, and sometimes attaining the stature of a genuine castle. In the enclosed courtyard of the manor were workshops in which cloth might be spun or woven, grapes pressed, food stored, simple ironwork or blacksmith work performed, coarse grain ground. Extending out around the manor was a patchwork of fields, typically subdivided into acre or half-acre strips, each with its own cycle of crops and rest. Half or more of all these belonged directly to the lord; the remainder "belonged," in various senses of that legal term, to the hierarchy of free, half-free, and unfree families who made up an estate.

The exact meaning of the word *belonged* hinged on the obligations and rights accrued to a serf, a freeman, or whatever other category one might be born into. Note, however, that even a freeman who "owned" his land could not sell it to another feudal lord. At best, his ownership meant that he could not himself be displaced from his land short of extraordinary circumstances. A lesser personage than a freeman did not even have this security. A typical serf was literally tied to "his" plot of land. He could not, without specific permission, and, usually, without specific payment, leave his homestead for another, either within the domain of the manor or within that of another. With his status came, as well, a series of obligations that lay at the very core of the manorial economic organization. These consisted of the necessity to perform labor for the lord—to till his fields, to work in his shops, to provide him with a portion of one's own crop. From manor to manor, and from age to age, the labor dues varied: In some localities, they amounted to as much as 4 or even 5 days of labor a week, which meant that only by the labor of a serf's wife or children could his own fields be maintained. Finally, the serfs

---

[13]That is, the lord might be the abbot or the bishop of the locality, or he might be a secular personage, a baron who came into his possessions by inheritance or by being made a knight and given lands for exceptional service in battle or for other reasons.

owed small money payments: head taxes, like the *chevage;* death duties, like the *heriot; merchet,* a marriage fee; or dues to use the lord's mill or his ovens.

Providing Security

There was, however, an extremely important quid pro quo for all this. If the serf gave the lord his labor and much of the fruits of his toil, in exchange the lord provided some things that the serf by himself could not have obtained.

The most important of these was a degree of physical security. It is difficult for us to reconstruct the violent tenor of much of feudal life, but one investigator has provided a statistic that may serve to make the point: Among the sons of English dukes, 46 percent of those born between 1330 and 1479 died violent deaths. Their life expectancy when violent death was excluded was 31 years; when violent death was included, it was but 24 years.[14] The peasant, although not a warrior and therefore not occupationally exposed to the dangers of continual combat, assassination, and so on, was preeminently fair prey for the marauding lord, defenseless against capture, unable to protect his poor possessions against destruction. Hence we can begin to understand why even freemen became serfs by "commending" themselves to a lord who, in exchange for their economic, social, and political subservience, offered them the invaluable cloak of his military protection.

In addition, the lord offered a certain element of economic security. In times of famine, it was the lord who fed his serfs from the reserves in his own manorial storehouses. Although he had to pay for it, the serf was *entitled* to use the lord's beasts and equipment in cultivating his own strips as well as those of the lord. In an age when the average serf possessed almost no tools himself, this was an essential boon.[15]

These facts should not incline us to an idyllic picture of feudal life. The relation between lord and serf was often, even usually, exploitative in the extreme. Yet we must see that it was also mutually supportive. Each provided for the other services essential for existence in a world where overall political organization and stability had virtually disappeared.

Economics of Manorial Life

Despite the extreme self-efficiency of manorial life, there is much here that resembles the economic organization of antiquity.

---

[14]T. H. Hollingsworth, "A Demographic Study of the British Ducal Families," *Population Studies,* XI (1957–58).

[15]For a picture of life among the various classes in medieval Europe, one might turn to Eileen Power's *Medieval People* (Garden City, NY: Doubleday, Anchor Books, 1954), a scholarly but charming account of the reality of human existence that lies behind history. For a sense of the violent tenor of the times, see J. Huizinga, *The Waning of the Middle Ages* (Garden City, NY: Doubleday, Anchor Books, 1954), Chap. 1. Let us call attention also to two other books that convey a vivid sense of feudal economic life: One is by H. S. Bennett, *Life on the English Manor* (Cambridge, England: Cambridge University Press, 1965); the other, by Marc Bloch, *French Rural History* (Berkeley, CA: University of California Press, 1966). *French Rural History,* especially, is one of the real masterworks of economic history. Less concerned with economic life (one has to read between the lines to ferret it out), but marvelous as a microhistory of medieval life, is the account of a tiny, heresy-ridden town in fourteenth-century southern France, by Emmanuel Le Roy Ladurie, *Montaillou: The Land of Promised Error* (New York: George Braziller, 1978). Last, by Georges Duby, *The Three Orders: Feudal Society Imagined* (Chicago: University of Chicago, 1980), a modern classic.

To begin with, like those earlier societies, this was clearly a form of economic society organized by tradition. Indeed, the hand of custom—the famous "ancient customs" of the medieval manor court, which served frequently as the counsel for the otherwise undefended serf—was never stronger. Lacking strong, unified central government, even the exercise of command was relatively weak. As a result, the pace of economic change, of economic development, although by no means lacking, was extremely slow during the early years of the medieval period.

Second, even more than with antiquity, this was a form of society that was characterized by a striking absence of money transactions. Unlike the latifundium of Rome, which sold its output to the city, the manor supplied only itself, and perhaps a local town. No manorial estate was ever quite so self-sufficient that it could dispense with monetary links with the outside world; even serfs bought a few commodities and sold a few eggs; and the lord, on occasion, had to buy considerable supplies he could not produce for himself. But on the whole, very little money changed hands. As Henri Pirenne, an authority on medieval economic history, has put it:

> . . . the tenants paid their obligations to their lord in kind. Every serf . . . owed a fixed number of days of labour and a fixed quantity of natural products or of goods manufactured by himself, corn, eggs, geese, chickens, lambs, pigs, and hempen, linen or woollen cloth. It is true that a few pence had also to be paid, but they formed such a small proportion of the whole that they cannot prevent the conclusion that the economy of the domain was a natural economy . . . since it did not engage in commerce it had no need to make use of money. . . .[16]

Town and Fair

It would, however, be a misrepresentation of medieval life to conclude that cash and cash transactions and the bargaining of a market society were wholly foreign to it. Rather, as was the case with antiquity, we must think of medieval economic society as consisting of a huge, static, largely moneyless foundation of agricultural production atop which flourished a considerable variety of more dynamic activities.

For one thing, in addition to manors, there also existed the shrunken descendants of Roman towns (and as we shall later see, the nuclei of new towns), and these small cities obviously required a network of markets to serve them. Every town had its stalls to which peasants brought some portion of their crop for sale. More important, towns were clearly a different social unit from manors, and the laws and customs of the manors did not apply to their problems. Even when towns fell under manorial protection, townspeople little by little won for themselves freedom from feudal obligations of labor and, more important, from feudal obligations of law.[17] In contrast to the "ancient customs" of the manor, a new, evolving "law of merchants" regulated much of the commercial activity within the town walls.

---

[16]Henri Pirenne, *Economic and Social History of Medieval Europe,* translated by I. E. Clegg (New York: Harcourt, Harvest Books, 1956), p. 105.

[17]Hence the saying, "City air makes men free," because the serf who escaped to a city and remained there a year and a day was usually considered to have passed from the jurisdiction of his lord to that of the city burghers. Running away was one of the very few means open to serfs to protest against their condition. Run-

fair

Another locus of active economic life was the fair. The fair was a kind of traveling market, established in fixed localities for fixed dates, in which merchants from all over Europe conducted a genuine international exchange. Held usually but once a year, the great fairs were tremendous occasions, a mixture of social holiday, religious festival, and intense economic activity. At some fairs, like those at Champagne in France or Stourbridge in England, a wide variety of merchandise was brought for sale: silks from the Levant, books and parchments, horses, drugs, and spices. Anyone who has ever been to the Flea Market, the famous open-air bazaar outside Paris, or to a country fair in New England or the Midwest, for example, has savored something of the atmosphere of such a market. One can imagine the excitement that fairs must have engendered in the still air of medieval life.

Guilds

Finally, within the towns themselves, we find the tiny but highly important centers of medieval "industrial" production, because even at its grandest, the manor could not support every craft needed for its maintenance, much less its extension. The services or products of glaziers and masons, expert armorers and metalworkers, and fine weavers and dyers had to be bought when they were needed, and typically they were to be found in the medieval institutions as characteristic of town life as the manors were of life in the country.

These institutions were the *guilds*—trade, professional, and craft organizations of Roman origin. Such organizations were the "business units" of the Middle Ages; in fact, one could not usually set oneself up in "business" unless one belonged to a guild. Thus, the guilds were a kind of exclusive union, but not a union of workers so much as of masters. The dominant figures in the guild were the guildmasters—independent manufacturers, working in their own houses and banding together to elect their own guild government, which then laid down the rules concerning the internal conduct of affairs.[18] Under the master guildsmen were their few journeymen (from the French *journée,* or "day"), who were paid by the day, and their half-dozen or so apprentices, 10 to 12 years old, who were bound to them for periods of 3 to 12 years as their legal wards. In time, an apprentice could become a journeyman and then, at least in medieval romance, graduate to the status of a full-fledged guildmaster on completion of his "masterpiece."

Any survey of medieval town life delights in the color of guild organizations: the broiders and glovers, the hatters and scriveners, the shipwrights and upholsterers, each with its guild hall, its distinctive livery, and its elaborate set of rules. But if life in the guilds and at the fairs provides a sharp contrast with the stodgy life on the manor, we must not be misled by surface resemblances into thinking that it represented a foretaste of modern life in medieval dress. It is a long distance from the guild to the modern business firm, and it is well to fix in mind some of the differences.

Functions of the Guild

In the first place, the guild was much more than just an institution for organizing production. Although most of its regulations concerned wages and conditions of work and

---

away serfs, like runaway slaves, were ferociously punished. Yet serfs did continuously escape to the cities, in this tiny, desperate way exerting economic pressure against their masters. For a debate on the importance of this issue, see *The Transition from Feudalism to Capitalism,* ed. Rodney Hilton (London: NLB, 1978).

[18]Note "his." There were no women in guilds except as servants.

specifications of output, they also dwelt at length on "noneconomic" matters: on the charitable contributions expected from each member, on his civic role, on his appropriate dress, and even on his daily deportment. Guilds were the regulators not only of production but also of social conduct: When one member of the mercer's guild in London "broke the hed" of another in an argument over some merchandise, both were fined £10 and bonded for £200 not to repeat the disgrace. In another guild, members who engaged in a brawl were fined a barrel of beer, to be drunk by the rest of the guild.

But between guild and modern business firm there is a much more profound gulf than this pervasive paternalism: *Unlike a modern firm, the purpose of a guild was not first and foremost to make money.* Rather, it was to preserve a certain orderly way of life—a way that envisaged a decent income for its master craftsmen but that was certainly not intended to allow any of them to become a "big" businessman or a monopolist. On the contrary, guilds were specifically designed to ward off any such outcome of an uninhibited struggle among their members. The terms of service, the wages, and the route of advancement of apprentices and journeymen were all fixed by custom. So, too, were the terms of sale: A guild member who cornered the supply of an item was guilty of *forestalling,* for which rigorous penalties were invoked, and one who bought wholesale to sell at retail was similarly punished for the faults of *engrossing* or *regrating.* Thus, competition was strictly limited and profits were held to prescribed levels. Advertising was forbidden, and even technical progress in advance of one's fellow guildsmen was considered disloyal.

In the great cloth guilds of Florence in the fourteenth century, for instance, no merchant was permitted to tempt a buyer into his shop or to call out to a customer standing in another's doorway, nor even to process his cloth in a manner different from that of his brethren. Standards of cloth production and processing were subject to the minutest scrutiny. If a scarlet dye, for instance, was found to be adulterated, the perpetrator was condemned to a crushing fine and, failing payment, to loss of his right hand.[19]

Surely the guilds represent a more "modern" aspect of feudal life than the manor, but the whole temper of guild life was still far removed from the goals and ideals of modern business enterprise. There was no free play of price, no free competition, no restless probing for advantage. Existing on the margin of a relatively moneyless society, the guilds perforce sought to take the risks out of their slender enterprises. Their aim was not increase, but preservation, stability, and orderliness. As such, they were as drenched in the medieval atmosphere as the manors.

Medieval Economics

Beyond even these differences, we must note a still deeper chasm between medieval economic society and that of a market economy. This is the gulf between a society in which economic activity is still inextricably mixed with social and religious activity, and one in which economic life has, so to speak, emerged into a special category of its own. In our next chapter, we talk about the ways in which a market society creates a special sphere of economic existence, but as we complete our introduction to medieval economic society, the main point to which we should pay heed is that no such special sphere then existed. *In medieval society, economics was a subordinate, not a dominant aspect of life.*

---

[19]Georges F. Renard, *Histoire du Travail à Florence* (Paris: 1913), pp. 190ff.

And what was dominant? The answer is, of course, that in economic matters, as in so many other facets of medieval life, the guiding ideal was religious. It was the Catholic Church, the great pillar of stability in an age of disorder, that constituted the ultimate authority on economics, as on most other matters.

But the economics of medieval Catholicism was concerned not with the credits and debits of successful business operation so much as with the credits and debits of the souls of business operators. As R. H. Tawney, one of the great students of the problem, has written:

> . . . the specific contributions of medieval writers to the technique of economic theory were less significant than their premises. Their fundamental assumptions, both of which were to leave a deep imprint on social thought of the sixteenth and seventeenth centuries, were two: that economic interests are subordinate to the real business of life, which is salvation; and that economic conduct is one aspect of personal conduct, upon which, as on the other parts of it, the rules of morality are binding. Material riches are necessary . . . since without them men cannot support themselves and help one another. . . . But economic motives are suspect. Because they are powerful appetites, men fear them, but they are not mean enough to applaud them. Like other strong passions, what they need, it is thought, is not a clear field, but repression. . . .[20]

Thus, what we find throughout medieval religious thought is a pervasive uneasiness with the practices of economic society. Essentially, the Church's attitude toward trade was wary and nicely summed up in the saying, "*Homo mercator vix aut numquam Deo placere potest*"—"The merchant can scarcely or never be pleasing to God."

The Just Price

We find such a suspicion of business motives in the Church's concern with the idea of a "just price." What was a just price? It was selling a thing for what it was worth, and no more. "It is wholly sinful," wrote Thomas Aquinas, "to practise fraud for the express purpose of selling a thing for more than its just price, inasmuch as a man deceives his neighbor to his loss."[21]

But what *was* a thing "worth"? Presumably, what it cost to acquire it or make it. Suppose, however, that a seller had himself paid too much for an article—then what was a "just price" at which he might resell it? Or suppose a man paid too little—was he then in danger of spiritual loss, offsetting his material gain?

These were the questions over which the medieval "economist-theologians" mulled, and they testify to the mixture of economics and ethics characteristic of the age. But they were not merely theoretical questions. We have records of the dismay that economic theology brought to actual participants in the economic process. One St. Gerald of Aurillac in the tenth century, having bought an ecclesiastical garment in Rome for an unusually low price, learned from some itinerant merchants that he had picked up a

---

[20]R. H. Tawney, *Religion and the Rise of Capitalism* (New York: Harcourt, 1947), p. 31.
[21]A. E. Monroe, ed., "Summa Theologica," in *Early Economic Thought* (Cambridge, MA: Harvard University Press, 1924), p. 54.

"bargain"; instead of rejoicing, he hastened to send to the seller an additional sum, lest he fall into the sin of avarice.[22]

St. Gerald's attitude was no doubt exceptional. Yet if the injunction to charge fair prices did not succeed in staying men's appetites for gain, it did bridle their enthusiasm. Men in ordinary business frequently stopped to assess the condition of their moral balance sheets. Whole towns would, on occasion, repent of usury and pay a heavy amend, or merchants like Gandoufle le Grand would, on their deathbeds, order restitution made to those from whom interest had been extracted. Men of affairs in the twelfth and thirteenth centuries occasionally inserted codicils in their wills urging their sons not to follow their footsteps into the snares of trade, or they would seek to make restitution for their commercial sins by charitable contributions. One medieval merchant of London founded a divinity scholarship with £14, "forasmoche as I fynde myn conscience aggrugged that I have deceived in this life divers persons to that amount."[23]

The Disrepute of Gain

Therefore, the theological cast of suspicion injected a wholly new note into the money-making process. For the first time, it associated the making of money with *guilt.* Unlike the acquisitor of antiquity who unashamedly reveled in his treasures, the medieval profiteer counted his gains in the knowledge that he might be imperiling his soul.

Nowhere was this disapproval of moneymaking more evident than in the Church's horror of usury—lending money at interest. Moneylending had, since Aristotle's day, been regarded as an essentially parasitic activity, an attempt to make a "barren" commodity, money, yield a return. But what had always been a vaguely disreputable and unpopular activity became, under Church scrutiny, a deeply evil one. Usury was decreed to be a *mortal* sin. At the Councils of Lyons and Vienne in the thirteenth and fourteenth centuries, the usurer was declared a pariah of society, to whom no one, under pain of excommunication, might rent a house; whose confession might not be heard; whose body might not have Christian burial; whose very will was invalid. Anyone even defending usury was to be suspected of heresy.

These powerful churchly sentiments were not produced merely by theological scruples. On the contrary, many of the Church's injunctions against both usury and profiteering arose from the most secular of realities. Famine, the endemic scourge of the Middle Ages, brought with it the most heartless economic gouging; loans commanded 40 to 60 percent—for bread. Much of the dislike of profit seeking and interest taking rose from its identification with just such ruthless practices, with which medieval times abounded.

Finally, another, perhaps even more fundamental, reason underlay the disrepute of gain and profit. This was the essentially static organization of economic life itself. Let us not forget that that life was basically agricultural and that agriculture, with its infinite complexity of peasant strips, was far from efficient. To quote once more from Henri Pirenne:

---

[22]Henri Pirenne, *Economic and Social History of Medieval Europe,* p. 27.
[23]S. L. Thrupp, *The Merchant Class in Medieval London* (Chicago: University of Chicago Press, 1948), p. 177. Also Georges F. Renard, *Histoire du Travail à Florence,* pp. 220ff.

. . . the whole idea of profit, and indeed the possibility of profit, was incompatible with the position occupied by the great medieval landowner. Unable to produce for sale owing to the want of a market, he had no need to tax his ingenuity in order to wring from his men and his land a surplus which would merely be an encumbrance, and as he was forced to consume his own produce, he was content to limit it to his needs. His means of existence was assured by the traditional functioning of an organization which he did not try to improve.[24]

What was true of the country was also true of the city. The idea of an *expanding* economy, a *growing* scale of production, an *increasing* productivity, was as foreign to the guildmaster or fair merchant as to the serf and lord. Medieval economic organization was conceived of as a means of reproducing, but not enhancing, the material well-being of the past. Its motto was perpetuation, not progress. There is little wonder that in such a static organization profits and profit seeking were viewed as essentially disturbing rather than welcome economic phenomena.

PREREQUISITES OF CHANGE

We have traced the broad outlines of the economic organization of the West roughly up to the tenth or twelfth century. Once again, it is wise to emphasize the diversity of currents concealed within a landscape we have too often been forced to treat as undifferentiated. At best, our journey into antiquity and the Middle Ages can give us a glimpse of the prevailing flavor of the times, a sense of the ruling economic climate, of the main institutions and ideas by which people organized their economic efforts.

But one thing is certain. We are very far from the temper and tempo of modern economic life. The few stirrings we have witnessed in the slow world of the manor and the town are but the harbingers of a tremendous change, which, over the course of the next centuries, would dramatically alter the basic form of economic organization itself, replacing the old ties of tradition and command with new ties of market transactions.

We shall have to wait until our next chapter to witness the actual process of change itself. But perhaps it will help us put into focus both what we have already seen and what we are about to witness if we anticipate our line of advance. We now have an idea of a premarket society, a society in which markets exist but that does not yet depend on a market mechanism to solve the economic problem. What changes will be required to transform such a society into a true market economy?

1. A New Attitude Toward Economic Activity Will Be Needed

For such a society to function, men must be free to seek gain. The suspiciousness and unease that surrounded the ideas of profit, of change, and of social mobility must give way to new ideas that would encourage those very attitudes and activities. In turn, this meant, in the famous words of the mid–nineteenth-century legal historian Sir Henry Maine, that the *society of status* must give way to the *society of contract,* that the society

---

[24]*Economic and Social History of Medieval Europe,* p. 63.

in which men were born to their stations in life must give way to a society in which they were free to define those stations for themselves.

Such an idea would have seemed to the medieval mind without any possible rationale. The idea that a general free-for-all should determine men's compensations, with neither a floor to prevent them from being ground down nor a ceiling to prevent them from rising beyond all reason, would have appeared senseless—even blasphemous. If we may turn again to R. H. Tawney:

> To found a science of society upon the assumption that the appetite for economic gain is . . . to be accepted, like other natural forces . . . would have appeared to the medieval thinker as hardly less irrational or less immoral than to make the premise of social philosophy the unrestrained operation of such necessary human attributes as pugnacity or the sexual instinct.[25]

Yet some such freeing of the quest for economic gain, some such aggressive competition in the new contractual relationship of person to person would be essential for the birth of a market society.

2. The Monetization of Economic Life Will Have to Proceed to Its Ultimate Conclusion

One prerequisite of a market economy should by now be clear: Such an economy must involve the process of exchange, of buying and selling, at every level of society. However, for this to take place, men must have the wherewithal to enter a market; that is, they must have cash. In turn, if society is to be permeated with cash, men must earn money for their labors. In other words, *for a market society to exist, nearly every task must have a monetary reward.*

Even in our highly monetized society, we do not pay for every service: most conspicuously not for the housekeeping or childcare services performed in the household. But all through the premarket era, unpaid service—the amount of work performed by law without monetary compensation—was vastly larger than it is in our society. Slave labor was, of course, unpaid; so was most serf labor. Even the labor of apprentices was remunerated more in kind, in food and lodging, than in cash. Therefore, probably 70 to 80 percent of the actual working population of an ancient or medieval economy labored without anything resembling regular payment in money.

Clearly, in such a society, the possibilities for a highly involved exchange economy were limited, but a still more important consequence must be noted. The absence of a widespread monetization of tasks meant *the absence of a widespread market for producers.* Nothing like the flow of "purchasing power" that dominates and directs our own productive efforts could be forthcoming in a society in which money incomes were the exception rather than the rule.

3. The Pressure of a Free Play of Market "Demand" Will Have to Take Over the Regulation of the Economic Tasks of Society

All through antiquity and the Middle Ages, as we have seen, tradition or command solved the economic problem. These were the forces that regulated the distribution of

---

[25]*Religion and the Rise of Capitalism,* pp. 31–32.

social rewards. But in a market society, another means of control must rise to take their place: *An all-encompassing flow of money demand, itself stemming from the monetization of all economic tasks, must become the great propulsive mechanism of society.* Men must go to their tasks not because they are ordered there, but because they will make money there, and producers must decide on the volume and the variety of their output not because the rules of the manor or the guild so determine, but because there is a market demand for particular things. From the top to the bottom of society, a new marketing orientation must take over the production and distribution tasks. The whole replenishment, the steady provisioning, the very progress of society must now be subject to the guiding hand of a universal demand for labor and goods.

What forces would ultimately drive the world of medieval economic organization into a world of money, of universal markets, of profit seeking? The stage is now set for us to attempt to answer this profoundly important and difficult question. Our next chapter will bring us to a consideration of the causes capable of affecting so vast a change.

Key Concepts and Key Words

Markets
1. We must differentiate between markets, which have a very ancient pedigree, and market societies, which do not. *In a market society, the economic problem itself—both production and distribution—is solved by means of a vast exchange between buyers and sellers.* Many ancient societies had markets, but these markets did not organize the fundamental activities of those societies.

2. The economic societies of antiquity had several features in common, many of which contrast sharply with those of modern market economies:

Peasant farming
- They rested on an agricultural base of *peasant farming.*
- Their cities were—from an economic point of view—parasitic *centers of consumption, not active centers of production.*

Slavery
- *Slavery* was a common and very important form of labor.

Surplus
- In addition they produced very considerable *surpluses,* as do modern economic systems.

Wealth and power
3. As a result, in the economic societies of antiquity, we find the economic side of life subservient to the political side. Priest, warrior, and statesman were superior to merchant or trader; *wealth followed power,* not—as in the market societies to come—the other way around.

Feudalism
4. Medieval economic life emerged from the catastrophic disorganization that followed the decline of Roman law and order. It was characterized by a new form of organization called the *manorial system* in which:

Lords
Serfs
- *Local lords were the centers of political, military, economic, and social power.*
- *Most peasants were bound as serfs* to a particular lord, for whom they were required to work and to whom they owed both labor and taxes or dues.
- *Physical security* against brigands or other lords was provided by the lord, who also gave some economic security in times of distress.

Manorial system
5. *The manorial system,* particularly in its earlier days (sixth to tenth centuries), *was a static economic system,* in which monetary payments played only a minor role. Self-sufficiency was the main purpose and the most outstanding characteristic of the manor.

Fairs
6. Side by side with the manor existed the economic life of the *towns.* Here monetary exchange always played a more important role, as did the organization of a more active economic life in the institution of *fairs.*

Guilds

7. The *guild* was the main form of organizing production in the towns and cities. *Guilds were very different from modern-day businesses,* insofar as they discouraged competition or profit seeking and sought to impose general rules on the methods of production, rates of pay, practices of marketing, and so on.

Usury

8. All through medieval times, the Catholic Church—the main social organization of the age—was suspicious of buying and selling activity. In part, this reflected a dislike of the exploitative practices of the times; in part, it was a consequence of an ancient contempt for moneymaking (remember Aristotle's dislike of *chrematistiké*) and especially for moneylending (usury). The religious leaders of the day worried about "just prices," and did not admit that unregulated buying and selling could give rise to just prices.

Market society

9. Three profound and pervasive changes would be needed to convert medieval society into a market society:
   * *A new attitude toward moneymaking* as a legitimate activity would have to replace the medieval suspicion of profit seeking.

Monetization

   * *The web of monetization would have to expand* beyond its narrow confines—that is, buying and selling would have to control the output of all products and the performance of nearly all tasks.
   * The flux of *"demand" and "supply" would have to be allowed to take over the direction of economic activity* from the dictates of lords and the usages of custom.

Questions

1. What differences, if any, characterize the economic attitudes and behavior of the American farmer and the American businessperson? Can this comparison also describe the behavior and attitude of the Egyptian peasant and the Egyptian merchant? What accounts for the difference between the two societies?
2. Julius Caesar and J. P. Morgan were both wealthy and powerful men. What is the difference in the origins of their wealth and their power? Does power still follow wealth in modern economic societies? Does wealth still follow power in non-market societies?
3. To what uses was the surplus of society put in ancient Rome? in feudal society? in the modern United States? in the People's Republic of China? What significance attaches to these different uses? What do they tell us about the structure of these societies?
4. What do you think of the validity of Aristotle's distinction between economic activity for *use* and for *gain?*
5. In what ways is a serf a different *economic* creature from a modern farm worker? How is a slave different from an industrial worker?
6. What changes would have to take place within a guild before it resembled a modern business?
7. The Bible has numerous hostile references to moneymaking—"It is easier for a camel to go through the eye of a needle than for a rich man to enter into the kingdom of God." How do you account for this ancient churchly antipathy toward wealth? Is religion today still suspicious of moneymaking? Why?
8. Is the idea of a "just" price (or a "just" wage) still encountered in our own society? What is usually meant by these terms? Do you think these ideas are compatible with a market system?
9. The manorial system persisted for nearly 1,000 years. Why do you think change was so slow in coming?
10. Ancient Greece and Rome were a great deal more "modern" in their temper than feudal Europe, yet neither was remotely a modern economic system. Why not?

Thinking Back, Looking Ahead

WHAT IS ECONOMIC HISTORY?

In our last "Thinking Back, Looking Ahead" box, we pondered the not-altogether-clear meaning of the word economics. Just to get you started, could the word "economical" have been used before the concept of an *economy* existed? That's an interesting question, which so far as we know, has never been asked. How would *you* answer it?

Now, however, let us try to clarify that oddly elusive word by watching the actual emergence in history of what we today call economic society. If you look carefully at the last sentence, we think you will spot another term on whose meaning much will depend. What is that term? Right! It is history.

What meanings does history have? Surely the first is suggested (in English, anyway) by "story." Is history the story of something? It can be, yes—but there is an interesting wrinkle here, too: There is often more than one story in history—that is, more than one possible reading of the events we seek to organize into a large-scale whole. Thus consider the history of progress, or its opposite, decline. Do you think the gradual extension of the right to vote, beginning some four centuries ago in England, was regarded as "progress" by the upper classes of that country, or as the first signs of imminent decline? Yet is it not also true that this same story was even then welcomed by a few farsighted aristocrats and is today universally celebrated as a triumph for those who see the advent of democracy as

the very process by which progress has been brought into being?

The past chapter concerns a remarkable change in European society, beginning from a point of view almost literally that of the Bible, where the love of money was described as the "root of all evil" (Timothy 6:10) and where merchants themselves, not surprisingly, were generally looked down on, not up to. By the end of the chapter, we begin to see a new social order in which money was more and more identified with respectability, and merchants more and more seen as practitioners of an honorable calling.

The change itself does not take place overnight but over a few centuries; we will examine some of their more dramatic aspects in our next chapter. Perhaps, however, this chapter will have already made you aware that history is often presented as a chapter to be read in half an hour although it took three centuries to enact. Yet our next chapter will show that history can also be understood by concentrating on its climactic "moments"—a mere 50 years in the making—which come to life in the context of the grander story you have now begun to see. Our focus until now has been on an era in which history dominates economics. Coming up is the beginning of an age in which that order of things will begin to change. Now the background of merchant institutions—especially trade and profit seeking—move to the fore to give shape and direction to history.

CHAPTER

The Emergence
of Market Society

Tradition, changelessness, order—these were the key concepts of economic society in the Middle Ages, and our preceding chapter introduces us to this unfamiliar and static way of economic life. But our purpose in this chapter is different. It is not to describe the factors that preserved the economic stability of medieval society, but to identify those forces that eventually burst it asunder.

Once again, we begin with a word of caution. Our chapter spans an immense variety of historical experience. We must beware of thinking that the forces of change that dominate this chapter were identical from region to region or from century to century, or that the transition they effected was uniform throughout the broad expanse of Europe. On the contrary, the great evolution that we will witness in these pages was not sharp and clear, but muddy and irregular. At the same time that the first evidences of a truly modern market society were beginning to manifest themselves in the medieval cities of Italy and Holland, archaic forms of feudal relationship still persisted in the agricultural sectors of these nations and, indeed, in the city life of other nations. We must bear in mind that the historic processes of this chapter extended from the tenth to the seventeenth centuries (and even to the eighteenth and nineteenth centuries, in some places) and manifested themselves in no two countries in precisely the same way.

With these warnings in mind, let us now turn to the great evolution itself. What agents were powerful enough to effect the major historic changes needed to bring about a market society?

FORCES OF CHANGE

The Itinerant Merchant

We meet the first of these forces of change in an unexpected guise. It is a small irregular procession of armed men, jogging along one of the rudimentary roads of medieval Europe: standard-bearer with colors in the lead, then a military chief, then a group of riders carrying bows and swords, and finally a caravan of horses and mules laden with casks and bales, bags, and packs.

Someone unacquainted with medieval life might easily take such a troop for part of the baggage train of a small army. But the observer would be mistaken. These were not soldiers but merchants, the traveling merchants whom the English of the twelfth century called "pie-powders," from *pieds poudreux,* dusty feet. No wonder they were dusty: Many of them traveled immense distances along routes so bad that we know of one instance where only the intervention of a local ecclesiastical lord prevented the "road" from being ploughed up as arable land. In their bags and packs were goods that had somehow made a perilous journey across Europe, or even all the way from Arabia or India, to be sold from town to town, or from halt to halt, as these merchant adventurers wound their way across the medieval countryside.

Adventurers they were. In the fixed hierarchies of the great manorial estates of Europe, there was no natural place for these unlanded peddlers of goods, with their unfeudal attributes of calculation and (often very crude) bookkeeping and their natural insistence on trade in money. The traveling merchants ranked very low in society. Some of them, without doubt, were the sons of serfs, or even runaway serfs themselves. Because no one could prove their bondage, they had, if only by default, the gift of "freedom." It is no wonder that in the eyes of the nobility, the merchants were upstarts and a disturbing element in the normal pattern of things.

However, no one would have dispensed with their services. To their brightly canopied stalls at the fairs flocked the lords and ladies of the manors as well as the Bodos and Ermentrudes of the fields. After all, where else could one buy pepper or purple dye, or acquire a guaranteed splinter from the Cross? Where else could one buy the marvelous cloths woven in Tuscany or hear such esoteric words, derived from the Arabic, as "jar" or "syrup"? If the merchant was a disturbing leaven in the mix of medieval life, he was also a pinch of active ingredient without which the mixture would have been very dull indeed.

We first note the traveling merchant in Europe in the eighth and ninth centuries, and we can follow his progress until the fourteenth and fifteenth centuries. By this time, largely through the merchants' own efforts, commerce was sufficiently organized so that it no longer required these itinerant journeyers.[1] For what these travelers brought, together with their wares, was the first breath of commerce and commercial intercourse to a Europe that had sunk to an almost tradeless and self-sufficient manorial stagnation. Even to towns as minuscule and isolated as Forcalquier in France—a dot on the map without so much as a road to connect its few hundred souls to the outer world—these hardy traders beat their path: We know from a primitive book of accounts that in May 1331, 36 itinerant merchants visited Forcalquier to transact business at the home and "shop" of one Ugo Teralh, a notary.[2] And so, in a thousand isolated communities, did they slowly weave a web of economic interdependence.

Urbanization

An important by-product of the rise of the itinerant merchant was the slow urbanization of medieval life, the creation of new towns and villages. When the traveling merchants stopped, they naturally chose the protected site of a local castle or burg, or of a church. So we find growing up around the walls of advantageously situated castles—in the *foris burgis,* whence *faubourg,* the French word for "suburb"—more or less permanent trading places, which in turn became the inner core of small towns. Nestled close

---

[1]Records of an order for goods placed on the occasion of a funeral of a Swedish nobleman in 1328 include saffron from Spain or Italy, caraway seed from the Mediterranean, ginger from India, cinnamon from Ceylon, pepper from Malabar, anise from southern Europe, and Rhine and Bordeaux wines. The order was placed for immediate delivery from one local merchant, despite the fact that Sweden was then a laggard and even primitive land. Cf. Fritz Rorig, *Mittelalterliche Weltwirtschaft* (Jena: 1933), p. 17. (We are indebted to Goran Ohlin for this reference.)

[2]*Cambridge Economic History of Europe* 2nd Edition, M. M. Postan and H. J. Hubakkuk, general editors (Cambridge, England: Cambridge University Press, 1952), II, pp. 325–326.

to the castle or cathedral wall for protection, the new burgs were still not "of" the manor. The inhabitants of the burg—the burgesses, burghers, bourgeois—had at best an anomalous and insecure relation to the manorial world. As we have seen, there was no way to apply the time-hallowed rule of "ancient customs" in adjudicating their disputes, because there *were* no ancient customs in the commercial quarters. Neither were there clear-cut rules for their taxation or for the particular degrees of fealty they owed their local masters. Worse yet, some of the growing towns began to surround themselves with walls. By the twelfth century, the commercial burg of Bruges, for example, had already swallowed up the old fortress like a pearl around a grain of sand.

Curiously, it was this very struggle for existence in the interstices of feudal society that provided much of the impetus for the development of a new social and economic order within the city. In all previous civilizations, cities had been the outposts of central government. Now for the first time, they existed as independent entities outside the main framework of social power. As a result, they were able to define for themselves—they *had* to define for themselves—a code of law and social behavior and a set of governing institutions that were eventually to displace those of the feudal countryside.

The process was long drawn out because the rate of growth of towns was often very slow. In the nearly two centuries between 1086 and 1279, for example, the town of Cambridge, England, added an average of but one house per year.[3] One important reason for this almost imperceptible rate of expansion was the difficulty of moving people or materials over the terrible roads. Not the least consequence of the decline of Roman power had been the decay of its once magnificent system of highways, the very stones of which were pilfered for building materials during the years of worst social disorganization. Until the roads recovered, economic movement was limited and limping. It is worth remarking that in many ports of Europe a system of transportation as efficient as that of ancient Rome was not enjoyed until the eighteenth or even nineteenth century. It took Napoleon almost as long to invade Italy from France as it had taken Caesar to go the other way.

Although growth was slow, it was steady; in some locales, it was much faster than in Cambridge. During the 1,000 years of the Middle Ages, nearly 1,000 towns were fathered in Europe, a tremendous stimulus to the commercialization and monetization of life. Each town had its local marts, its local toll gates, often its local mint, its granaries and shops, its drinking places and inns, and its air of "city life," which contrasted so sharply with that of the country. The slow, spontaneous growth of urban ways was a major factor in introducing a marketing flavor to European economic life.

The Crusades

The rise of the itinerant merchant and the town were two great factors in the slow evolution of a market society out of medieval economic life; a third factor was the Crusades.

It is ironic that the Crusades, the supreme religious adventure of the Middle Ages, should have contributed so much toward the establishment of a society to which the Church was vigorously opposed. If we consider the Crusades, however, not from the

---

[3]George Gordon Coulton, *Medieval Panorama* (New York: World Publishing, Medidian Books, 1955), p. 285.

point of view of their religious impulse, but simply as great expeditions of exploration and colonization, their economic impact becomes much more understandable.[4]

The Crusades served to bring into sudden and startling contact two very different worlds. One was the still slumbering society of European feudalism with all its rural inertia, its aversion to trade, and its naïve conceptions of business; the other was the brilliant society of Byzantium and Venice, with its urban vitality, its unabashed enjoyment of money-making, and its sophisticated business ways. The crusaders, coming from their draughty castles and boring manorial routines, thought they would find in the East only untutored heathen savages. They were astonished to be met by a people far more civilized, infinitely more luxurious, and much more money-oriented than they.

One result was that the simple-minded crusaders found themselves the pawns of commercial interests that they little understood. During the first three Crusades, the Venetians, who provided ships, gulled them as shamelessly as country bumpkins at a fair. The fact that they were fleeced, however, did not prevent the crusaders from reaching the Holy Land, albeit with inconclusive results. However, in the notorious Fourth Crusade (1202–1204), Dandolo, the wiley 94-year-old doge of Venice, managed to subvert the entire religious expedition into a gigantic plundering operation for Venetian profit.

First, Dandolo held up the voyagers for an initial transportation price of 85,000 silver marks, an enormous sum for the unmoneyed nobility to scrape up. Then, when the funds had been found, he refused to carry out his bargain until the crusaders agreed first to attack the town of Zara, a rich commercial rival of Venice. Because Zara was a Christian, not an "infidel," community, Pope Innocent III was horrified and suggested that the attack be directed instead against heathen Egypt. But Egypt was one of Venice's best customers, and this horrified Dandolo even more. The crusaders, stranded and trapped, had no choice: Zara soon fell—after which, at Dandolo's urging, Christian Constantinople was also sacked. The "heathen" Orient was never reached at all, but Venice profited marvelously.

It was not only Venice that gained, however. The economic impact on the crusaders themselves was much more formidable than the religious. On many, this impact was disastrous: Knights who had melted down their silver plate to join the Crusades came back penniless to their ruined manor houses. To others, however, the Crusades brought a new economic impetus. When in 1101, for example, the Genoese raided Caesarea, a Palestinian seaport, 8,000 soldiers and sailors reaped a reward of some 48 solidi each, plus 2 pounds of pepper—and 8,000 petty capitalists were born.[5] In 1204 when Constantinople fell, not only did each knight receive 20 marks in silver as his share of the booty, but even the squires and archers were rewarded with a few marks each.

The Crusades provided an immense fertilizing experience for Europe. The old, landed basis of wealth came into contact with a new moneyed basis that proved much more powerful. Indeed, the old conception of life itself was forcibly revised before a glimpse of an existence not only wealthier, but gayer and more vital. As a means of shaking a sluggish society out of its rut, the Crusades played an immense role in speeding the economic transformation of Europe.

---

[4]We might note some of the complex interaction of the process we are watching. The Crusades were not only a cause of European economic development, but also a symptom of the development that had previously taken place.

[5]*Cambridge Economic History of Europe*, II, p. 306.

Growth of National Power

Another factor in the slow commercialization of economic life was the gradual amalgamation of Europe's fragmented economic and political entities into larger wholes. As the disintegration of economic life following the breakup of the old Roman Empire had shown, a strong economic society requires a strong and broad political base. As political Europe began its slow process of reknitting, once again its economic tempo began to rise.

One of the most striking characteristics of the Middle Ages, and one of its most crippling obstacles to economic development, was the medieval compartmentalization of authority. Over a journey of 100 miles, a traveling merchant might fall under a dozen different sovereignties, each with different rules, regulations, laws, weights, measures, and money. Worse yet, at each border there was apt to be a toll station. At the turn of the thirteenth and fourteenth centuries, there were said to have been more than 30 toll stations along the Weser River and at least 35 along the Elbe; along the Rhine, a century later, there were more than 60 such toll stations, mostly belonging to local ecclesiastical princes. Thomas Eykes, an English chronicler, described the system as "the raving madness of the Teutons." But it was not only a German disease. There were so many toll stations along the Seine in France in the late fifteenth century that it cost half its final selling price to ship grain 200 miles down the river.[6] Indeed, among the European nations, England alone enjoyed an internally unified market during the middle and late Middle Ages. This was one powerful contributory factor to England's emergence as the first great European economic power.

The amalgamation of Europe's fragmented markets was essentially a political as well as an economic process; it followed the gradual centralization of power that changed the map of Europe from the infinite complexity of the tenth century to the more or less "modern" map of the sixteenth. Here, once again, the burgeoning towns played a central and crucial role. It was the city burghers who became the allies of the nascent monarchies, thereby disassociating themselves still further from their local feudal lords while, in turn, supplying the shaky monarchs with an absolutely essential prerequisite for kingship: cash.

Monarch and bourgeois combined to bring about the slow growth of centralized governments. From centralized government, in turn, came not only a unification of law and money but a direct stimulus to the development of commerce and industry, as well. In France, for example, manufacturing was promoted by royal patronage of the famous Gobelin tapestry and Sèvres porcelain works, and business was created for innumerable craftsmen and artisans by the demands of the royal palaces and banquet halls. In other fields, growing national power also imparted a new encouragement: Navies had to be built; armies had to be equipped; and these new "national" armed forces, many of whom were mercenaries, had to be paid. All this set into faster motion the pumps of monetary circulation.

Exploration

Another economic impetus given by the gradual consolidation of political power was the official encouragement of exploration. Through the long years of the Middle Ages, a few intrepid adventurers, like Marco Polo, had beaten their way to remote regions in

---

[6]*Cambridge Economic History of Europe*, II, pp. 134–135.

search of a short route to the fabled riches of India; by the early fourteenth century, the route to the Far East was well enough known so that silk from China cost but half the price of that from the Caspian area, only half the distance away.

However, the network of all these hazardous and brave penetrations beyond Europe formed only the thinnest of spiderwebs. There still remained the systematic exploration of the unknown, and this awaited the kingly support of state adventurers. Columbus and Vasco da Gama, Cabral and Magellan did not venture on their epoch-making journeys as individual merchants (although they all hoped to make their fortunes thereby) but as adventurers in fleets bought with, and equipped by, royal money, bearing the royal mark of approval, and sent forth in hope of additions to the royal till.

The economic consequences of those amazing adventures were incalculably great. For one thing, they opened up an invigorating flow of precious metals into Europe. Gold and silver, coming from the great Spanish mines in Mexico and Peru, were slowly redistributed to other nations as Spain paid in gold specie for goods it bought abroad. As a result, prices rose throughout Europe—between 1520 and 1650 alone, it is estimated that they doubled and quadrupled, bringing about both stimulus and stress to industry but setting in motion a great wave of speculation and commerce.

In addition, of course, the longer-run results of exploration brought an economic stimulus of still greater importance. The establishment of colonies in the sixteenth and seventeenth centuries and the subsequent enjoyment of trade with the New World provided a tremendous boost in propelling Europe into a bustling commercial society. The discovery of the New World was, from the beginning, a catalytic and revolutionizing influence on the Old.

Change in Religious Climate

The forces of change that we have thus far summarized were actually visible. At any time during the long transition from a nonmarket into a market society, we could have witnessed the traveling merchants, the expanding towns, the Crusades, the evidence of a growing national power, the far-flung explorations. Yet these were not the only forces that undermined the feudal system and brought into being its commercial successor. There were, as well, powerful but invisible currents of change, currents that affected the intellectual atmosphere, the beliefs, and the attitudes of Europe. One of these, of special importance, was a change in the religious climate of the times.

In the previous chapter, we saw how deeply the Catholic Church was imbued with theological aversions to the principle of gain—and especially to interest-taking or usury. An amusing story of the times sums up the position of the Church very well. Humbertus de Romanis, a Monk, tells of someone who found a devil in every nook and cranny of a Florentine cloister, although in the marketplace he found but one. The reason, Humbertus explains, was that it took only one to corrupt a marketplace, whereas every man harbored a devil in his own heart.[7] In such a disapproving climate, it was hard for the commercial side of life to thrive.

To be sure, for all its fulminations against gain and usury, the Church itself grew in time to a position of commanding economic importance. Through its tithes and benefices, it was the largest collector and distributor of money in all of Europe; in an age in which banks and safe deposit boxes did not exist, it was the repository of much

---

[7]Miriam Beard, *A History of the Business Man* (New York: Macmillan, 1938), p. 160.

feudal wealth. Some of its suborders, such as the Knights Templar, became immensely wealthy and served as banking institutions, lending to needy monarchs on stiff terms. Nonetheless, all this faintly disreputable activity was undertaken despite, and not because of, the Church's deepest convictions. For behind the ecclesiastical disapproval of wealth-seeking was a deep-seated theological conviction, a firm belief in the transient nature of this life on earth and the importance of preparing for the Eternal Morrow. The Church lifted its eyes and sought to lift the eyes of others above the daily struggle for existence. It strove to minimize the importance of life on earth and to denigrate the earthly activities to which an all-too-weak flesh succumbed.

Calvinism

What changed this dampening influence on the zest of wealth-making? According to the theories of the German sociologist Max Weber and the English economic historian R. H. Tawney, the underlying cause lay in the rise of a new theological point of view contained in the teachings of the Protestant reformer John Calvin (1509–1564).

Calvinism was a harsh religious philosophy. Its core was a belief in *predestination*—the idea that from the beginning God had chosen the saved and the damned and that nothing man could do on earth could alter that inviolable writ. Furthermore, according to Calvin, the number of the damned exceeded by a vast amount the number of the saved, so that for the average person the chances were great that this earthly prelude was but the momentary grace given before eternal Hell and Damnation commenced.

Perhaps only a man of Calvin's iron will could have borne life under such a sentence. We soon find that in the hands of his followers in the Lowlands and England, the inexorable and inscrutable quality of the original doctrine began to be softened. Although the idea of predestination was still preached, it was now allowed that in the tenor of one's worldly life there was a hint of what was to follow. Therefore, the English and Dutch divines taught that whereas even the saintliest-seeming man might end in Hell, the frivolous or wanton one was certainly headed there. Only in a blameless life lay the slightest chance of demonstrating that Salvation was still a possibility.

The Calvinists urged a life of rectitude, severity, and, most important of all, diligence. In contrast to the Catholic theologians, who tended to look upon worldly activity as vanity, the Calvinists sanctified and approved of endeavor as a kind of index of spiritual worth. Indeed, in Calvinist hands there grew up the idea of a man dedicated to his work: "called" to it, as it were. The fervid pursuit of one's calling, far from evidencing a distraction from religious ends, came to be taken as evidence of a dedication to a religious life. The energetic merchant was, in Calvinist eyes, a *godly* man, not an ungodly one; from this identification of work and worth, it was not long before the notion grew that the more successful a man was, the more worthy he was. Calvinism provided a religious atmosphere that, in contrast to Catholicism, encouraged wealth-seeking and the temper of a businesslike world.

Perhaps even more important than its encouragement of seeking wealth was the influence of Calvinism on the *use* of wealth. The prevailing attitude of the prosperous Catholic merchants had been that the aim of worldly success was the enjoyment of a life of ease and luxury; Catholic nobility displayed on occasion a positively grotesque disdain for wealth. In an orgy of gambling that gripped Paris at the end of the seventeenth century, a prince who sent his mistress a diamond worth 5,000 livres had it pulverized and strewn over her reply when she rejected it as being too small. The same prince eventually gambled away an income of 600,000 livres a year. A *maréchal* whose grandson turned up his nose at a gift of a purse of gold threw it into the street: "Let the street cleaner have it then."[8]

The Calvinist manufacturer or trader had a very different attitude toward wealth. If his religion approved of diligence, it most emphatically did not approve of indulgence. Wealth was to be accumulated and put to good use, not frittered away.

The Protestant Ethic

Calvinism promoted an aspect of economic life of which we have hitherto heard very little: thrift. It made saving, the conscious abstinence from the enjoyment of income, a virtue. It made investment, the use of saving for productive purposes, an instrument of piety as well as profit. It even condoned, with various *quids* and *quos,* the payment of interest. In fact, Calvinism fostered a new conception of economic life. In place of the old ideal of social and economic stability, of knowing and keeping one's "place," it brought respectability to an ideal of struggle, of material improvement, of economic growth.

Economic historians still debate the precise degree of influence that may properly be attributed to "the Protestant Ethic" in bringing about the rise of a new gain-centered worldly philosophy. After all, there was nothing much that a Dutch Calvinist would have been able to teach an Italian Catholic banker about the virtues of a businesslike approach to life. However, looking back on the subsequent course of economic progress, it is striking that without exception it was the Protestant countries with their "Puritan streak" of work and thrift that forged ahead in the economic race. As one of the powerful winds of change of the sixteenth and seventeenth centuries, the new religious outlook must be counted as a highly favorable stimulus for the evolution of the market society.

Breakdown of the Manorial System

The enumeration of all these currents does not exhaust the catalog of forces bearing against the old fixed economic order in Europe. The list could be expanded and greatly refined.[9] Yet, with all due caution, we can now begin to comprehend the immense coalition of events—some as specific as the Crusades, some as diffuse as a change in religious ideals—that jointly cooperated to destroy the medieval framework of economic life and to prepare the way for a new dynamic framework of market transactions.

One important aspect of this profound alteration was the gradual monetization of feudal obligations. In locality after locality, we can trace the conversion of the old feudal payments in *kind*—the days of labor or chickens or eggs a lord received from his tenants—into payments of *money* dues and money rents with which they now discharged their obligations to him.

---

[8]Werner Sombart, *Luxury and Capitalism* (New York: Columbia University Press, 1938), pp. 120ff. Also Thirion, *La Vie Privée des Financiers au XVIIIe Siècle* (Paris: 1895), p. 292.

[9]An extremely important influence (to which we will turn in our next chapter) was the rise of a new interest in technology, founded on scientific inquiry into natural events. Another important causative factor was the development of modern business concepts and techniques. The German economic historian Werner Sombart has said that if he were forced to give a single date for the "beginning" of modern capitalism, he would choose 1202, the year in which appeared the *Liber Abaci,* a primer of commercial arithmetic. Similarly, the historian Oswald Spengler has called the invention of double-entry bookkeeping in 1494 an achievement worthy of being ranked with that of Columbus or Copernicus.

A number of causes lay behind this commutation of feudal payments. One was the growing urban demand for food, as town and city populations began to swell. In concentric circles around the town, money filtered out into the countryside, simultaneously raising the capacity of the rural sector to buy urban goods and whetting its desire to do so. At the same time, in a search for larger cash incomes to buy a widening variety of goods, the nobility looked with increasing favor on receiving its rents and dues in money rather than in kind. In so doing, however, it unwittingly set into motion a cause for the further serious deterioration of the manorial system. Usually, the old feudal services were converted into fixed sums of money payments. This temporarily eased the cash position of the lord but soon placed him in the squeeze that always hurts the creditor in times of inflation. When dues were not fixed, rents and money dues lagged sufficiently behind the growing monetary needs of the nobility so that still further feudal obligations were magnetized to keep the lord in cash. But as prices rose and the monetized lifestyle expanded still further, these too failed to keep him solvent. This process of economic decline was considerably hastened by the ineptitude of the nobility as managers of their estates. The descendants of the crusaders were not much more businesslike than their ancestors.

The result was that the rural nobility, which now depended increasingly on rents and dues for its income, steadily lost its economic power. Indeed, beginning in the sixteenth century, we find a new class coming into being—the impoverished nobility. In the year 1530 in the Gevaudan district of France, 121 lords had an aggregate income of 21,400 livres, but one of these seigneurs accounted for 5,000 livres of the sum, another for 2,000—and the rest averaged but a mean 121 livres apiece.[10] In fact, the shortage of cash afflicted not only the lesser nobility but even the monarchy itself. Maximilian I, Emperor of the Holy Roman Empire, on occasion lacked the cash to pay for even the overnight lodgings of his entourage on tour; when two of his grandchildren married children of the King of Hungary, all the trappings of the weddings—2,000 caparisoned horses, jewels, and gold and silver plate—were borrowed from merchant bankers to whom Maximilian had written wheedling letters begging them not to forsake him in his moment of need.

Rise of the Cash Economy

Clearly, the manorial system was incompatible with a cash economy; although the nobility was pinched between rising prices and costs and static incomes, the merchant classes, to whom cash naturally gravitated, steadily increased their power. In the Gevaudan district, for example, where the richest lord had his income of 5,000 livres, the richest town merchants had incomes up to 65,000 livres. In Italy, the Gianfigliazzi of Florence, who began as "nobodies" lending money to the Bishop of Fiesole, ended up stripping him of his possessions and leaving him a pauper; in Tuscany, the descendants of lords who looked down their noses at usurers in the tenth century lost their estates to them in the twelfth and thirteenth. In Germany, while Maximilian scratched for cash, the great banking families of Augsburg commanded incomes far larger than Maximilian's entire kingly revenue. All over Europe men of no social standing turned the monetary economy to good account. One Jean Amici of Toulouse made a fortune in English booty during the Hundred Years War; Guillaume de St.-Yon grew rich by

---

[10]*Cambridge Economic History of Europe*, I, 557–558.

selling meat at rapacious prices to Paris; and Jacques Coeur, the most extraordinary figure of all, rose from merchant to King's coiner, then to King's purchasing agent, then to financier not for, but *of,* the King, during the course of which he accumulated a huge fortune, estimated at 27 million écus.[11]

APPEARANCE OF THE ECONOMIC ASPECT OF LIFE

Behind all these profoundly disturbing events, we can discern an immense process of change that literally revolutionized the economic organization of Europe. Whereas in the tenth century, cash and money transactions were only peripheral to the solution of the economic problem, by the sixteenth and seventeenth centuries, cash and money transactions were already beginning to provide the very molecular force of economic cohesion.

But over and above this general monetization of life, another and perhaps even more profound change was taking place. This was the emergence of a separate economic sphere of activity visible within, and separable from, the surrounding matrix of social life. It was the creation of a whole aspect of society that had never previously existed but was thenceforth to constitute a commanding facet of human existence.[12]

In antiquity and feudal times, one could not easily separate the economic motivations or even the economic actions of the great mass of humankind from the normal round of existence itself. The peasant following his immemorial ways was hardly conscious of acting according to "economic" motives; indeed, he did not—he heeded the orders of his lord or the dictates of custom. Nor was the lord himself economically oriented. His interests were military or political or religious, and not basically oriented toward the idea of gain or increase. Even in the towns, as we have seen, the conduct of ordinary business was inextricably mixed with noneconomic concerns. The undeniable fact that men were acquisitive, not to say avaricious, did not yet impart its flavor to life in general; the making of money, as we have been at some pains to indicate, was a tangential rather than a central concern of ancient or medieval existence.

Labor, Land, and Capital Come into Being

With the ever-widening scope of monetization, however, a genuinely new element of life came slowly to the fore. Labor, for example, emerged as an activity quite different from what it was in the past. No longer was "labor" part of an explicit social relationship in which one man (serf or apprentice) worked for another (lord or guildmaster) in return for at least an assurance of subsistence. Labor was now a mere quantum of effort, a "commodity" to be disposed of in the marketplace for the best price it could bring, quite devoid of any reciprocal responsibilities on the part of the buyer, beyond the payment of wages. If those wages were not enough to provide subsistence—well, that was not the buyer's responsibility. He had bought his "labor," and that was that.

This emergence of "abstract" labor—labor as a quantity of effort detached from a man's life and bought on the market in fixed amounts—had a parallel in two other main elements of economic life. One of these was land. Formerly conceived as the territory

---

[11]Note, however, that Coeur eventually fell from power, was imprisoned, and died in exile. The countinghouse was not yet fully master of the castle.

[12]The following section owes much to the insights of Karl Polanyi's famous *The Great Transformation* (Boston: Beacon Press, 1957, paperback ed.), Part II.

of a great lord, as inviolable as the territory of a modern nation-state, land was now also seen in its economic aspect as something to be bought or leased for the economic return it yielded. An estate that was once the core of political and administrative power became a "property" with a market price, available for any number of uses, even as a site for a factory. The dues, the payments in kind, the intangibles of prestige and power that once had flowed from the ownership of land gave way to the single return of rent; that is, to a money return derived from putting land to profitable use.

The same transformation became true of property. As it was conceived in antiquity and throughout most of the Middle Ages, property was a sum of tangible wealth, a hoard, a treasury of plate, bullion, or jewels. Very logically, it was realized in the form of luxurious homes, in castles and armaments, in costly robes and trappings. However, with the monetization and commercialization of society, property, too, became expressible in a monetary equivalent: A man was now "worth" so many livres, or écus, or pounds, or whatever. Property became capital, manifesting itself no longer in specific goods, but as an abstract sum of infinitely flexible use whose "value" was its capacity to earn interest or profits.

None of these changes, it should be emphasized, was planned, clearly foreseen, or for that matter, welcomed. It was not with equanimity that the feudal hierarchies saw their prerogatives nibbled away by the mercantile classes. Neither did the tradition-preserving guildmaster desire his own enforced metamorphosis into a "capitalist," a man of affairs guided by market signals and beset by competition. But perhaps for no social class was the transition more painful than for the peasant, caught up in a process of history that dispossessed him from his livelihood and made him a landless laborer.

Enclosures

This process, which was particularly important in England, was the *enclosure movement,* a by-product of the monetization of feudal life. Starting as early as the thirteenth century, the landed aristocracy, increasingly squeezed for cash, began to view its estates not merely as ancestral fiefs but as potential sources of cash revenue. In order to raise larger cash crops, lords therefore began to "enclose" the pasture that had previously been deemed "common land." Communal grazing fields, which had in fact always belonged to the lord despite their communal use, were now claimed for the exclusive benefit of the lord and turned into sheepwalks. Why sheepwalks? Because a rising demand for woolen cloth was making sheep-raising a highly profitable occupation. The medieval historian Eileen Power writes:

> The visitor to the House of Lords, looking respectfully upon that august assembly, cannot fail to be struck by a stout and ungainly object facing the throne—an ungainly object upon which in full session of Parliament, he will observe seated the Lord Chancellor of England. The object is a woolsack, and it is stuffed as full of pure history as the office of the Lord Chancellor itself. . . . The Lord Chancellor of England is seated upon a woolsack because it was upon a woolsack that this fair land rose to prosperity.[13]

---

[13]Eileen Power, *Medieval People* (Garden City, N.Y.: Doubleday, Anchor Books, 1954), p. 125.

The enclosure process in England proceeded at an irregular pace over the long centuries; not until the late eighteenth and early nineteenth centuries did it reach its engulfing climax.[14] By its end, some 10 million acres, nearly half the arable land of England, had been "enclosed"—in its early Tudor days by the more or less highhanded conversion of the "commons" to sheep-raising; in the final period, by the forcible consolidation of strips and plots into tracts suitable for commercial farming, for which tenants presumably received "fair compensation."

From a strictly economic point of view, the enclosure movement was unquestionably salutary in that it brought into productive employment land that had hitherto yielded only a pittance. Indeed, particularly in the eighteenth and nineteenth centuries, enclosure was the means by which England "rationalized" its agriculture and finally escaped from the inefficiency of the traditional manorial strip system. But there was another, crueler side to enclosure. As the common fields were enclosed, it became ever more difficult for the tenant to support himself. In the fifteenth and sixteenth centuries, when the initial enclosure of the commons reached its peak, as many as three-fourths to nine-tenths of the tenants of some estates were simply turned off the farm. Whole hamlets were thus wiped out. Sir Thomas More described it savagely in Book I of his *Utopia*:

> Your sheep that were wont to be so meek and tame, and so small eaters, now, as I hear say, be become so great devourers and so wild, that they eat up and swallow down the very men themselves. They consume, destroy and devour whole fields, houses and cities. For look in what parts of the realm doth grow the finest, and therefore dearest wool, there noblemen and gentlemen, yea and certain abbots, holy men God wot, not contenting themselves with the yearly revenues and profits that were wont to grow to their forefathers and predecessors of their land . . . leave no ground for tillage, they enclose all into pastures, they throw down houses, they pluck down towns and leave nothing standing, but only the church to make of it a sheep house. . . .

The enclosure process provided a powerful force for the dissolution of feudal ties and the formation of the new relationships of a market society. By dispossessing the peasant, it created a new kind of labor force—landless, without traditional sources of income, however meager, impelled to find work for wages wherever it might be available.

Emergence of the Proletariat

Together with this agricultural proletariat, we begin to see the emergence of an urban proletariat, partly brought about by a gradual transformation of guilds into more "businesslike" firms, partly by the immigration into the cities of some of the new landless peasantry. To exacerbate the situation, from the middle of the eighteenth century, a rising population (itself traceable in large measure to the increase in food output resulting from the enclosures) began to pour growing numbers into the labor market. As a result of this complicated interplay of causes and effects, we find England plagued with the problem of the "wandering poor." One not untypical proposal of the eighteenth century was that they be confined in what a reformer candidly termed "Houses of Terror."

---

[14]In other European nations, an enclosure process also took place, but at a much slower pace. In France, Italy, and southern Germany, the small-holder peasant persisted long after he had virtually ceased to exist in England; in northeastern Germany, on the other hand, the small peasant was deprived of his holdings and turned into a landless proletarian.

The emergence of a market-oriented system brought into being a "labor force," and though the process of adjustment for other classes of society was not so brutal, it, too, extracted its social price. Tenaciously the guildmasters fought against the invasion of their protected trades by manufacturers who trespassed on traditional preserves or who upset established modes of production with new machinery. Doggedly, the landed nobility sought to protect its ancient privileges against the encroachment of the moneyed *nouveaux riches.*

However, the process of economic enlargement, breaking down the established routines of the past, rearranging the power and prestige of all social classes, could not be stopped. Ruthlessly it pursued its historic course and impartially it distributed its historic rewards and sacrifices. Although stretched out over a long period, it was not an evolution but a slow revolution that overtook European economic society. Only when that society had run its gauntlet, suffering one of the most wrenching dislocations of history, would the world of transactions appear "natural" and "normal" and the categories of "land," "labor," and "capital" become so matter-of-fact that it would be difficult to believe they had not always existed.

Factors of Production

As we have seen, it was not at all "natural" and "normal" to have free, wage-earning, contractual labor or rentable, profit-producing land or fluid, investment-seeking capital. They were creations of the great transformation of a premarket into a market society. Economics calls these creations the *factors of production,* and much of economics is concerned with analyzing the manner in which these three basic constituents of the productive process are combined in the market mechanism.

What we must realize at this stage of our inquiry, however, is that "land," "labor," and "capital" do not exist as eternal categories of social organization. Admittedly, they are categories of nature, but these eternal aspects of the productive process—the soil, human effort, and the artifacts that can be applied to production—do not take on, in every society, the specific separation that distinguishes them in a market society. In premarket economies, land, labor, and capital are inextricably mixed and mingled in the figure of slave and serf, lord and guildmaster—none of whom enters the production process as the incarnation of a specific economic function offered for a price. The slave is not a "worker," the guildmaster is not a "capitalist," nor is the lord a "landlord." *Only when a social system has evolved in which labor is sold, land is rented, and capital is freely invested do we find the categories of economics emerging from the flux of life.*

Nowhere do we see this astonishing social process more clearly illustrated than in the evolution of the concept of property in humankind itself. In ancient society, as we have seen, people owned people. That is, a slave was literally the chattel of his or her owner, to be used, abused, or even put to death under certain circumstances. In the Middle Ages, this idea of human property evolved into the concept of serfdom. A serf was also the property of his or her master and subject to the ties and bonds we have discussed, but the ownership was not so all-embracing and entailed reciprocal obligations on the part of the lord.

Finally, we reach modern commercial society, in which each person has property in himself or herself. A worker who has become a "factor of production" owns his own labor, which he or she is free to sell as advantageously as possible, something that no slave or serf could do. At the same time, the free worker, who is no man's property, is also no man's obligation. The employer buys his or her employees' labor, not their lives. All responsibility for the laborer ends when he or she leaves his or her employer's office or factory, which is the owner's "property."

Wage Labor and Capitalism

The employer also gains a unique economic advantage when labor becomes a commodity offered for sale. In exchange for buying labor power for a payment called a *wage,* the employer becomes entitled to all the output that "his" workers produce. To put it differently, men and women who enter into a waged relationship with their employers give up all claims to any output they will create while fulfilling their labor stint.

Waged (or salaried) labor is so normal a part of modern market society that it always comes as a surprise to reflect on the curious arrangement under which labor power is sold without any rights of ownership in its product. However, consider for a moment who owns the cars coming off an assembly line. Is it the working force that has made them? The engineers who have designed them? The managers who have superintended the production process? The president of the company or its stockholders? The answer is that none of these persons owns the cars. Even the president of General Motors, or the biggest stockholder in the company, cannot lay claim to a vehicle coming off the line, without paying for it.

Who, then, does own the cars? Any worker or manager can tell you: They are "company property." That means they are owned by the company, the fictive legal "person" who employs the president, the managers, and the engineers, as well as the workers. The stockholders legally own and control the company, but it is the company itself that enters into the wage contract, and, therefore, it is the company that owns the cars. In a simpler establishment run by a single proprietor—say, a bakery—we see the same thing when the boss takes home baked products without paying for them because—as he says, perfectly correctly—they *belong* to him.

The wage contract, therefore, becomes a critical landmark, identifying a new kind of economic society, organized along entirely different lines from the older lord-and-peasant or master-and-apprentice arrangements. In these older societies, surplus had taken the form of great monuments or edifices or luxuries that had gone directly into the hands of the ruling classes, where they remained, or were used, as objects of prestige. In the new capitalist form, the surplus generated by society—that is, all wealth over and above that needed to replenish the working force and the other factors of production—accrued to the employer-capitalist.

Two changes attended this shift in surplus allocation. First, the surplus now took the much humbler forms of commodities produced in workshops, farms, or nascent factories, rather than impressive monuments, courtly trappings, and the like. Second, the commodities, unlike those monuments and trappings, had to be sold before they counted as "wealth."

The emergence of capitalism, with its central wage-labor relationship, signaled much more than a change in ruling classes, from aristocrats to capitalists. It signaled as well a new meaning for wealth: as commodities for sale, not as objects for display. Unlike the pyramids, cathedrals, and edifices of previous societies, the wealth of capitalism had no status until it was "realized" on the marketplace. This necessity for sale introduced a new note of urgency, a nervous intensity, into the economic life of capitalism.

In a word, capitalism was more than just a change in social institutions; it was also a completely new economic order.

Capitalism and the Profit Motive

Much of this book is concerned with examining how this new order works—what problems inhere in its complicated process of commodity production and sale. This takes us to an examination of the changing institutional forms that capitalism has created, as well as into an inquiry into some of the economic mechanisms by which the system works.

But it is useful to focus immediately on one aspect of capitalism that would occupy a central and indispensable place in its scheme of things. This was a new form of behavior that capitalism generalized throughout society: a drive to maximize income (as the economists would describe it) by concluding the best possible bargain on the marketplace into which everyone ventured, either to sell his or her labor power or other resources, or to purchase goods. In the language of business, the same behavioral drive was described as the *profit motive*.

The market society had not, of course, invented this motive. Perhaps it did not even intensify it. But it did make it a ubiquitous and necessitous aspect of social behavior. Although men may have felt acquisitive during the Middle Ages or antiquity, they did not enter en masse into market transactions for the basic economic activities of their livelihoods. When, for instance, a peasant sold his few eggs at the town market, rarely was the transaction a matter of overriding importance for his continued existence. Market transactions in a fundamentally nonmarket society were a subsidiary activity, a means of supplementing a livelihood that, however sparse, was largely independent of buying or selling.

With the monetization of labor, land, and capital, however, transactions became universal and critical activities. Now everything was for sale, and terms of transactions were anything but subsidiary to existence itself. To a man who sold his labor on a market, in a society that assumed no responsibility for his upkeep, the price at which he concluded his bargain was all-important. So it was with the landlord and the budding capitalist. For each of these a good bargain could spell riches—and a bad one, ruin. The pattern of economic maximization was generalized throughout society and given an inherent urgency that made it a powerful force for shaping human behavior. The drive to maximize income became a new mode of social coordination and control.

THE INVENTION OF ECONOMICS

The new market society did more than merely bring about an environment in which men were not only free, but *forced,* to follow their self-interest. It also brought a puzzle of great importance and considerable difficulty. The puzzle was to understand the workings of a world in which profit-seeking persons were no longer constrained to follow the ways of their forefathers or to shape their economic activities according to the dictates of a ruling lord or king.

The "Philosophy" of Trade

The new order needed a "philosophy"—a reasoned explanation of how such a society would hang together, would "work." Such a philosophy was by no means self-evident. In many ways, the new world of profit-seeking persons appeared as perplexing and fraught with dangers to its contemporaries as it did to the imaginary leaders of a traditional society to whom we described it in our first chapter.

It is not surprising that the philosophers of trade disagreed. In England, a group of pamphleteers and merchants, the so-called Mercantilists, put forward an explanation of economic society that stressed the importance of gold and extolled the role of the merchant, whose activities were most likely to bring "treasure" into the state by selling goods to foreigners. In France, a school of thinkers we call the *Physiocrats* held quite different ideas. They exalted the virtues of the farmer, not the merchant. All wealth ultimately came from nature's bounty, the Physiocrats argued, dismissing merchants and even manufacturers as belonging to a "sterile" class that added nothing to the wealth produced by the farmer. Labor was assumed to be poor, although not necessarily "wretched."

With such diverse views, it is obvious that nothing like unanimity prevailed concerning proper economic policy. Should competition be regulated or left alone? Should the export of gold be prohibited, or should "treasure" be permitted to enter or leave the kingdom as the currents of trade dictated? Should agricultural producers be taxed because they were the ultimate source of all wealth, or should taxes fall on the prosperous merchant class? The answers to these perplexing questions awaited the advent of Adam Smith (1723–1790), patron saint of our discipline and a figure of towering intellectual stature. His masterwork, *The Wealth of Nations*, published in 1776, the year of the American Revolution, gave to the Western world the first full account of something it dearly wanted to know—how its own economic mechanism worked.

Division of Labor

The world that Smith described was very different from our own. It was a world of very small enterprises: Smith's famous description of a pin factor involves a manufacturing establishment that employs 10 people. It was still hampered by medieval guild restrictions: In Smith's time, no master hatter in England could employ more than two apprentices; in the famous Sheffield silver trade, no master cutler could employ more than one. Still more important, it was a world in which government-protected monopolies were accorded to certain fields of commerce, such as the trade with the East Indies. However, for all the differences from modern economic society, the basic vision that Smith gave to his time can still elucidate the tasks of economics in our own time.

Two main problems occupied Smith's attention. The first is implicit in the title of the book. This is Smith's theory of the most important tendency of a society of "perfect liberty"—its tendency to grow.[15]

Economic growth—that is, the steady increase in the output of goods and services enjoyed by a society—was hardly a concern for philosophers of tradition-bound societies, or even of societies ruled by imperial-minded emperors. But what Smith discerned amid the seeming turmoil of a market society was a hidden mechanism that would

---

[15]By "perfect liberty," Smith emphasized that all agents in such a society were free to enter, or not to enter, into economic arrangements such as the wage contract, in sharp contrast to the *obligations* imposed on serfs and slaves. That "liberty" may not have appeared very precious to the "freely contracting" owner of labor in a London slum. Nonetheless, there was a difference—a legal difference, not yet invented in his time—that Smith correctly identified as crucial for the system of capitalism. Incidentally, *capitalism* was a word even Karl Marx used only once or twice.

operate to enlarge the "wealth of nations"—at any rate, those nations that enjoyed a system of perfect liberty and did not tamper with it.

What was it that drove society to increase its riches? Basically, it was the tendency of such a society to encourage a steady rise in the *productivity* of its labor, so that, over time, the same number of working people could turn out a steadily larger output.

And what lay behind the rise in productivity? The answer, according to Smith, was the gain in productiveness that was to be had by achieving an ever-finer *division of labor.* Here Smith's famous pin factory serves as an example:

> One man draws out the wire, another straits it, a third cuts it, a fourth points it, a fifth grinds it at the top for receiving the head; to make the head requires two or three distinct operations; to put it on is a peculiar business; to whiten it is another; it is even a trade by itself to put them into paper. . . . I have seen a small manufactory of this kind where ten men only were employed and where some of them consequently performed two or three distinct operations. But though they were poor, and therefore but indifferently accommodated with the necessary machinery, they could, when they exerted themselves, make among them about twelve pounds of pins in a day. There are in a pound upwards of four thousand pins of middling size. Those ten persons, therefore, could make among them upwards of forty-eight thousand pins in a day. . . . But if they had all wrought separately and independently . . .they could certainly not each of them make twenty, perhaps not one pin in a day.

Adam Smith's Growth Model

This begins to unravel the reasons why a society of free enterprise tends to grow. But it does not fully explain the phenomenon. For what is it that drives such a society to a division of labor? How do we know that the tendency to growth will not peter out, for one reason or another?

This leads us to the larger picture that Smith had in mind. We would call it a "growth model," although Smith used no such modern term himself. What we mean by this is that Smith shows us both a propulsive force that will put society on an upward growth path and a self-correcting mechanism that will keep it there.

First the driving force. One of the fundamental building blocks of Smith's conception of human nature was what he called the "desire for betterment"—what we have already described as the profit motive. What does the desire for betterment have to do with growth? The answer is very important: *It impels every manufacturer to expand his or her business in order to increase his or her profits.*

How does this business expansion result in a higher division of labor? The answer is very neat. The main road to profit consists in equipping workers with the necessary machinery that Smith mentions in his description of the pin factory, for it is this machinery that will increase their productivity. Therefore, the path to growth lies in what Smith called *accumulation,* or in more modern terminology, the process of *capital investment.* As capitalists seek money, they invest in machines and equipment. As a result of the machines and equipment, their workers can produce more. Because they produce more, society's output grows.

The Dynamics of the System

This answers the first part of our query. However, there is still the question of how we know that society will continue to grow, that its trajectory will not flatten out. Here we come to the cleverest part of Smith's model. At first look, it might seem as if the drive to increase capital investments would be self-defeating. The steady increase in the demand for workers to run the new machines would drive up their wages; as wages rose, they would cut into the manufacturer's profits. In turn, as profits were eaten away, the very source of new investment would evaporate, and the growth curve would soon level off.

Not so, according to Smith. To be sure, the rising demand for workers *would* tend to drive up wages, but this was only half the picture. The same upward tendency of wages would also tend to increase the supply of workers. The reason is not implausible. In Smith's day, infant mortality was shockingly high: "It is not uncommon," Smith remarked, ". . . in the Highlands of Scotland for a mother who has borne twenty children not to have two alive." But as wages rose, infant and child mortality would tend to diminish, and therefore more of the population would survive to working age (10 or younger in Smith's day).

The outcome must already be clear. Along with an increase in the demand for workers (and working children) comes an increase in their supply. This increase in the number of available workers meant that the competition for jobs would increase. Therefore, the price of labor would *not* rise, at least not enough to choke further growth. Like a vast self-regulating machine, the mechanism of capital accumulation would provide the very thing it needed to continue unhampered: a force to prevent wages from eating up profits. The growth process could go on undisturbed.

We will not concern ourselves here with the full details of Smith's growth model. Of course, his "model" is not directly applicable to the modern world, where (at least in industrialized nations) most children do not die before they reach working age and where his "safety valve" therefore has no relevance. Nonetheless, in Smith's depiction we get a sense of the imaginative reach and capacity for enlightenment that economic analysis can bring.[16]

The Market Mechanism

The wealth (we would say the output) of nations was not, however, the only major problem on which Smith's treatise threw a clarifying light. There was also the question of how a market system held together, of how it provided an orderly solution to the problems of production and distribution.

This brings us to Smith's description and explanation of the market mechanism. Here Smith begins by elucidating a perplexing problem. The actors in Smith's drama, as we know, are driven by the desire for self-betterment and guided mainly by their

---

[16]It seems necessary to add a word to the student who gets sufficiently interested in Smith's model to look into the *Wealth* itself. The student will look in vain in this vast, discursive book for a clear-cut exposition of the interactions we have just described. The model is implicit in Smith's exposition, but it lies around the text like a disassembled machine, requiring us to put it together in our minds. Nonetheless, it is there, if one fits together the pieces. For a fuller exposition, see R. Heilbroner, *The Essential Adam Smith* (New York: W. W. Norton, 1986).

self-interest. "It is not from the benevolence of the butcher, the brewer or the baker that we expect our dinner," writes Smith, "but from their regard to their self-interest. We address ourselves not to their humanity, but to their self-love, and never talk to them of our necessities, but of their advantages."[17]

The problem here is obvious. How does a market society prevent self-interested, profit-hungry men from holding up their fellow citizens for ransom? How does a socially workable arrangement emerge from such a socially dangerous set of motivations?

The answer introduces us to a central mechanism of a market society, the mechanism of competition. For each person, out to do the best for himself with no thought of others, is faced with a host of similarly motivated persons who are in exactly the same position. Each is only too eager to take advantage of his or her competitor's greed if it urges the competitor to raise his or her price above the level "set" by the market. If a pin manufacturer tried to charge more than its competitors, they would take away its trade; if a worker asked for more than the going wage, he or she would not be able to find work; if a landlord sought to exact a rent steeper than another with land of the same quality, he or she would get no tenants.

The Market and Allocation

But the market mechanism does more than impose a competitive safeguard on the price of products. It also arranges for the production of the right *quantities* of the goods that society desires. Suppose that consumers want more pins than are being turned out and fewer shoes. The public will buy out the existing supply of pins, while business in the shoe stores will be dull. Pin prices will tend to rise as the public scrambles for shrinking supplies, and prices of shoes will tend to fall as merchants try to get rid of their burdensome stocks.

Once again, a restorative force comes into play. As pin prices rise, so will the profits of the pin business, and as shoe prices sag, so will profits in shoemaking. Again, self-interest and the desire for betterment go to work. Pin manufacturers will expand their output to take advantage of higher prices; shoe factories will curtail production to cut their losses. Employers in the pin business will seek to hire more factors of production—more workers, more space, more capital equipment; employers in the shoe business will reduce their use of the factors of production—letting workers go, giving up leases on land, cutting down on their capital investment.

Therefore, pin output will rise and shoe output will fall, *but this is exactly what the public wanted in the first place!* Through what Smith called, in a famous phrase, an "invisible hand," the selfish motives of people are transmuted by the market mechanism to yield the most unexpected of results: social well-being.

The Self-Regulating System

Smith showed that a market system, far from being chaotic and disorderly, is in fact the means by which a solution of the strictest discipline and order is provided for the economic problem.

---

[17]Adam Smith, *The Wealth of Nations* (New York: Modern Library, 1937), p. 14.

First, he explained how the motive of self-interest provides the necessary impetus to set the mechanism to work. Next, he showed how competition prevents any individual person from exacting a price higher than that set by the marketplace. Third, he made clear how the changing desires of society lead producers to increase production of wanted goods and to diminish the production of goods that are no longer as highly desired.

Not least, he showed that the market system is a self-regulating process. The beautiful consequence of a competitive market is that it is its own guardian. If prices or profits or wages stray away from their "natural" levels determined by cost, forces exist to drive them back into line. Therefore, a curious paradox emerges: The competitive market, which is the acme of individual economic freedom, is at the same time the strictest of economic taskmasters. One may appeal the ruling of a planning board or win the dispensation of a minister, but there is no appeal, no dispensation, from the anonymous pressures of the competitive marketplace. Economic freedom is more illusory than it appears. You may do as you please, but if you please to do that which the market disapproves, the price of freedom is ruin.

The Market System and the Rise of Capitalism

Does the market system really work as Smith's great treatise suggests? Much of the rest of this book is devoted to that question—that is, to tracing the growth and the internal order of the system whose prospects Smith's model described so brilliantly. The fact that we have suffered business cycles and depressions, and that giant business firms and labor unions have taken the place of pin factories and child workers, is evidence enough that Smith's model alone will certainly not serve as a dependable guide through economic history. The fact that our economy has grown prodigiously and that it has hung together, despite all its problems, is also evidence that there is an important kernel of truth in Smith's conception.

Let us return to our historical narrative, to see how much of what Smith foresaw came true and how much did not, and for what reasons. *The Wealth of Nations* appeared before capitalism assumed anything like its current industrial guise. After all, serfdom was not formally abolished in Germany until a half century later. Even in Adam Smith's England, the market society had not yet reached the stage in which capitalism achieved full legal and political status. For example, the guild regulations that irked Smith did not vanish until the medieval Statute of Artificers was repealed in 1813. Likewise in France, until the revolution of 1789, an immense web of regulations bound the would-be capitalist. Rules and edicts, many of them seeking to standardize production, laid down the exact number of threads to be woven into the cloths of the French textile manufacturers, and to disregard these laws was to risk pillorying—first for the cloth, then for the manufacturer.

Well into the eighteenth century, we find the great revolution of the market still incomplete; or rather, we find the nearly complete process of monetization and commercialization contained uncomfortably within a frame of legal and social organization not yet fully adapted to it. We will have to observe how capitalism burst through the restrictions of the precapitalist, mercantilist era before we can see Adam Smith's marvelous market mechanism in full operation.

Key Concepts and Key Words

Feudalism

1. *Powerful forces of change* were operative within European feudalism and served gradually to introduce the structure of a market society. Primary among these forces were:

   - The role of the *itinerant merchant* in introducing trade, money, and the acquisitive spirit into feudal life.
   - The *process of urbanization* as a source of economic activity and as the locus of a new, trade-centered seat of power.
   - *The Crusades* as a force for the disruption of feudal life and the introduction of new ideas.
   - The rise of unifying, commerce-supporting *national states.*
   - The stimulus of the *Age of Exploration* and of the *gold* it brought into Europe.
   - The emergence of *new religious ideas* more sympathetic to business activity than Catholicism had been.
   - The *monetization of dues* within the manorial system.

Economic life

2. As a consequence of these forces, we begin to see the *separation of economic from social life.* The processes of production and distribution were no longer indistinguishably melded into the prevailing religious, social, and political customs and practices, but now began to form a sharply distinct area of life in themselves.

Enclosures

3. With the rise of the economic aspect of life, we see *deep-seated transformations* taking place. The peasant-serf is no longer bound to the land but becomes a free mobile laborer; the guildmaster is no longer hobbled by guild rules but becomes an independent entrepreneur; the lord of the land becomes (in the modern sense of the word) a landlord. The transformation was a long and often violent one, especially in the complex case of the *enclosures.*

Factors of production

4. The advent of free laborers, capitalists, and landlords, each selling his or her services on the market for land and capital and labor, made it possible to speak of the *"factors of production."* By this was implied two things: the *physical categories* of land, labor, and capital as distinguishable agents in the production process; and the *social relationships* among laborers, landowners, and capitalists as distinct groups or classes entering the marketplace.

Wage labor

5. Central among these new relationships was that of *wage labor.* In the wage-labor relationship, a worker is paid a wage for his or her labor time, and the ownership of the entire product is vested in the hands of the employer-capitalist.

Wealth in capitalism

6. The emergence of capitalism changes the conception of wealth from objects for display or prestige into commodities that must be brought to market and sold. This necessity to sell introduces a hitherto unknown urgency into the economic system.

Profit motive

7. As part of this process of change, we find the emergence of the *profit motive* at all levels of society, not as an acquisitive drive (which may have existed for centuries), but as the pervasive necessity for all people in a *monetized society* to strive for higher incomes for economic survival.

Adam Smith's Wealth of Nations

8. Along with the new economic society came a new interest in the mechanism of a market society. The greatest of the early economists was *Adam Smith,* author of *The Wealth of Nations.* Essentially a philosopher, Smith turned his powerful and far-ranging inquiry to the understanding of a society of "perfect liberty" (a society of freely contracting agents).

Growth

9. In *Wealth,* Smith describes two attributes of such a society. The first is its *tendency to grow.* Smith shows how growth results from the increase in labor *productivity* that comes from the ever-finer *division of labor.* This enhancement in productivity is

brought about by capitalists' *investment* in *capital equipment* as a means to higher profit.

Self-regulation

10. Smith also describes the *market mechanism.* In this mechanism, *competition* plays a key role in preventing people from exacting whatever price they please from buyers. The *market mechanism* also reveals how changing demands for goods would change the production of goods, to match that demand. Therefore, the capstone of Smith's treatise is the demonstration of the *self-regulating* nature of a competitive market, in which an "invisible hand" brings socially useful ends from selfish and private means.

Questions

1. What activities of the merchant were so disruptive to feudal life? Are business activities today also the causes of social stress?
2. Why is wage labor completely incompatible with feudalism?
3. The underdeveloped nations today often resemble the economies of antiquity or of the Middle Ages, at least insofar as their poverty and stagnation are concerned. Discuss what relevance, if any, the forces of change mentioned in this chapter have on the modernization of these areas. Are there new forces of change?
4. The leading nations in the world, so far as per capita income is concerned, are the United States, Germany, and the Scandinavian states. Among the less affluent Western nations are Greece and Portugal. Do you think this proves the validity of the Weber-Tawney thesis as to the importance of the Protestant Ethic in economic growth? Does the addition of Japan change the argument?
5. The process of monetization and commercialization was often a violent one in Europe. Do you think the Civil War, which ended slavery and displaced the southern semifeudal plantation system, could be considered part of the same transformation in America?
6. Is economic life distinctly separate from social and political life in America?
7. Do you think most people in the United States obey the profit motive? Do you know anyone who has changed his or her residence because of economic considerations? His or her profession? Do you know anyone who has deliberately chosen to change his or her time of work although it would cut their income?
8. Acquisitiveness is certainly as old as man. Can we speak of the origins of capitalism as being equally old?
9. Describe what Smith meant by the "invisible hand." What is the mechanism by which selfish interests are made compatible with—indeed, made the agent for—successful social provisioning?
10. Can you see a relation between Smith's growth model and his market model? Would the growth model work if the forces of the market did not operate?

Thinking Back, Looking Ahead

VISIONS OF THE FUTURE

Market society did not appear overnight; it took hundreds of years for market society to take hold as a dominant form of organizing economic society. Moreover, the great engine of market society—machinery and the mass production it would allow—only appears at the end of this period of "emergence," indicating that technological change itself had preconditions in the social realm, as we will see in our next chapter. In this chapter, our focus has been on the process of the emergence and appearance of new forms of social organization. This is more difficult to understand than an era in which a clear set of social relations has already been well established.

Part of the difficulty of understanding this period is that much of the process of creation also involved some destruction, like religious beliefs in the sinfulness of making money. Amidst this disarray and breaking up of existing social structures, it was very difficult to see the emergence of a new coherent entity, a "market society" with all the implications of harmony that such a phrase implies. Therefore, historical change is more difficult to grasp than more or less stationary "periods." Not until the Industrial Revolution does change become a norm, with all the disturbances we can image. Do you think that the increasing presence of automated production processes might pose a similar challenge in our time? This question takes us to our next chapter.

CHAPTER

The Industrial
Revolution

4

In our survey of economic history, we have concentrated almost entirely on two main currents of economic activity: agriculture and commerce. However, from earliest days there was a third essential source of economic wealth—industry—which we deliberately let slip by unnoticed. In contrast to agriculture and commerce, industrial manufacture did not leave a major imprint on economic society itself. As a peasant, serf, merchant, or guildsman, the actors in the economic drama directly typified the basic activities of the times, but this would not have been true of someone in industry. Such a person as a "factory worker"—indeed, the very idea of an *industrial* "proletarian"—was absent from the long years before the late seventeenth century. Only with the advent of Adam Smith's pin factory does this concept begin to enter the scene.

The "industrial capitalist" was also lacking. Most of the moneymakers of the past gained their fortunes by trading, or transporting, or lending—not by making. It is amusing—more than amusing; instructive—to mark the best ways of getting rich enumerated by Leon Battista Alberti, a fifteenth-century architect, musician, and courtier. They are (1) wholesale trade; (2) seeking for treasure trove; (3) ingratiating oneself with a rich man to become his heir; (4) usury; and (5) the rental of pastures, horses, and the like. A seventeenth-century commentator adds to this royal service, soldiering, and alchemy. Manufacturing is conspicuously absent from both lists.[1] It, too, enters the economic world only about the time of Smith.

In ancient Greece, Demosthenes had an armor and a cabinet "factory"; from long before his time, in ancient Egypt, we even have the attendance record of workers in "factories" for the production of cloth. Yet it is clear that this form of production was far less important in shaping the economic texture of the times than either agriculture or commerce. For one thing, the typical scale of manufacture was small. Note that the very word *manufacture* (from the Latin *manus,* "hand," and *facere,* "to make") implies a system of hand, rather than machine, technology. Demosthenes' enterprises, for example, employed no more than 50 men. It is true that from time to time we do come across quite large manufacturing operations; already in the second century A.D., a Roman brickworks employed 46 foremen; by the time we reach the seventeenth century, enterprises with several hundred workers are not unheard of. However, such operations were the exception rather than the rule. In 1660, for instance, a steelsmith in France needed no more than 3 tons of pig iron a year for his output of swords or sickle blades or artistic cutlery. Similarly, most guild operations, as we have seen, were small. As late as 1843, a Prussian census showed only 67 working people for every 100 masters.[2] In the past—as today in the East and Near East—most "industry" was carried on in the backs

---

[1] Werner Sombart, *The Quintessence of Capitalism* (New York: Dutton, 1915), pp. 34–35.
[2] *Cambridge Economic History of Europe,* 2nd Edition, M. M. Postan and H. J. Hubakkuk, general editors, (Cambridge: Cambridge University Press, 1952), II, 34; John U. Nef, *Cultural Foundations of Industrial*

of small shops or the dim cellars of houses, in sheds behind bazaars, or in the scattered homes of workers to whom materials would be supplied by an organizing "capitalist."

A GREAT TURNING POINT

Pace of Technical Change

In addition to its small scale of industry, another aspect of the times delayed industrial manufacture from making known its social presence. This was the absence of any sustained interest in the development of an *industrial technology.* Throughout antiquity and the Middle Ages, little of society's creative energy was directed toward a systematic improvement of manufacturing techniques. It is indicative of the lack of interest attached to productive technology that so simple and important an invention as the horse collar had to await the Middle Ages for discovery; the Egyptians, Greeks, and Romans, who were capable of a magnificent technology of architecture, were simply not concerned with the techniques of everyday production itself.[3] Even well into the Renaissance and Reformation, the idea of industrial technology hardly attracted serious thought. With the principal exception of Leonardo da Vinci, whose fecund mind played with inventions of the most varied kind, the serious thinkers of Europe, until well into the seventeenth century, were both ignorant of and uninterested in the technology of basic production.

There was good reason for this prevailing indifference: In the societies of the pre-market world, the necessary economic base for any large-scale industrial manufacture was totally lacking. In economies sustained by the labor of peasants, slaves, and serfs, economies in which the stream of money was small and the current of economic life—accidents of war and nature aside—relatively changeless from year to year, who could dream of a process in which avalanches of goods would be turned out? The very idea of industrial production on the large scale was inconceivable in such an unmonetized, static setting.

For all these reasons, the pace of industrialization was slow. It is a question whether Europe in the year 1200 was significantly more technologically advanced than it had been in the year 200 b.c. The widespread use of waterpower in industry did not appear until the fifteenth century, and it would be still another century before windmills provided a common means for tapping the energy of nature. The mechanical clock dates from the thirteenth century, but not for 200 years would significant improvements be made in instruments for navigation, surveying, or measuring. Movable type, that indispensable forerunner of mass communication, did not appear until 1450.

In short, despite important pockets of highly organized production, notably in the thirteenth-century Flanders cloth industry and in Northern Italian towns, not until the late sixteenth century can we discern the first signs of a general groundswell of industrial technology. Even in that time it would have been impossible to foresee that one day industry would be the dominant form of productive organization. Indeed, as late as the eighteenth century, when manufacturing had already begun to reach respectable

---

Civilization (New York: Harper, Torchbooks, 1960), p. 131; R. H. Tawney, *Equality,* 4th ed. (London: Macmillan, 1952), p. 59.

[3] E. M. Jope, in *History of Technology,* ed. Charles J. Singer et al. (New York: Oxford University Press, 1956), II, 553. There was, however, considerable improvement in mining techniques, especially for silver and copper.

proportions as a form of social endeavor, it was not generally thought of as inherently possessing any but secondary importance. Agriculture, of course, was the visible foundation of the nation itself. Trading was regarded as useful insofar as it brought a nation gold. At best, industry was seen as a handmaiden of the others, providing the trader with the goods to export, or serving the farmer as a secondary market for the products of the earth.[4]

What finally conspired to bring manufacturing into a position of overwhelming prominence?

It was a complex concatenation of events that brought about the eruption we call the Industrial Revolution. As with the Commercial Revolution and the Mercantile era, which preceded it and formed its indispensable preparation, it is impossible in a few pages to do justice to the many currents that contributed to that final outburst of industrial technology. However, if we cannot trace the process in detail, we can at least gain an idea of its impetus and of the main forces behind it if we turn now to England around 1750. Here, for the first time, industrial manufacture as a major form of economic activity began to work its immense social transformations.

England in 1750

Why did the Industrial Revolution originally take place in England and not on the Continent? Why did the pin factory attract Smith's attention? To answer these questions, we must look at the background factors that distinguished England from most other European nations in the eighteenth century.

The first of these factors was simply that England was relatively wealthy. In fact, a century of successful exploration, slave trading, piracy, war, and commerce had made her the richest nation in the world. Even more important, her riches had accrued not solely to a few nobles, but also to a large upper-middle stratum of commercial *bourgeoisie*. England was thus one of the first nations to develop, albeit on a tiny scale, a prime requisite of an industrial economy: a "mass" consumer market. As a result, a rising pressure of demand inspired a search for new techniques. Very typically, the Society for the Encouragement of Arts and Manufacturers (itself a significant child of the age) offered a prize for a machine that would spin six threads of cotton at one time, thus enabling the spinner to keep up with the technologically more advanced weaver. It was this that led, at least in part, to Arkwright's spinning jenny, of which we shall hear more shortly.

Second, England was the scene of the most successful and thoroughgoing transformation of feudal into commercial society. The process of enclosures was a significant clue to a historic change that sharply marked England from the Continent. In England, the aristocracy had early made its peace with (and more than that, found its profits in) commerce. Although sharp conflicts of interest remained between the "old" landed power and the "new" monied power, by 1700, the ruling orders in England had decisively opted for adaptation rather than resistance to the demands of the market economy.[5]

---

[4]In the mid-eighteenth century, when the French doctor François Quesnay propounded one of the first systematic explanations of economic production and distribution (called *Physiocracy*), only the farmer was regarded as a producer of net worth; the manufacturer, although his utility was not ignored, was nonetheless relegated to the "sterile" (i.e., non–wealth-producing) classes.

[5]See Barrington Moore, *Social Origins of Dictatorship and Democracy* (Boston: Beacon Press, 1966), Chap. 1.

Third, England was the locus of a unique enthusiasm for science and engineering. The famous Royal Society, of which Newton was an early president, was founded in 1660 and was the immediate source of much intellectual excitement. Indeed, a popular interest in gadgets, machines, and devices of all sorts soon became a mild national obsession: *Gentlemen's Magazine,* a fashionable periodical of the time, announced in 1729 that it would henceforth keep its readers "abreast of every invention"—a task that the mounting flow of inventions soon rendered quite impossible. No less important was the enthusiasm of the British landed aristocracy for scientific farming: English landlords displayed an interest in matters of crop rotation and fertilizer that their French counterparts would have found quite beneath their dignity.

Then there were a host of other background causes, some as fortuitous as the immense resources of coal and iron ore on which the British sat; others were as purposeful as the development of a national patent system that deliberately sought to stimulate and protect the act of invention itself.[6] As the revolution came into being, it fed upon itself. The new techniques (especially in textiles) simply destroyed their handicraft competition around the world and thus enormously increased their own markets. What finally brought all these factors into operation was the energy of a group of New Men who made of the latent opportunities of history a vehicle for their own rise to fame and fortune.

Rise of the New Men

One such, for instance, was John Wilkinson. The son of an old-fashioned, small-scale iron producer, Wilkinson was a man possessed by the technological possibilities of his business. He invented a dozen things: a rolling mill and a steam lathe, a process for the manufacture of iron pipes, and a design for machining accurate cylinders. Typically, he decided that the old-fashioned leather bellows used in the making of iron itself were not efficient, so he determined to make iron ones. "Everybody laughed at me," he later wrote. "I did it and applied the steam engine to blow them and they all cried: 'Who could have thought of it?' "

He followed his success in production with a passion for application; everything must be made of iron: pipes, bridges, even ships. After a ship made of iron plates had been successfully launched, he wrote a friend: "It answers all my expectations, and has convinced the unbelievers, who were nine hundred and ninety-nine in a thousand. It will be a nine-days wonder, and afterwards, a Columbus' egg."[7]

But Wilkinson was only one of many. The most famous was, of course, James Watt—well known to Adam Smith—who, together with Matthew Boulton, formed the first

---

[6]Phyllis Deane, in *The First Industrial Revolution* (paperback ed., Cambridge: Cambridge University Press, 1965), ascribes the onset of industrialism in England to a somewhat different set of causes: a rise in population, better food-producing techniques, a boom in foreign trade, and vast improvement in transportation. There is no doubt that these were also indispensable elements in the process. I mention Deane's book so that a student will not think that there is only one "right" way of accounting for very complex historical transformations. For another excellent account of the process, one might turn to the fascinating book by David Landes, *Prometheus Unbound* (Cambridge: Cambridge University Press, 1969); for still another interesting account, see Joel Mokyr, *The Lever of Riches: Technological Creativity and Economic Progress* (New York: Oxford University Press, 1990).

[7]Paul Mantoux, *The Industrial Revolution in the Eighteenth Century,* 2nd ed. (New York: Harcourt, 1928), pp. 313*n*, 315.

company for the manufacture of steam engines. Watt was the son of an architect, shipbuilder, and maker of nautical instruments. At 13 he was already making models of machines, and by young manhood he was an accomplished artisan. He planned to settle in Glasgow, but the guild of hammermen objected to his making mathematical instruments—the last remnants of feudalism thus coming into an ironic personal conflict with the man who, more than any other, would create *the* invention that would destroy guild organization. At any rate, Watt found a haven at the university and there, in 1764, had his attention turned to an early and very unsatisfactory steam engine invented by Newcomen. In his careful and systematic way, Watt experimented with steam pressures, cylinder designs, and valves, until by 1796 he had developed a truly radical and (by the standards of those days) extraordinarily powerful and efficient engine. Interestingly, Watt could never have done so well with his engines had not Wilkinson perfected a manner of making good piston-cylinder fits. Previously, cylinders and pistons were made of wood and rapidly wore out. Typically, too, it was Wilkinson who bought the first steam engine to be used for purposes other than pumping: It worked the famous iron bellows.

There was needed, however, more than Watt's skill. The new engines had to be produced and sold, and the factory that made them had to be financed and organized. Watt at first formed a partnership with John Roebuck, another iron magnate, but it shortly failed. Thereafter, luck came his way. Matthew Boulton, already a wealthy and highly successful manufacturer of buttons and buckles, took up Roebuck's contract with Watt, and the greatest combination of technical skill and business acumen of the day was born.

Even then the firm did not prosper immediately. Expenses of development were high, and the new firm was not out of debt for 12 years. Yet from the beginning, interest was high. By 1781, Boulton was able to claim that the people of London, Birmingham, and Manchester were all "steam mill mad"; by 1786, when two steam engines were harnessed to 50 pairs of millstones in the largest flour mill in the world, all London came to see the marvel.

The steam engine was the greatest single invention, but by no means the sole mainstay, of the Industrial Revolution. Hardly less important were a group of textile inventions, of which the most famous was Arkwright's jenny, or water frame, as it was called to distinguish it from other hand-operated spinning jennies.[8]

Arkwright's career is, in itself, interesting. A barber, he plied his trade near the weaving districts of Manchester and so heard the crying need for a machine that would enable the cottage spinners to keep up with the technically more advanced weavers. Good fortune threw him into contact with a clockmaker named John Kay, whom he hired to perfect a machine that Kay had already begun with another employer–inventor. What happened thereafter is obscure: Kay left the business accused of theft and embezzlement, and Arkwright appeared as the "sole inventor" of a spinning jenny in 1769.

He now found two rich hosiers, Samuel Need and Jedediah Strutt, who agreed to set up business with him to produce water frames, and in 1771, the firm built its own spinning mill. It was an overnight success; by 1779, it had several thousand spindles,

---

[8]Essentially, what the water frame did was enable cotton thread of much greater strength to be produced. As a result, for the first time it was possible to use cotton thread instead of linen thread for the warp (the vertical threads that take most of the strain in weaving) as well as for the weft. Not until Arkwright's invention was "cotton cloth" made wholly of cotton. The new cloth was incomparably superior to the old and instantly enjoyed a huge demand.

more than 300 workers, and ran night and day. Within not many years, Arkwright had built an immense fortune for himself and founded an even more immense textile industry for England. "O reader," wrote Carlyle, looking back on his career, "what a historical phenomenon is that bag-cheeked, pot-bellied, much enduring, much inventing barber! . . . It was this man that had to give England the power of cotton."[9]

The Industrial Entrepreneur

It is interesting, as we watch the careers of these New Men, to draw a few generalizations concerning them. This was an entirely new class of economically important persons. Peter Onions, who was one of the inventors of the puddling process, was an obscure foreman; Arkwright was a barber; Benjamin Huntsman, the steel pioneer, was originally a maker of clocks; Henry Maudslay, who invented the automatic screw machine, was a bright young mechanic at the Woolwich Arsenal. None of the great industrial pioneers came of noble lineage; with few exceptions, such as Matthew Boulton, none even possessed money capital. In agriculture, the new revolutionary methods of scientific farming enjoyed aristocratic patronage and leadership, especially from the famous Sir Jethro Tull and Lord Townshend; but in industry, the lead went to men of humble origin and descent.

This required a social system flexible enough to permit the rise of such obscure "adventurers." It is not until we see the catalytic effect of unleashing and harnessing the energies of talented men in the lower and middle ranks of the social order that we begin to appreciate the immense liberating effect of the preceding economic and political revolutions. In the medieval hierarchy, the meteoric careers of such New Men would have been unthinkable. In addition, the New Men were the product of the unique economic preparation of England itself. They were, of course, the beneficiaries of the rising demand and the technical inquisitiveness of the times. Beyond that, many of the small manufacturers were themselves former small proprietors who had been bought out during the late period of the enclosure movement and who determined to use their tiny capital in the promising area of manufacture.

The New Rich

Many of these New Men made great sums of money. A few, like Boulton and Watt, were modest in their wants. Despite an iron-clad patent, they charged for their engines only the basic cost of the machine and installation plus one-third the saving in fuel the customer got. Some, like Josiah Wedgwood, founder of the great china works, actually refused on principle to take out patents, but most of them did not display such fine sensibilities. Arkwright retired a multimillionaire, living in ostentatious splendor: Huntsman, Wilkinson, and Samuel Walker (who began life as a nailsmith and stole the secret of cast steel) all went on to roll up huge fortunes.[10] Indeed, Wilkinson's iron business became a minor industrial state with credit stronger than many German and Italian principalities. It even coined its own money, and its copper and silver tokens (with a profile and legend of John Wilkinson, Ironmaster) were much in use between 1787 and 1808.

---

[9]Mantoux, *The Industrial Revolution in the Eighteenth Century,* p. 225.
[10]In contrast to the manufacturers, the inventors did not usually fare successfully. Many of them, who did not have Watt's good fortune in finding a Boulton, died poor and neglected, fruitlessly suing for stolen inventions, unpaid royalties, or ignored claims.

Besides being avaricious, the manufacturers have been described by the economic historian Paul Mantoux as

> tyrannical, hard, sometimes cruel: their passions and greeds were those of up-starts. They had the reputation of being heavy drinkers and of having little re-gard for the honour of their female employees. They were proud of their newly acquired wealth and lived in great style with footmen, carriages and gorgeous town and country houses.[11]

It is not surprising, then, that Adam Smith, although recognizing their usefulness, looked with distrust on the "mean rapacity, the monopolizing spirit" of merchants and manu-facturers, warning that "they neither are, nor ought to be, the rulers of mankind."[12]

Pleasant or unpleasant, these men's personal characteristics fade beside one over-riding quality: These were all interested in expansion, in growth, in investment for in-vestment's sake. All of them were identified with technological progess, and none of them disdained contact with the physical process of production. An employee of Maud-slay once remarked, "It was a pleasure to see him handle a tool of any kind, but he was *quite splendid* with an 18-inch file."[13] Watt was tireless in experimenting with his ma-chines; Wedgwood stomped about his factory on his wooden leg, scrawling "This won't do for Jos. Wedgwood" wherever he saw evidence of careless work. Richard Arkwright was a bundle of ceaseless energy in promoting his interests as he jounced about Eng-land over execrable roads in a post chaise driven by four horses, pursuing his corre-spondence as he traveled.

"With us," wrote a French visitor to a calico works in 1788, "a man rich enough to set up and run a factory like this would not care to remain in a position which he would deem unworthy of his wealth."[14] This was an attitude entirely foreign to the rising Eng-lish industrial capitalist. His work was its own dignity and reward; the wealth it brought was quite aside. Boswell, on being shown Watt and Boulton's great engine works at Soho, declared that he never forgot Boulton's expression, as the latter declared, "I sell here, sir, what all the world desires to have—Power."[15]

The New Men were first and last *entrepreneurs*—organizers. They brought with them a new energy, as restless as it proved to be inexhaustible. In an economic, if not a political, sense, they deserve the epithet "revolutionaries," for the change they ushered in was nothing short of total, sweeping, and irreversible.

Industrial and Social Repercussions

The first and most striking element of that change was a sharp rise in the output of the newly industrialized industries. The import of raw cotton for spinning weighed 1 million pounds in 1701; 3 million pounds in 1750; 5 million in 1781. That was a respectable rate of increase, but then came the sudden burst in textile technology. By 1784, the figure was over 11 million pounds; by 1789, it was three times greater yet, and still it grew: to 43 million pounds in 1799; 56 million in 1800; 60 million in 1802.[16] So was it with much else

---

[11]Mantoux, *The Industrial Revolution in the Eighteenth Century,* p. 397.
[12]Adam Smith, *The Wealth of Nations* (New York: Modern Library, 1937), p. 460.
[13]Lewis Mumford, *Technics and Civilization* (New York: Harcourt, 1934), p. 210.
[14]Mantoux, *The Industrial Revolution in the Eighteenth Century,* p. 404.
[15]H. R. Fox Bourne, *English Merchants* (London: 1866), p. 119.
[16]Mantoux, *The Industrial Revolution in the Eighteenth Century,* p. 258.

where the new technology penetrated. The output of coal increased tenfold in 40 years; that of pig iron leaped from 68,000 tons in 1788 to 1,347,000 tons in 1839.[17]

The first impact of the Industrial Revolution was an immense quickening of the pace of production in the new industrial sector of the economy, an effect we find repeated in every nation that goes through an "industrial revolution." In France, for example, the impact of industrial techniques did not make its influence felt until about 1815; between that date and 1845, the French output of pig iron grew fivefold; her coal production, sevenfold; her rate of importation, tenfold.[18]

The Industrial Revolution itself did not immediately exert a comparable leverage on the *overall* increase of output. The industrial sector was small; the phenomenal rates of increase in those industries where its leverage was first and most fruitfully applied were by no means mirrored in every industry. What is of crucial importance, however, is that the Industrial Revolution ushered in the technology by which large-scale, sustained growth was eventually to take place. This is a process into which we must look more carefully at the end of this chapter.

Rise of the Factory

But first we must pay heed to another immediate and visible result of the Industrial Revolution in England. We can describe it as the transformation of an essentially commercial and agricultural society into one in which industrial manufacture became the dominant mode of organizing economic life. The Industrial Revolution was characterized by the rise of the factory to the center of social as well as economic life. After 1850, the factory was not only the key economic institution of England, it was also the economic institution that shaped its politics, its social problems, and the character of its daily life just as decisively as the manor or the guild had done a few centuries earlier.

It is difficult for us today to realize the pace or the quality of change that this rise of factory work created. Until the mid-eighteenth century, Glasgow, Newcastle, and the Rhondda Valley were mostly wasteland or farmland, and Manchester in 1727 was described by Daniel Defoe as "a mere village." Forty years later, there were 100 integrated mills and a whole cluster of machine plants, forges, leather and chemical works in the area. A modern industrial city had been created.

By the 1780s, the shape of the new environment was visible. A French mineralogist visiting England in 1784 wrote:

> [The] creaking, the piercing noise of the pulleys, the continuous sound of hammering, the ceaseless energy of the men keeping all this machinery in motion, presented a sight as interesting as it was new. . . . The night is so filled with fire and light that when from a distance we see, here a glowing mass of coal, there darting flames leaping from the blast furnaces, when we hear the heavy hammers striking the echoing anvils and the shrill whistling of the air pumps, we do not know whether we are looking at a volcano in eruption or have been miraculously transported to Vulcan's cave. . . .[19]

---

[17]J. L. and B. Hammond, *The Rise of Modern Industry* (New York: Harcourt, 1937), p. 160.
[18]A. Dunham, *The Industrial Revolution in France, 1815–48* (New York: Exposition Press, 1955), p. 432.
[19]Mantoux, *The Industrial Revolution in the Eighteenth Century,* p. 313.

The factory provided not merely a new landscape but a new and uncongenial social habitat. In our day, we have become so used to urban industrial life that we forget what a wrench is the transition from farm to city. For peasants, this transfer requires a drastic adjustment. No longer do they work at their own pace, but at the pace of a machine. No longer are slack seasons determined by the weather, but by the state of the market. No longer is the land, however miserable its crop, an eternal source of sustenance close at hand, but only the packed and sterile earth of the industrial site.

It is little wonder that the English laborer, still more used to rural than urban ways, feared and hated the advent of the machine. Throughout the early years of the Industrial Revolution, workers literally attacked the invading army of machinery, burning and wrecking factories. During the late eighteenth century, for instance, when the first textile mills were built, whole hamlets rose in revolt rather than work in the mills. Headed by a mythical General Ludd, the Luddites constituted a fierce but fruitless opposition to industrialism. In 1813, in a mass trial that ended in many hangings and transportations, the movement came to an end.[20]

Conditions of Labor

Distasteful as was the advent of the factory itself, even more distasteful were the conditions within it. Child labor, for instance, was commonplace and sometimes began at age 4; hours of work were generally dawn to dusk; abuses of every kind were all too frequent. A Committee of Parliament, appointed in 1832 to look into conditions, gives this testimony from a factory overseer.

Q. At what time in the morning, in the brisk time, did these girls go to the mills?

A. In the brisk time, for about six weeks, they have gone at three o'clock in the morning and ended at ten or nearly half past at night.

Q. What intervals were allowed for rest and refreshment during those nineteen hours of labour?

A. Breakfast a quarter of an hour, and dinner half an hour, and drinking a quarter of an hour.

Q. Was any of that time taken up in cleaning the machinery?

A. They generally had to do what they call dry down; sometimes this took the whole time at breakfast or drinking.

Q. Had you not great difficulty in awakening your children to the excessive labour?

A. Yes, in the early time we had to take them up asleep and shake them.

Q. Had any of them any accident in consequences of this labour?

A. Yes, my eldest daughter . . . the cog caught her forefinger nail and screwed it off below the knuckle.

Q. Has she lost that finger?

A. It is cut off at the second joint.

Q. Were her wages paid during that time?

A. As soon as the accident happened the wages were totally stopped.[21]

---

[20]Even in our day, however, we use the word *Luddite* to describe an attempt to "fight back" at the threat of machinery.

[21]Tawney, Bland, and Brown, *English Economic History, Selected Documents* (London: Bell, 1914), p. 510.

It was a grim age. The long hours of work, the general dirt and clangor of the factories, the lack of even the most elementary safety precautions, all combined to give early industrial capitalism a reputation from which, in the minds of many people of the world, it has never recovered. Worse yet were the slums to which the majority of workers returned after their travail. Life expectancy at birth in Manchester was 17 years—a figure that reflected a child mortality rate of over 50 percent. This is not so surprising when we read this government commissioner's report of 1839 on one such workers' quarter in Glasgow called "the wynds."

> The wynds . . . house a fluctuating population of between 15,000 and 30,000 persons. The district is composed of many narrow streets and square courts and in the middle of each court there is a dunghill. Although the outward appearance of these places was revolting, I was nevertheless quite unprepared for the filth and misery that were to be found inside. In some bedrooms we visited at night we found a whole mass of humanity stretched on the floor. There were often 15 to 20 men and women huddled together, some being clothed and others naked. There was hardly any furniture there and the only thing which gave these holes the appearance of a dwelling was fire burning on the hearth. Thieving and prostitution are the main sources of income of these people.[22]

Early Capitalism and Social Justice

Without question, the times were marked by tremendous social suffering. But it is well, in looking back on the birth years of industrial capitalism, to bear several facts in mind:

1. It Is Doubtful if the Poverty Represented a Deterioration in Life for the Masses in General.

In at least some sections of England, industrialism brought immediate benefits. Wedgwood (an exceptionally good employer, it is true) used to tell his employees to ask their parents for a description of the country as *they* first knew it and to compare their present state. So, too, the 12-hour day in Arkwright's mills was a 2-hour *improvement* over previous Manchester standards. Furthermore, the existing poverty was not by any means new. As we know from Hogarth's etchings, long before the Industrial Revolution, "Gin Lane" already sported its pitiful types. As one reformer of the mid-nineteenth century wrote, those whose sensibilities were revolted by the sight of suffering factory children thought "how much more delightful would have been the gambol of free limbs on the hillside; the sight of the green mead with its spangles of buttercups and daisies; the song of the bird and the humming of the bee . . . [but] we have seen children perishing from sheer hunger in the mud hovel or in the ditch by the wayside."[23]

---

[22]Quoted in F. Engels, *The Condition of the Working Class in England* (New York: Macmillan, 1958), p. 46.
[23]Friedrich Hayek, ed., *Capitalism and the Historians* (Chicago: University of Chicago Press, 1954), p. 180.

2. Much of the Harsh Criticism to Which Early Industrial Capitalism Was Subjected Was Derived Not So Much from Its Economic as from Its Political Accompaniments.

Coincident with the rise of capitalism, and indeed contributory to it, was a deep-seated change in the vantage point of political criticism. New ideas of democracy, of social justice, of the "rights" of the individual charged the times with a critical temper of mind before which *any* economic system would have suffered censure.

To be sure, the political movements by which capitalism was carried to its heights were not working-class movements, but middle-class, bourgeois movements; the rising manufacturers in England and France had little social conscience beyond a concern for their own rights and privileges. However, the movement of political liberalism that they set in motion had a momentum beyond the narrow limits for which it was intended. By the first quarter of the nineteenth century, the condition of the working classes, now so exposed to public view in the new factory-slum environment, had begun to curry public sympathy.

Thus, one of the unexpected consequences of the Industrial Revolution was a sharp reorientation of political ideas. In the creation of an industrial working class and an industrial environment, the revolution bequeathed a new economic framework to politics.[24] Karl Marx and Friedrich Engels were to write in 1848 that "all history" was the history of class struggle, but never did that struggle emerge so nakedly into the open as after the industrial environment had been brought into being.

Equally important was that the rise of political liberalism not only aroused feelings of hostility toward the prevailing order, but initiated the slow process of amelioration. From the outset, a reform movement coincided with capitalism. In 1802, pauper apprentices were legally limited to a 12-hour day and barred from night work. In 1819, the employment of children under nine was prohibited in cotton mills; in 1833, a 48- to 69-hour week was decreed for workers under 18 (who comprised about 75 percent of all cotton-mill workers), and a system of government inspection of factories was inaugurated; in 1842, children under 10 were barred from the coal mines; in 1847, a 10-hour daily limit (later raised to 10½) was set for children and women.

The nature of the reforms is itself eloquent testimony to the conditions of the times, and the fact that the reforms were bitterly opposed and often observed in the breach is testimony to the prevailing spirit. Yet capitalism, unlike feudalism, was from the beginning subject to the corrective force of democracy. Using the material of the 1830s, Karl Marx drew a mordant picture of the capitalist process in all its economic squalor, but he overlooked (or shrugged off) this countervailing force whose power was steadily to grow.

3. The Most Important Effect of the Industrial Revolution We Have Left for Last: Its Long-Term Leverage on Economic Well-Being.

The ultimate impact of the Industrial Revolution was to usher in a rise of living standards on a mass scale unlike anything that the world had ever known.

This did not happen overnight. In 1840, according to the calculations of Arnold Toynbee, Sr., the wage of an ordinary laborer came to 8 shillings a week, which was

---

[24]For a stirring account of the birth of a self-conscious working-class movement, see E. P. Thompson, *The Making of the English Working Class* (New York: Pantheon, 1964).

6 shillings less than he needed to buy the bare necessities of life.[25] He made up the deficit by sending his children or his wife, or both, to work in the mills. If, as we have noted, some sections of the working class gained from the early impact of industrialization, others suffered a decline from the standard of living enjoyed in 1795 or thereabouts. A Committee of Parliament in the 1830s, for example, discovered that a hand weaver at that earlier date could have bought more than three times as many provisions with his wages as at the later date. Although not every trade suffered equally, the first flush of the Industrial Revolution brought its hardships to bear full force, though its benefits were not as immediately noticeable.

By 1870, however, the long-run effects of the Industrial Revolution were beginning to make themselves felt. The price of necessities had by then risen to 15 shillings, but weekly earnings had crept up to meet and even exceed that sum. Hours were shorter, too. At the Jarrow Shipyards and the New Castle Chemical Works, the workweek had fallen from 61 to 54 hours; even in the notoriously long-working textile mills, the stint was down to "only" 57 hours. It was still a far cry from an abundant society, much less an "affluent" one, but the corner had been turned.

THE INDUSTRIAL REVOLUTION IN THE PERSPECTIVE OF THEORY

We have reviewed very briefly the salient historic features of the rise of industrial capitalism. Now we must reflect on the great economic and social changes we have witnessed and ask a pertinent economic question: How did the process of industrialization raise material well-being? To answer the question, we must turn to economic theory to elucidate systematically the insights we have already gained from Smith's *Wealth of Nations*.

Let us begin by asking what is necessary for a rise in the economic well-being of a society. The answer is not difficult. If we are to enjoy a greater material well-being, generally speaking, we must produce more. This is particularly true when we begin at the stage of scarcely-better-than-subsistence that characterized so much of Europe before the Industrial Revolution. For such a society to raise the standard of living of its masses, the first necessity is unquestionably higher production. Despite all the inequities of distribution that attended the society of serf and lord, capitalist and child-employee, underlying the meanness of the times was one overriding reality: the sheer inadequacy of output. There was simply not enough to go around, and if less lopsided distributive arrangements might have lessened the moral indignity of the times, they would not have contributed much to a massive improvement in basic economic well-being. Even assuming that the wage of the city laborer and the income of the peasant could have been doubled had the rich been deprived of their share—and this is a wildly extravagant assumption—still, the prime characteristic of rural and urban life would have been its poverty.

We must add only one important qualification to this emphasis on increased output as the prerequisite of economic improvement. Overall living standards will not improve if a country's population is growing even faster than its increased output. The production of goods and services must rise faster than population if individual well-being is to improve.

---

[25] Arnold Toynbee, *The Industrial Revolution* (Boston: Beacon Press, 1956), p. 113.

How does a society raise its per capita output?

We cannot fully analyze this problem here, but our glimpse into the pin factory and our study of the Industrial Revolution in England enable us to understand a great deal about the problem. For clearly, *the key to higher output lies in enhancing the human energies of the community with the leverage of industrial capital.* Our analytic understanding of the growth must begin by looking further into this extraordinary power that capital possesses.

Capital and Productivity

We have frequently used the word *capital,* but we have not yet defined it. We can see that, in a fundamental sense, capital consists of anything that can enhance a person's power to perform economically useful work. An unshaped stone is capital to the caveman who can use it as a hunting implement. A hoe is capital to a peasant; a road system is capital to the inhabitants of a modern industrial society. Knowledge is capital, too—indeed, perhaps the most precious part of society's stock of capital.

When economists talk of capital, however, they usually confine their meaning to *capital goods*—the stock of tools, equipment, machines, and buildings that society produces in order to expedite the production process.[26] All these capital goods have one common effect on the productive process: They all operate to make human labor more productive. They make it possible for a worker to produce more goods in an hour (or a week, or a year) than he or she could produce without the aid of that capital. Capital is therefore a method of raising per capita productivity, which is an individual person's output in a given span of time; it is the lesson of the pin factory extended to all branches of output. For example, in a 40-hour week, a typical modern worker using power-driven mechanical equipment can physically outproduce at least a half dozen persons working 70 hours a week with the simpler tools available at the beginning of this century. To put it differently, in one day, a modern worker will turn out more output than his or her counterpart of 1900 did in a full week—not because the modern worker works harder, but because he or she commands thousands of dollars' worth of capital equipment rather than the few hundred dollars' worth available to a worker in 1900.[27]

Why does capital make labor so much more productive?

The most important reason is that capital goods enable people to use principles and devices such as the lever and the wheel, heat and cold, and combustion and expansion in ways that the unaided body cannot. *Capital goods give people mechanical and physico-chemical powers of literally transhuman dimensions.* They enormously magnify muscular strength; they refine powers of control; they embody intelligence; they endow men and women with endurance and resilience far beyond those of flesh and bone. In using capital, human beings utilize the natural world as a supplement to their own feeble capacities.

---

[26]There is also another meaning to the word *capital.* This is the social relationship that binds the wage-worker and the capitalist, the owner of the capital goods (the factory) where the worker seeks employment. Capital as a social relationship establishes the prerogatives of both capitalist and worker in their mutual dealings. First proposed by Marx, it is perhaps the most important meaning of the word if we seek to define *capitalism* as a distinct period of social history. In this book, we stay with the conventional economic usage, however, and speak of capital in terms of capital goods.

[27]We need an important qualifier here. Very few commodities remain unchanged over a century-long span. We have searched for items—nails? pins? bricks?—that have been unchanged since 1900. We found none with reliable statistics attached. Therefore, our figures are "guesstimates" of the rise in productivity.

Capital and Specialization

Another reason for the augmentation of production lies in the fact that capital facilitates the specialization of human labor. Once again, Smith's example serves us well. A team of people working together, each one tending to one job alone in which he or she is expert, can usually far outproduce the same number of people, each of whom does a variety of jobs. The prime example is, of course, the auto production line, in which a thousand workers cooperate to produce an immensely larger output of cars than could be achieved if each one built a car alone. Auto assembly lines, of course, use prodigious quantities of capital in the overhead conveyor belts, the inventories of parts on hand, the huge factory with its power system, and so on. Although not all specialization of labor depends on capital, capital is usually necessary for the large-scale industrial operations in which specialization becomes most effective.

In our next chapter, we return to these important matters in the context of the development of modern industry. While we are still discussing the basic question of the rise of industry itself, there is a fundamental problem to consider: This is the question of how capital is made in the first place, of how a society generates the capital equipment it needs in order to grow.

Capital and Saving

The question brings us for the first time to a relationship that we will encounter many times in our study of economics, both from a perspective of history and from a later vantage point of theory. The relationship is between the creation of those physical artifacts that we call capital and the inescapable prior act that we call *saving*.

When we think of saving, we ordinarily picture it in financial terms; that is, as a decision not to spend part of our money income. Behind this financial act, however, lies a "real" act that we must now clearly understand: When we save money, we also abstain from using a certain quantity of goods and services we might have bought. To be sure, our money savings represent a claim on goods and services, a claim that we may later exercise. Until we do, however, we have freed resources that would otherwise have been used to satisfy our immediate wants. When Smith's pin manufacturer "accumulated," he deliberately denied himself the higher standard of living that he could have enjoyed by spending his profits on riotous living. From these freed resources—the unused labor and capital that might have produced silks and coaches—society builds its capital, or, in more technical language, carries out the act of investment. Note that *investment* in economics means devoting labor and other inputs to the creation of capital goods. It does not mean putting money into stocks and bonds, although that may lead to, or assist, the capital-building process. Economists call the process of making money investments *financial* investment, to distinguish it from real investment in capital goods.

Saving and Investment

The acts of saving and investment are inextricably linked: Saving is the releasing of resources from consumption; investment is the employment of these resources in making capital. Indeed, from society's point of view, saving and investment are only two sides of the same coin. Why do we then separate them in economic discourse? The reason is that different people may perform the saving and investing functions, especially in modern societies. Those who release the resources of society are often not the same persons as those who gather up those resources for investment purposes. Nonetheless, we can see that every act of capital building, no matter who performs it, requires that resources be devoted to that purpose.

This does not mean that investment necessarily entails a diminution of consumption. A rich society does not feel its normal, recurrent saving as a "pinch" on its spending, and Smith's manufacturers were not known for their modest ways. More important, a society with unemployed factors can put its idle resources to work building capital without diminishing its expenditure on consumption. It is still saving, insofar as it is not using these newly employed resources to make consumption goods. However—and this is a crucial point—when a society is fully employed, for instance in the midst of war, it can only spend more for capital if it curtails its consumption. Put differently, at full employment, consumption spending and capital spending are competitive; when there is unemployment, both consumption and capital spending can increase.

We can now see that the rate at which an economy can invest—that is, the size of the yearly addition it can make to its stock of capital goods—depends on its capacity to save. If its living standards are already close to the margin of existence, it will not be able to transfer much labor from consumption effort to capital-building effort. However badly it may wish for more tools, however productive those tools would prove to be, it cannot invest beyond the point at which its remaining consumption activity would no longer be adequate to maintain subsistence. At the other extreme, if a society is well-to-do, it may be able to abstain from a great deal of current consumption effort to provide for the future. Accordingly, its growth will be fast. *Whether growth is fast or slow, it is a hard economic reality that the amount of investment can never exceed the amount of resources and effort that are unused for other purposes, mainly consumption.*

Growth in Early Capitalism

This seems to imply that the process of economic growth must perforce be very slow in a poor economy, and so it is. In England, as we have already seen, nearly three-quarters of a century elapsed before the new process of industrialization brought about an increase in productivity sufficiently large to be felt as a general improvement in the lot of the worker. In the underdeveloped nations, as we shall see in Chapter 13, the prospect is equally or even more sluggish. At its best, growth is a gradual and cumulative rather than an instant phenomenon; where the initial level of savings is low because of poverty, the rate of advance is correspondingly slower.

Perhaps we can better appreciate this overall determinant of the pace of growth if we examine the actual social circumstances under which saving arose in early nineteenth-century England.

Who did the saving? Who abstained from consumption? Well-to-do agriculturalists and manufacturers (for all their ostentatious ways) were certainly important savers who plowed substantial sums into more new capital investments. Yet the savers were not just the manufacturers or the gentry but also another class—the industrial workers. Here, in the low level of industrial wages, a great sacrifice was made—not voluntarily, by any manner of means, but made just the same. From the resources the workers could have consumed was built the industrial foundation for the future.

We can also see something that is perhaps even more significant. This is the fact that England had to hold down the level of its working-class consumption in order to free productive effort for the accumulation of capital goods. In point of historic actuality, the "holding down" was accomplished largely by the forces of the marketplace—with a liberal assist, to be sure, from the capitalists and from a government quick to oppose the demands of labor in the interests of its upper classes. But social inequities aside, the hard fact remains that had industrial wages risen very much, a vast demand for consumer goods would have turned the direction of the English economy away from capital building, toward the satisfaction of current wants. This would certainly have redounded to the immediate welfare of the English worker (although the increase in per capita consumption would have been small). At the same time, however, it would have postponed the day when society's overall productive powers were capable of generating an aggregate output of very large size.

This bitter choice must be confronted by every industrializing society, capitalist or socialist, democratic or totalitarian. To assuage the needs of today or to build for tomorrow is *the* decision a developing society must make.

Incentives for Growth

There remains but one last question. We have gained some insight into the mechanics of growth, but we have not yet answered the question: How are these mechanics brought about? How does society arrange the reallocation of its factors of production to bring about the creation of the capital it needs?

This query brings us again to a consideration of our original division of economic societies into three types: traditional, command, and market. It also leads to some very important conclusions.

The first of these is obvious: Tradition-bound societies are not apt to grow. In such societies, there is no direct social means of inducing the needed reallocation of factors. Worse yet, there are often strong social and religious barriers that create obstacles to the needed shifts in employment.

The situation is very different, however, when we turn to command societies. We have seen a striking use of command as the industrializing agency in modern times. In at least one country at one time, the Soviet Union, command was the principal mechanism for a dramatic transition from peasanthood to industrialization, and in many other collectivist economies, command has been used, with varying results, to bring into effect such a transition. China is the big case in point today, with command being used to create a dynamic market sector.

Command was also one of the principal ways by which Europe began its industrialization. In the state-directed establishment of shipyards and armories, the construction of royal palaces and estates, tapestry works and chinaware factories, a very important organizing impetus was given to the creation of an industrial sector in the Mercantile era. True, in those days, command was never so ruthlessly applied nor so widely directed as with the communist states. But however much milder the dosage, the medicine was in essence the same: The *initial* transfer of labor from the traditional pursuits of the land to the new tasks of the factory depended on a commanding authority that ordered the new pattern into being. A few years ago Barbara Ward wrote in *India and the West:* "A developing society must at some point begin to save, even though it is still poor. This is the tough early stage of growth which Marx encountered in Victorian England and unfortunately took to be permanent. It is a difficult phase in any economy—so difficult that most societies got through it by *force majeure*. . . . No one asked the British laborers moving into the Manchester slums whether they wanted to save. . . .

The Soviet workers who came to Sverdlovsk and Magnitogorsk from the primitive steppes had no say in the scale or the condition of their work. Nor have the Chinese in their communes today."[28]

The Market as a Capital-Building Mechanism

Command was by no means the main agency for the final industrialization of the West. Rather, the organizing force that put people to work in making capital equipment was the market.

How did the market bring about this remarkable transformation? It achieved its purposes by the lure of monetary rewards. It was the hope of profits that lured manufacturers into turning out more capital goods. It was the attraction of better wages (or sometimes of *any* wages) that directed workers into the new plants. It was the signal of rising prices that encouraged, and falling prices that discouraged, the production of this or that particular capital good. Here is Smith's market mechanism, joined to his growth model.

What, we may next ask, opened the prospect of profits large enough to induce entrepreneurs to risk their savings in new capital goods? The answer brings us full circle to the focal point of this chapter, for it is to be found primarily in the body of technological advance constituting the core of the Industrial Revolution. It was the pin-making machinery that opened the possibility of a profitable and expanding pin industry.

Not that every new invention brought with it a fortune for its pioneering promoters, or that every new product found a market waiting for it. The path of technical advance is littered with inventions born too soon and with enterprises founded with great hopes and closed down 6 months later. Looking back over the vast process of capital accumulation that, beginning in the late eighteenth century, lifted first England and then America into the long flight of industrial development, there is little doubt that the impelling force was the succession of inventions and innovations that successfully opened new aspects of nature to human control. Steam power, the cheap and efficient spinning and weaving of cloth, the first mass production of iron and, later, steel—these were the great breakthroughs of industrial science that opened the way for the massive accumulation of capital. When the great inventions had marked the channel of advance, secondary improvements and subsidiary inventions took on an important supporting role. To the entrepreneur with a cost-cutting innovation went the prize of a market advantage in costs and correspondingly higher profit. More than that, when one pioneer in a field had gained a technical advantage, competition quickly forced everyone else in the field to catch up as quickly as they could. Most of the cost-cutting innovations involved adding machinery to the production process—and this in turn boosted the formation of capital.

Capitalism as a whole proved an unparalled machine for the accumulation of capital. In its development, we find the first economic system in history in which economic growth became an integral part of daily life. As Marx and Engels were to write in the *Communist Manifesto:* "The bourgeoisie, during its scarce one hundred years, has created more massive and more colossal productive forces than have all preceding generations together." The compliment, all the more meaningful coming from the two archenemies of its social order, was true.

---

[28]From Barbara Ward, *India and the West* (New York: W. W. Norton, 1964), p. 113.

Key Concepts and Key Words

Industrial Revolution

1. The Industrial Revolution was *a great turning period* in history, during which manufacturing and industrial activity became primary forms of social production.

2. The Industrial Revolution began in England in the mid- to late-eighteenth century (although its roots are far deeper). There are numerous reasons why it occurred there and then:

   - England was *a wealthy trading nation* with a well-developed middle class.
   - England's *aristocracy was much more commerce-minded* than the aristocracies of the Continent.
   - England was the home of a widespread vogue of *scientific investigation* and of "gentlemen farmers" interested in agricultural innovation.
   - England's relatively *open social structure* permitted the rise of New Men, such as Watt and Wilkinson, who brought to manufacturing a burst of new social energies.
   - Many other causes could be cited as well. The Industrial Revolution was a *many-sided, complex chain of events.*

Output

3. The Industrial Revolution brought with it changes of the greatest importance in society.

   - It ushered in a slow but cumulative *rise in output* that was eventually to lift the industrial world out of an age-old poverty.
   - It brought the *factory* (and the *industrial slum*) as a new environment for work and life.
   - It gave rise to new kinds of *social abuses,* but it also greatly sharpened the general *awareness of economic conditions.*

Capital building

4. The Industrial Revolution was essentially a *capital-building process* (machines, buildings, canals, railways), as a result of which the productivity of labor was greatly increased.

Productivity

5. *Capital generally enhances productivity* because it gives people far greater physical and technical capabilities than they enjoy with unaided labor alone. It also enables people to combine and *specialize* their labor, as in modern factory production lines.

Saving

6. *Capital building requires saving.* Capital can be built only if society has the use of resources normally used for filling its consumption needs. Saving releases these resources; investing puts them to use.

Investment

7. Society cannot devote more resources or energies to capital building than those it releases from other uses (or those it has available as unemployed resources). By and large, *saving regulates the pace at which investment can proceed.* Poor societies, in which it is difficult to give up consumption, accordingly have great problems in amassing enough resources for investment.

Consumption

8. The saving necessary for investment can come from agriculture, manufacturing enterprises, and many other sources. In poor nations, it must also often be wrung from workers or peasants, by denying them the use of all the nation's economic potential to fill their consumption needs.

9. *Saving in poor nations is usually an involuntary process.* Capital building in many developing nations today, particularly those under authoritarian regimes, is attempted by the agency of command, not very successfully, on the whole. In the Industrial Revolution, it was accomplished in part by command, but mainly by the market system. The remarkable inventions of the Industrial Revolution served as sources of profits that resulted in great accumulations of capital.

Questions

1. It is interesting to note that technical improvements in agriculture or manufacturing have generally been slow to arise in countries that have relied on slave labor. Can you think of a reason why this might be so?
2. What forces do you think would be necessary to bring a new "industrial revolution" to the underdeveloped world today? Is an industrial revolution there apt to resemble the one that took place in England in the eighteenth century?
3. Industrialization in England was marked by a sharp growth of bitter political feeling on the part of the new factory proletariat. Do you think this must be an accompaniment of industrialization everywhere, or was it a particular product of early capitalism?
4. How does capital help human productivity? Discuss this in relation to the following kinds of labor: farm labor, office help, teaching, government administration.
5. When General Motors devotes $1 billion to new investment (e.g., building new factories, warehouses, offices), who does the saving that is required? Stockholders? Workers? The public? Buyers of cars?
6. It is estimated that the value of our private capital structures and equipment in the United States in 1992 was some $18 trillion. Assume that half of it were wiped out in some catastrophe. What would happen to U.S. productivity? To average U.S. well-being? How could the damage be repaired?
7. Does all investment require saving? Why?
8. Is capital building in the United States today directed by the market alone? Does the government accumulate capital? Does public capital improve productivity as well as private capital?
9. Is building a school an "investment"? Is building a hospital? A sports stadium? A housing project? A research lab? What do you think distinguishes investment, in general, from consumption?

Thinking Back, Looking Ahead

THE EMBEDEDNESS OF ECONOMICS

The fact-packed pages behind us lead to a question central to economics that is curiously hard to answer. It is whether there is an inner core to that complicated thing we call "economic history"—the "story," if you will, that lies behind the title of our book.

Is technology the theme of that larger story? It certainly seems to be just such a core in the period we have just studied. If so, however, what was the shaping force of economic history during the thousands of years before that dynamic technology was born? Kinship obligations were surely the organizing force of hunting and gathering societies, and relations of command and obedience were the core of the social formations that followed them. What have kinship, or command and obedience, to do, though, with economics as we know it? Does economics always rest on some fundamental sociological, or psychological, or political aspect of society? Is there no *economic* organizing force, as such? Does that mean that to be an economic historian we need to know a great deal about engineering and social and political relationships? Or, looking ahead to the world of market systems, does it mean that economists have to be experts on the psychol-ogy of buyers and sellers of all kinds, not least of stocks and bonds? If so, what is left for economics to add?

Here is our answer: We see economics as a unique field of social inquiry that helps us understand why human history has gone in the directions of the past and in whatever directions it may move in the imaginable future.

That certainly does not make us one-track thinkers who see production and distribution, or markets, or even the powerful dynamics of capitalism behind everything, important as these forces have been and are likely to continue to be. There can be more than one way to describe the nature and impact of capitalism on politics or national cultures or the human imagination. Looking forward in economics is no more cut and dried than we hope looking backward has been.

We ask you to read the following chapters with a sharpened awareness of our interest in the ways in which economics may help us see both the past and the future more clearly. By now, you must have determined the degree to which economics has helped you understand the past. Beginning with Chapter 5, you should be looking for ways in which economics may—or may not—be useful in shedding light on the future.

CHAPTER

The Impact
of Industrial Technology

W ith this chapter, we enter a new period of economic history. Until now, we
have largely dealt with the past, giving only an occasional glance to later
echoes of the problems we encountered. Our focus now turns toward the present. We have reached the stage of economic history whose nearest boundary is our own
time. Simultaneously, our point of geographic focus shifts. As economic history enters
the mid-nineteenth century, the dynamic center of events begins to shift toward the
United States. Not only do we now begin to enter the modern world, but the economic
trends in which we will be interested take us directly into our own society.

What is the theme of this chapter? Essentially, it continues a motif we began with
the Industrial Revolution—the impact of technology on economic society. Looking
back, we can see that the burst of inventions that marked the revolution was not in any
sense the completion of a historic event. Rather, it was merely the inception of a change
process that would continually accelerate to the present time.

We can distinguish three or even four stages of this continuous process. The first industrial revolution was largely concentrated in new textile machinery, improved methods of coal production and iron manufacture, revolutionary agricultural techniques, and
steam power. It was succeeded in the mid-nineteenth century by a second industrial
revolution: a clustering of industrial inventions centering on steel, railroad and steamship transportation, agricultural machinery, and chemicals. By the early twentieth century, there was a third wave of inventions: electrical power, automobiles, and the
gasoline engine. In our own time, there is a fourth: the revolution of electronics, air
travel, and nuclear energy. Some people speak of today's computerization of the world
as constituting a fifth such revolution, perhaps the most important of all.

It is difficult, perhaps impossible, to exaggerate the impact of this continuing advance. Now moving rapidly, now slowly; now on a broad front, now on a narrow
salient; now in the most practical of inventions, again in the purest of theoretical discoveries, the cumulative application of science and technology to the productive
process was *the* great change of the nineteenth and twentieth centuries. The initial Industrial Revolution was therefore in retrospect a kind of discontinuous leap in human
history, a leap as important as that which had lifted the first pastoral settlements above
the earlier hunting communities. We have already noted that in the factory the new
technology brought a new working place for people, but its impact was vastly greater
than that alone. The enormously heightened powers of transportation and communication, the far more effective means of wresting a crop from the soil, the hugely enhanced ability to apply power for lifting, hauling, shaping, binding, cutting—all this
conspired to bring about a literal remaking of the human environment, and by no
means an entirely benign one.

IMPACT OF ONE INVENTION

In this book, we cannot do more than inquire into some of the economic consequences of the incursion of industrial technology into modern society. However, it may help us gain some insight into the dimensions of that penetrative process if we follow for a short distance the repercussions of a single invention introduced more than a century ago.

Let us therefore look in on the Paris Exposition of 1867, where curious visitors are gathered around an interesting exhibit: a small engine in which illuminating gas and air are introduced into a combustion chamber and ignited by a spark. The resulting explosion pushes a piston; the piston turns a wheel. There is but one working stroke in every four, and the machine requires a large flywheel to regularize its movement, but, as the historian Allan Nevins writes, the effect of the machine "was comparable to the sudden snapping on of an electric globe in a room men had been trying to light with smoky candles."[1] It was the world's first internal combustion engine.

It was not long before the engine, invented by Dr. N. A. Otto of Germany, was a regular feature of the American landscape. Adapted to run on gasoline, a hitherto uninteresting by-product of kerosene manufacture, it was an ideal stationary power plant. Writes Nevins, "Soon every progressive farm, shop, and feed-mill had its one-cylinder engine chugging away, pumping water, sawing wood, grinding meal, and doing other small jobs."[2] By 1900, there were more than 18,500 internal combustion engines in the United States; whereas the most powerful model in the Chicago World's Fair in 1893 was 35 horsepower, at the Paris Exposition 7 years later, it was 1,000 horsepower.

The internal combustion engine was an extraordinary means of increasing, diffusing, and giving mobility to a basic requirement of material progress: power. Soon the new engine opened the way for a yet more startling advance. In 1886, Charles E. Duryea of Chicopee, Massachusetts, had already decided that the gasoline engine was a far more promising power source than steam for a self-propelling road vehicle. By 1892, he and his brother had produced the first gas-powered "automobile," a weak and fragile toy. The next model in 1893 was a better one, and by 1896, the Duryea brothers actually sold 13 cars. In that same year, a 32-year-old mechanic named Henry Ford sold his first "quadricycle." The history of the automobile industry had begun.

The Automobilization of America

Its growth was phenomenal. By 1905, there were 121 establishments making automobiles, and 10,000 wage earners were employed in the industry. By 1923, the number of plants had risen to 2,471, making the industry the largest in the country. In 1960, its annual payroll was as large as the national income of the United States in 1890. Not only that, but the automobile industry had become the single greatest customer for sheet steel, zinc, lead, rubber, and leather. It was the buyer of one out of every three radios produced in the nation. It absorbed 25 billion pounds of chemicals a year. It was the second largest user of engineering talent in the country, bowing only to national defense. It was the source of one-sixth of all the patents issued in the nation and the object of one-tenth of all consumer spending in the country. By the 1980s, it was estimated that roughly one job out of every seven owed its existence directly or indirectly to the car,

---

[1]Allan Nevins, *Ford* (New York: Scribner's, 1954), I, p. 96.
[2]Allan Nevins, *Study in Power, John D. Rockefeller* (New York: Scribner's, 1953), II, p. 109.

as did one business out of every six—not just factories, of course, but repair shops, garages, gas stations, and traffic police departments.

Even this impressive array of figures by no means exhausts the impact of the internal combustion engine and its vehicular mounting. By 2001, 96 million U.S. households own 151 million passenger cars; more than one in two own two or more cars. As a result, some 50,000 towns manage to flourish without rail or water connections, an erstwhile impossibility. At least seven out of ten workers no longer live within walking distance of their places of employment but drive to work. To an extraordinary extent, our entire economy has become "mobilized"—which is to say, dependent for its very functioning on the existence of wheeled, self-propelled transportation. If by some strange occurrence our automotive fleet were put out of commission—say by a spontaneous change in the nature of the gasoline molecule, rendering it incombustible—the effect would be as grave and socially disastrous as a catastrophic famine in the Middle Ages.[3] No wonder that the Arab oil embargos of 1974 and 1979 shook the industrialized world!

THE GENERAL IMPACT OF TECHNOLOGY

We dwell on the impact of the car to stress the economic consequences of technology. These may not be its most ultimately important consequences. Ours is a world threatened in many ways by the extraordinary disruptive power of man's inventive capacity. Technology has progressed to the point at which whole species (including humankind itself) are endangered by the poisons we manufacture and carelessly spew into the air and water, by the vast quantities of heat we throw into the atmosphere, and of course by the capacity for explosive disintegration that has come with the mastery of the atomic nucleus.

Later we examine some of these problems when we turn to the immediate issues confronting the United States. But at this point, while we are studying the general effects of man's gradually increasing technological powers, we leave aside these very large problems to focus on the ways in which technology has silently affected our economic system. Let us look into some of these effects.

Urbanization

The first has been a vast increase in the degree of urbanization of society. To an extraordinary extent, technology has enhanced the ability of the farmer to support the nonfarmer. As a result, society has increasingly taken on the aspects and problems of the city rather than the country. In 1790, only 24 towns and cities in all of the United States had a population of more than 2,500, and together they accounted for only 6 percent of the total population. By 1860, the 392 biggest cities held 20 percent of the population; 130 years later, more than three-quarters of the nation's people lived in 268 great "standard or consolidated metropolitan areas," and the belt from Boston to Washington was in fact, if not in government, one vast sprawling "city." Industrial technology has literally refashioned the human environment, bringing with it all the gains—and all the terrible problems—of city life on a mass scale.

---

[3]The economist Kenneth Boulding once suggested that if the United States were to be visited by intelligent beings from another part of the universe, their initial impression would probably be that the dominant form of life here consists of creatures with hard shells and soft pulpy insides, who are propelled by wheels, although the creatures are capable of sluggish motion on their own when not encased in their natural exoskeletons.

Interdependence

Second, the steady growth of industrial technology has greatly lessened the degree of economic independence of the average citizen. In our opening chapter, we note the extreme vulnerability of the "unsupported" inhabitants of a modern society, dependent on the work of a thousand others to sustain their own existence. This, too, we can now trace to the effect of the continuing industrial revolution. Technology has not only moved people off the soil and into the city, but has vastly increased the specialized nature of work. Unlike the person of all trades of the early nineteenth century—the farmers who could perform so many of their necessary tasks themselves—the typical factory worker or office worker is trained and employed to do only one small part of a social operation that now achieves staggering complexity. Technology has vastly increased the degree of economic interdependence of the modern community and has made the solution of the economic problem hinge on the smooth coordination of an ever-widening network of delicately connected activities.

Sociological Effects

Third, the expansion of industrial technology has radically changed the character of work itself. For the greater part of human history, work was a strenuous physical activity, largely carried on alone or in small groups in the open air, requiring considerable dexterity to match human strength to the infinite variations of the natural environment, and culminating in an end product as unambiguously identifiable as the grain in the field or the cloth on a loom.

The Industrial Revolution profoundly altered these attributes of work. Work now consisted more and more of repetitive movements that, however exhausting after a full day, rarely involved more than a fraction of a person's full muscular ability. In place of the judgments and aptitudes required to meet the variations of nature, it demanded only the ability to repeat a single task adapted to a changeless work surface. No longer alone in nature, workers performed their jobs in vast sheds with regiments like themselves. Most wrenching of all, in place of "their" product, what they saw emerging from the factory was an object in which they could no longer locate, much less appreciate, their own contribution:

> I work on a small conveyor which goes around in a circle. We call it a "merry-go-round." I make up zigzag springs for front seats. Every couple of feet on the conveyor there is a form for the pieces that make up the seat springs. As the form goes by me, I clip several pieces together, using a clip gun. I then put the pieces on the form, and it goes around to where other men clip more pieces together. . . . The only operation I do is work the clip gun. It takes just a couple of seconds to shoot six or eight clips into the spring and I do it as I walk a few steps. Then I start right over again. . . .[4]

It is not surprising that this change in the character of work had deep sociological repercussions to which we return in later chapters. But we have yet to pay heed to two much more immediate "economic" effects of the continuing industrial revolution.

---

[4]Charles R. Walker and Robert H. Guest, *The Man on the Assembly Line* (Cambridge, MA: Harvard University Press, 1952), p. 46.

MASS PRODUCTION

The first of these is already implicit in our description of the new technology. It is the development of a new method of continuous throughput—so-called mass production—that far exceeded the productivity gains of Adam Smith's pin factory, which depended only on the division of labor.

The historian Allan Nevins has described what mass-production techniques looked like in the early Ford assembly lines:

> Just how were the main assembly lines and lines of component production and supply kept in harmony? For the chassis alone, from 1,000 to 4,000 pieces of each component had to be furnished each day at just the right point and right minute; a single failure, and the whole mechanism would come to a jarring standstill. . . . Superintendents had to know every hour just how many components were being produced and how many were in stock. Whenever danger of shortage appeared, the shortage chaser—a familiar figure in all automobile factories—flung himself into the breach. Counters and checkers reported to him. Verifying in person any ominous news, he mobilized the foreman concerned to repair deficiencies. Three times a day he made typed reports in manifold to the factory clearing-house, at the same time chalking on blackboards in the clearing-house office a statement of results in each factory-production department and each assembling department.[5]

Such systematizing in itself resulted in astonishing increases in productivity. With each operation analyzed and subdivided into its simplest components, with a steady stream of work passing before stationary people, with a relentless but manageable pace of work, the total time required to assemble a car dropped astonishingly. Within a single year, the time required to assemble a motor fell from 600 minutes to 226 minutes; to build a chassis, from 12 hours and 28 minutes to 1 hour and 33 minutes. A stopwatch man was told to observe a 3-minute assembly in which men assembled rods and piston, a simple operation. The job was divided into three jobs, and half the men turned out the same output.[6] Today this routinization of work is often called *Fordism.* It is on the wane, but it still exists.

Economies of Large-Scale Production

But what interests us in the context of our study is not the technical achievements of mass production as much as its economic results: Increases in the scale of production can bring great reductions in cost. Even though the machinery needed for mass production is extremely expensive, output increases so fast that costs per unit of output drop dramatically.

Imagine, for instance, a small plant turning out 1,000 items a day with the labor of 10 workers and a small amount of equipment. Suppose each worker is paid $50, each item of material before manufacture costs 50¢, and the daily amount of overhead—that is, the daily share of costs such as rent, plant maintenance, office salaries, and wear and tear on equipment—comes to $500. Our total daily cost of production is $1,500 ($500 of

---

[5] *Ford, the Times, the Man, the Company,* I, p. 507.
[6] *Ford,* pp. 504, 506.

payroll, $500 of material costs, and $500 of overhead). Divided among 1,000 items of output, our cost per item is $1.50.

Now imagine that our product lends itself to mass-production techniques. Our payroll may then jump to $1,000 and, with our much larger plant and equipment, our daily overhead to $5,000. Nevertheless, mass production may have boosted output as much as 100 times. Our total daily cost of production is $56,000 ($1,000 of payroll, $5,000 of overhead, and $50,000 of material costs). Divided among our 100,000 items of output, our cost per item has fallen to 56¢. Despite more than a 30-fold rise in overall expense, our cost per unit has been almost cut to one-third.

This is not a far-fetched example of what economists call the economies of large-scale production, or more simply, economies of scale. A glance at Table 5-1 shows how mass-production techniques did, in fact, boost output of Ford cars by more than 100 times while reducing their cost by seven-eighths.

Nor do the dynamics of the industrial process come to a halt with these formidable economies of large-scale production. This technological achievement brings into the market system itself a new element of primary importance: size.

It is not difficult to see why. When a firm—by virtue of adroit management, improved product, advantages of location, or whatever other reason—steps out decisively in front of its competitors in size, economies of large-scale production operate to push it out still further in front. Bigger size usually means lower cost, at least for a young, expanding industry. Lower cost means bigger profits. Bigger profits mean the ability to grow to still larger size. The techniques of large-scale manufacturing bring about a situation threatening to alter the whole meaning of competition. From a mechanism that prevents any single firm from dominating the market, competition now becomes a force that may drive an ever-larger share of the market into the hands of the largest and most efficient producer.[7]

AGENTS OF INDUSTRIAL CHANGE

The Great Entrepreneurs

We shall have more to say about the economics of large-scale production when we study the evolution of the market system at the end of this chapter. However, it may be helpful if we look once again at the actual historic scene in which this internal growth took place. The processes of economic change described in this chapter did not occur in a vacuum. They were brought about by a social "type" and a business milieu that powerfully accelerated and abetted the process of industrial enlargement, much as the New Men had influenced the initial industrializing process in England in the late eighteenth century.

The agents of change during the late nineteenth century in the United States were very much the descendants of their industrial forebears a century earlier. Like Arkwright and Watt, many of the greatest American entrepreneurs were men of

---

[7]In an important book, *The Visible Hand: The Managerial Revolution in American Business* (Cambridge, MA: Harvard University Press, 1977), Alfred D. Chandler looks into why some industries displayed a tendency toward the emergence of big business (such as autos) and others did not (such as furniture). The crucial elements, he shows, were a cost-cutting, mass-producing technology, which did not develop in all industries, and an equally important technology of mass distribution, also not available to every industry.

TABLE 5-1 Sales and Prices of Ford Automobiles, 1907–1917		
Year	**Unit Sales, Ford Cars**	**Price of Typical Model (Touring)**
1907–1908	6,398	$2,800 (Model K)
1908–1909	10,607	850 ⎫
1909–1910	18,664	950 ⎮
1910–1911	34,528	780 ⎮
1911–1912	78,440	690 ⎮
1912–1913	168,304	600 ⎬ Model T
1913–1914	248,307	550 ⎮
1914–1915	221,805 (10 mos.)	490 ⎮
1915–1916	472,350	440 ⎮
1916–1917	730,041	360 ⎭

Source: Compiled from Nevins, *Ford, the Times, the Man, the Company,* pp. 644, 646–647.

humble origin, endowed with an indomitable drive for business success. There was Carnegie in steel, Harriman in railroads, Rockefeller in oil, Frick in coke, Armour and Swift in meatpacking, and McCormick in agricultural machinery—to mention but a few. To be sure, the typical businessman was very different from these Horatio Alger stereotypes of the business hero. Economic historians, such as F. W. Taussig, looking back over the careers of the business leaders of the late nineteenth century, have discovered that the average entrepreneur was not a poor, industrious immigrant lad, but the son of well-circumstanced people often in business affairs themselves. Nor was the average businessman nearly so successful as a Carnegie or a Rockefeller.

Captains of Industry

In nearly every line of business, at least one "captain of industry" appeared who dominated the field by his personality and ability. Though few achieved their supreme degree of pecuniary success, the number who climbed into the "millionaire class" was impressive. In 1880, it was estimated that there were 100 millionaires in the country. By 1916, the number had grown to 40,000.

Interesting and significant differences distinguish these nineteenth-century business leaders from those a century earlier. The American captains of industry were not typically men whose leadership rested on inventive or engineering skills. With the growth of large-scale production, the engineering functions became the province of salaried production experts, of second-echelon plant managers. What was required now was the master touch in guiding industrial strategy, in making or breaking alliances, choosing salients for advance, or overseeing the logistics of the whole operation. Increasingly, the great entrepreneurs were concerned with the strategy of finance, of competition, of sales, rather than with the cold techniques of production itself.

Then, too, we must make note of the entrepreneurial tactics and tone of the period. In a phrase that has stuck, Matthew Josephson once called the great men of business in this era "the robber barons." In many ways, they did indeed resemble the predatory lords of the medieval era. For example, in the 1860s, a small group of California entrepreneurs under the guiding hand of Collis Huntington performed the astonishing feat of building a railroad across the hitherto impassable Rockies and Sierras. Aware that Huntington and his associates would thereby have a monopolistic control of all rail traffic to California, Congress authorized the construction of three competing lines. But the legislators had not taken the measure of the wily pioneers. Before their own line was completed, they secretly bought the charter of one competitive line; when the second proved somewhat harder to buy out, they simply built it out, recklessly flinging their lines into its territory until it, too, was forced to surrender. Thereafter, it was no great trick to buy out the third, having first blocked it at a critical mountain pass. Only one competitive source of transportation remained: the Pacific Mail Steamship Company. Fortunately, this was owned by the obliging Jay Gould, a famous robber baron in his own right; for the payment of a proper tribute, he agreed to eliminate San Francisco as a cargo port. There was now no way of bringing goods across the nation into southern California except those the Huntington group controlled. Counting the smaller lines and subsidiaries that passed into their grasp, 19 rail systems, in all, came under their domain. It was not surprising that to the residents of California, the resulting unified system was known as "the Octopus" and that its average freight rate was the highest in the nation.

The Omnipresent Trust

It was not just the railroad industry that used economic power to create a monopoly position. In whiskey and in sugar, in tobacco and cattle feed, in wire nails, steel hoops, electrical appliances, tinplate, in matches and meat, there was an octopus similar to that which fastened itself on California. One commentator of the late 1890s pictured the American citizen as born to the profit of the Milk Trust and dying to that of the Coffin Trust.

If the robber barons milked the public as consumers (and to an even greater extent bilked them as stockholders), they also had no compunctions about cutting each other down to size. In the struggle for financial control of the Albany and Susquehanna Railroad, for instance, James Fisk and J. P. Morgan found themselves in the uncomfortable position of each owning a terminal at the end of a single line. Like their feudal prototypes, they resolved the controversy by combat, mounting locomotives at each end and running them full tilt into each other—after which the losers still did not give up, but retired, ripping up the line and tearing down trestles as they went. In similar spirit, the Huntington group that built the Central Pacific hired General David Colton to run a subsidiary enterprise for them, and the general wrote to his employers:

> I have learned one thing. We have got *no true* friends outside of us five. We cannot depend upon a human soul outside of ourselves, and hence we must all be good-natured, stick together, and keep to our own counsels.

Whereupon he proceeded to swindle his friends out of several millions.

With this buccaneering went as well another identifying mark of the times: what the economist Thorstein Veblen was to call Conspicuous Consumption. One repentant member of the Gilded Age recalled in his memoirs parties at which cigarettes were wrapped in money for the sheer pleasure of inhaling wealth; a dog that was presented with a $15,000 diamond collar; an infant, resting in a $10,000 cradle, attended by four doctors who posted regular bulletins on the baby's (excellent) health; the parade of fabulous chateaux stuffed with fabulous and not-so-fabulous works of art on

New York's Fifth Avenue; and the collection of impecunious European royalty as sons-in-law of the rich.

The age was a rollicking, sometimes cruel, but always dynamic one. However, our task here is not to recount its colorful social history as much as to understand its deeper economic consequences. It is impossible to consider the period with which we have been concerned without taking into account the social type of robber barons and the milieu in which they operated. Bold, aggressive, acquisitive, competitive, the great entrepreneur was the natural agent to speed along the process for which the technology of the day prepared the way. But as yet we have only begun to sketch the changes wrought by the joint impact of strong men and ever-more-complex machinery. Hitherto we have mainly looked at the direct technical effects of mass production; now we must investigate its broader economic effects.

THE CHANGE IN MARKET STRUCTURE

We can describe those effects very simply. Under the joint influence of the drive of bold entrepreneurs and the self-feeding tendencies of mass production, dramatic changes began to appear in the structure of the market itself. A production system originally characterized by large numbers of small enterprises increasingly gave way to one in which production was concentrated in the hands of a relatively few, very big and powerful business units.

A look at the economy shows how dramatic was the transformation. By 1900, for example, the number of textile mills, although still large, had dropped by a third from the 1880s; over the same period, the number of manufacturers of agricultural implements had fallen by 60 percent, and the number of leather manufacturers by three-quarters. In the locomotive industry, two companies ruled the roost in 1900, contrasted with nineteen in 1860. The biscuit and cracker industry changed from a scatter of small companies to a market in which one producer had 90 percent of the industry's capacity by the turn of the century. Meanwhile, in steel, there was the colossal US Steel Corporation, which alone turned out more than half the steel production of the nation. In oil, the Standard Oil Company tied up between 80 to 90 percent of the nation's output. In tobacco, the American Tobacco Company controlled 75 percent of the output of cigarettes and 25 percent of cigars. Similar control rested with the American Sugar Company, the American Smelting and Refining Company, the United Shoe Machinery Company, and dozens more.

From an overall view, the change was even more impressive. In the early 1800s, according to the calculations of Myron W. Watkins, no single plant controlled as much as 10 percent of the output of a manufacturing industry. By 1904, 78 enterprises controlled more than half the output of their industries; 57 controlled 60 percent or more; and 28 controlled 80 percent or more. From industry to industry, this degree of concentration varied—from no significant concentration at all in printing and publishing, for instance, to the highly concentrated market structure of industries like copper or rubber. There was no mistaking the overall change. In 1896, railroads excepted, there were not a dozen $10 million companies in the nation. By 1904, there were more than 300 of them, with a combined capitalization of more than $7 billion. Together, these giants controlled more than two-fifths of the industrial capital of the nation and affected four-fifths of its important industries.[8]

Clearly, something akin to a major revolution in market structure had taken place, not just in the United States, but in all capitalist nations. Let us examine more closely the course of events that led up to it.

THE RISE OF BIG BUSINESS

Change in Competition

The initial impact of the trend to big business was an unexpected one. Rather than diminishing the degree of competitiveness of the market structure, it extended and intensified it. In the largely agricultural, handicraft, and small-factory economy of the early nineteenth century, "the market" consisted mainly of small, localized markets, each insulated from the next by the high cost of transportation and each supplied by local producers who had neither the means nor the motivation to invade the market on anything resembling a national scale.

The rise of mass production radically changed this fragmented market structure and, with it, the type of competition within the market. As canals and railroads opened the country and as new manufacturing techniques vastly increased output, the parochial quality of the market system changed. Increasingly, one unified and interconnected market bound together the entire nation, and the petty semimonopolies of local suppliers were invaded by products from large factories in distant cities.

Quickly, a second development followed. As the new production techniques gained momentum, aggressive capitalists typically not only built, but overbuilt. "[C]onfident entrepreneurs raced to take advantage of every ephemeral rise in prices, of every advance in tariff schedules, of every new market opened by the railroads and puffed up immigration," write Thomas Cochran and William Miller in a history of these industrializing times, "they recklessly expanded and mechanized their plants, each seeking the greatest share of the new melon."[9]

The result was a phenomenal burst in output but, simultaneously, a serious change in the nature of competition. Competition now became not only more extensive, but more expensive. As the size of the plant and the complexity of equipment grew, so did the "fixed charges" of a business enterprise—the interest on borrowed capital, the depreciation of capital assets, the cost of administrative staff, the rent of land, and overhead, generally. By the 1880s, for example, fixed costs averaged two-thirds of the total cost of railroad operation. These costs tended to remain fairly constant, regardless of whether sales were good or bad. Unlike the payment of wages to a working force, which dropped when workers were fired, there was no easy way to cut down the steady drain of payments for these fixed expenditures. The result was that the bigger the business, the more vulnerable its economic health when competition cut into its sales.

The ebullience of the age, plus the steady growth of a technology that required massive investments, made competition increasingly drastic. As growing giant businesses

---

[8]John Moody, *The Truth about Trusts* (Chicago: Moody, 1904). See also Ralph Nelson, *Merger Movements in American Industry, 1895–1956* (Princeton, NJ: National Bureau of Economic Research, 1959).
[9]Thomas Cochran and William Miller, *The Age of Enterprise,* rev. ed. (New York: Harper, Torchbooks, 1961), p. 139.

locked horns, railroad against railroad, steel mill against steel mill, each sought to en-sure the coverage of its fixed expenses by gaining for itself as much of the market as it could. The outcome was the emergence of cutthroat competition among massive pro-ducers, replacing the more restricted, local competition of the small-business, small-market world. In 1869, for example, the New York–Chicago railway freight rate on a hundredweight of grain crashed from $1.80 on February 4 to 40¢ 20 days later, climbed back to $1.88 in July, and then plummeted to 25¢ in August when another "war" broke out. In the oil fields, the coal fields, among the steel and copper producers, similar price wars repeatedly occurred as producers sought to capture the markets they needed to achieve a profitable level of production. All this was unquestionably favorable to the consumer, as competitive situations always are, but it threatened literal bankruptcy for the competing enterprises themselves—and furthermore, bankruptcy on a multimillion-dollar scale.

Limitation of Competition

In these circumstances, it is not difficult to understand the next phase of economic de-velopment. The giants decided not to compete.

But how were they to avoid competition? Because common law invalidated any contract binding a competitor to fixed prices or production schedules, there seemed no alternative but voluntary cooperation: trade associations, "gentleman's agreements" or "pools," informal treaties to divide the market. By the 1800s, there were a cordage pool and a whiskey pool, a coal pool, a salt pool, and endless rail pools, all calculated to relieve the individual producers from the mutually suicidal game of all-out competition. But to little avail. The division of the market worked well during good times, but when bad times approached, the pools broke down. As sales fell, the temptation to cut prices was irresistible, and thus began again the old, ruinous game of competition.

The robber-baron ethics of the day contributed to the difficulties. "A starving man will usually get bread if it is to be had," said James J. Hill, a great railway magnate, "and a starving railway will not maintain rates."[10] Typically, at a meeting of railroad heads called to agree upon a common freight schedule, the president of one road slipped out, during a brief recess, to wire the new rates to his road, so that it might be the first to undercut them. (By chance, his wire was intercepted, so that when the group next met, it was forced to recognize that even among thieves there is not always honor.)

Trusts, Mergers, and Growth

During the 1880s, a more effective device for control became available. In 1879, Samuel Dodd, lawyer for the new Standard Oil Company, had a brilliant idea for regulating the murderous competition that regularly wracked the oil industry. He devised the idea of a trust. Stockholders of companies that wished to join in the Standard Oil Trust were asked to surrender their actual shares to the board of directors of the new trust. They would give up working control over their companies, but in return they would get trust certificates that entitled them to the same share in the profits as their shares earned. In

---

[10]Cochran and Miller, *The Age of Enterprise,* p. 141.

this way, the Standard Oil directors wielded control over all the associated companies, while the former stockholders shared fully in the profits.

Eventually, as we shall see, the trusts were declared illegal. By that time, still more effective devices had been created. In 1888, the New Jersey legislature passed a law allowing a corporation chartered in the state to buy stock in another corporation. This was a privilege that had not previously been available to corporations chartered anywhere in the United States. The result was the rapid appearance of the corporate merger—the coming together of two corporations to form a new, bigger one. In manufacturing and mining alone, there were 43 mergers in 1895 (affecting $41 million worth of corporate assets); 26 mergers in 1896; and 69 mergers in 1897. In 1898, there were 303—and finally, in 1899, a climactic 1,208 mergers combined some $2.26 billion in corporate assets.[11] A further great wave of mergers occurred in the 1920s. In all, from 1895 to 1929, some $20 billion in industrial corporate wealth was merged into larger units.

At this point, we must call attention to a development that deserves a chapter in itself. This is the importance of the *corporation*, as a marvelously adaptive legal form of organizing production, in spurring on the growth of the economy. Unlike the personal proprietorship or partnership, the corporation existed quite independently of its owners, survived their deaths, and could enter into binding contracts in "its" own name. Further, by limiting the liability of its owners to the value of the stock they had bought, it protected a capitalist against limitless loss. Much has been written, quite rightly, about the abuses of corporations, but it is important to recognize how valuable was this ingenious legal innovation in encouraging the accumulation of capital and in creating the organizational means to supervise and direct that capital into production.

The holding company was another effective means of limiting competition. Having passed a law permitting its corporations to buy stock in one another, New Jersey now allowed its corporations to do business in any state. The legal foundation was laid for a central corporation that could control subsidiary enterprises by the simple means of buying a controlling share of their stock. By 1911, when the Standard Oil combine was finally dissolved, Standard Oil of New Jersey had used this device to acquire direct control over 70 companies and indirect control over 30 more.

However, we must not think that it was only the movement toward trustification and merger that brought about the emergence of the giant firm with its ability to limit—or eliminate—competition. Equally, perhaps more, important was simply the process of internal growth. Ford and General Motors, General Electric and AT&T, du Pont and Carnegie Steel (later to be the core of US Steel) grew essentially because their market was expanding and they were quick, able, efficient, and aggressive enough to grow faster than any of their competitors. All of them gobbled up some small businesses along the way, and most of them benefited from agreements not to compete. However, their gradual emergence to a position of dominance within their industries was not, in the last analysis, attributable to these facts. It was, rather, the dynamism of their own business leadership, coupled with a production technique that made enormous size both possible and profitable.

---

[11]*Historical Statistics of the United States: Colonial Times to 1970,* edited by Susan B. Carter, Series V, pp. 30–31, on CD-Rom (New York: Cambridge University Press).

Threat of Monopoly Capitalism

For the first time, business size began to rival the size of government units. By the end of the nineteenth century, some business units were already considerably larger than the states in which they were located. Charles William Eliot pointed out in 1888 that a single railway with headquarters in Boston not only employed three times as many people as the entire government of the Commonwealth of Massachusetts, but enjoyed gross receipts nearly six times that of the state government that had created it. By comparison with the findings of the Pujo Committee of the U.S. Senate, not quite 25 years later, the railway was rather small. The committee pointed out that the Morgan banking interests held 341 directorships in 112 corporations whose aggregate wealth exceeded by three times the value of all the real and personal property of New England. Not only was the process of trustification eating away at the competitive structure of the market, but the emergence of enormous financially controlled empires posed as well a political problem of ominous portent. As Woodrow Wilson declared, "If monopoly persists, monopoly will always sit at the helm of government. I do not expect to see monopoly restrain itself. If there are men in this country big enough to own the government of the United States, they are going to own it."[12]

Rise of Antitrust Legislation

Not surprisingly, from many quarters the trend to big business was vehemently opposed. From the 1880s on, a series of state laws strove to undo the trusts that squeezed their citizens. Louisiana sued the Cottonseed Oil Trust; New York, the Sugar Trust; Ohio, the Oil Trust—but to little avail. When one state, like New York, clamped down on its trusts, other states, seeking the revenue available from a change in corporate headquarters, virtually invited the trust to set up business there. When the Supreme Court ruled that corporations, as "persons," could not be deprived of property without "due process of law," state regulation became almost totally useless.

It was soon clear that if something further were to be done, the federal government would have to do it. "Congress alone can deal with the trusts," said Senator Sherman in 1890, "and if we are unwilling or unable, there will soon be a trust for every production and a master to fix the price for every necessity of life."[13]

The result was the Sherman Antitrust Act, which, on its surface, was an effective remedy for the problem. "Every contract, combination . . . or conspiracy, in restraint of trade" was declared to be illegal. Violators were subject to heavy fines and jail sentences, and triple damages could be obtained by persons who proved economic injury because of unfair price rigging.

Indeed, under the Sherman Act a number of trusts were prosecuted; in a famous action in 1911, the great Standard Oil Trust was ordered dissolved. Yet, despite the breakup of a few trusts, the act was singularly weak. Fines for violations were too small to be effective, and in any case, few were levied: Not until Franklin Roosevelt's time would the Antitrust Division of the Department of Justice have as much as a million dollars with which to investigate and control the affairs of a multibillion-dollar economy.

---

[12]Richard Hofstadter, *The Age of Reform* (New York: Knopf, 1955), p. 231.
[13]Cochran and Miller, *The Age of Enterprise*, p. 171.

In fact, during the first 50 years of its existence, only 252 criminal actions were instituted under the Sherman law. Then, too, the prevailing judicial opinion of the 1890s and early 1900s was not much in sympathy with the act. The Supreme Court early dealt it a severe blow by finding, in the American Sugar Refining case, that manufacturing was not "commerce," and therefore the American Sugar Refining Company, which had bought controlling stock interests in its four largest competitors, was not to be considered as acting "in restraint of trade." It is not surprising that the concentration of business was hardly slowed in such a climate of opinion. As a humorist of the times put it, "What looks like a stone wall to a layman is a triumphal arch to a corporation lawyer."

These weaknesses led to further acts in 1914: primarily, the Clayton Antitrust Act, prohibiting specific kinds of price discrimination and mergers by the acquisition of stock in competing corporations; and the Federal Trade Commission, which sought to define and prevent "unfair" business practices. These acts were not without their effect. Yet, undermining the entire antitrust movement was one critical and vitiating fact. The purpose of antitrust was essentially to restore competitive conditions to markets that were in danger of becoming monopolized by giant firms. Against this tendency, antitrust legislation could pose a deterrent only insofar as the monopolization process resulted from the outright *combination* of erstwhile competitors. Against a much more fundamental condition—the ability of large businesses to enjoy decisive advantages over small businesses in finance, merchandising, and research—it could offer no remedy. While antitrust effort concentrated its fire against collusion or amalgamation, it was powerless against the fact of spontaneous internal growth.

The Berle and Means Study

Therefore, growth continued. Through most of the first quarter of the twentieth century, the biggest corporations not only grew, but grew much faster than their smaller competitors. As Adolf Berle and Gardiner Means pointed out in a famous study in 1932, between 1909 and 1928, the 200 largest nonfinancial corporations increased their gross assets more than 40 percent more rapidly than all nonfinancial corporations.[14] Looking into the future, Berle and Means concluded:

> Just what does this rapid growth of the big companies promise for the future? Let us project the trend of the growth of recent years. If the wealth of the large corporations and that of all corporations should each continue to increase for the next twenty years at its average annual rate for the twenty years from 1909 to 1929, 70 percent of all corporate activity would be carried on by two hundred corporations in 1950. If the more rapid rates of growth from 1924 to 1929 were maintained for the next twenty years, 85 percent of corporate wealth would be held by two hundred huge units. . . . If the indicated growth of the large corporations and of the national wealth were to be effective from now until 1950, half of the national wealth would be under the control of big companies at the end of that period.[15]

---

[14]Adolf Berle and Gardiner Means, *The Modern Corporation and Private Property* (New York: Macmillan, 1948), p. 36.
[15]*The Modern Corporation and Private Property*, pp. 40–41.

Indeed, warned the authors, if the trend of the past continued unchecked, it was predictable that in 360 years, all the corporate wealth in the nation would have become fused into one gigantic enterprise, which would then have an expected life span equal to that of the Roman Empire.

Has the Berle and Means projection come true? We will come back to that momentous question. Before we can do so, we must examine an event of extraordinary importance. The event was to be called the Great Depression. As we shall see, it changed our perception of the economy fundamentally, including our view of the impact of technology on its workings.

Key Concepts and Key Words

Technical progress

1. The Industrial Revolution brought not one but *successive waves of technical progress* and economic advance.

2. In studying the impact of these industrial discoveries, we must broaden our lens to look beyond the effect on productivity alone (although that was no doubt the single most important result). Industrialization brought:

Urbanization

- A vast increase in *urbanization.*
- A cumulative rise in the degree of *economic interdependence* of individual persons within society.

Social effects

- A new climate for and character of work, including the disturbing problems of *monotonous industrial work* (alienation).

Mass production

3. The new technology brought as well a change in the character of both production and competition. Production became increasingly a process of highly integrated subassemblies, making possible the *mass production* of goods. The large amounts of capital required for mass production led to very great *economies of scale.*

Economies of scale

Destructive competition

4. With the advent of mass production, *the nature of competition also changed into a destructive force.* Economies of scale led to situations in which a leading firm could undersell all competitors and thus dominate a market.

Robber barrons

5. The dynamic potential of the new technology was given further impetus by the *aggressive "robber baron" era* of business leadership.

Concentration

6. A combination of aggressive entrepreneurship and the economies of scale typical of industrial technology brought about a *concentration of economic power* in many markets in the late nineteenth and early twentieth centuries.

Merger

7. The emergence of large firms with massive capital structures led to "cutthroat" competition that was exceedingly dangerous for the firms concerned. Hence there were *many attempts to stabilize the competitive struggle* by means of pools, trusts, holding companies, and mergers.

Antitrust

8. As the great trusts and combines rose to power, there was a "countervailing" thrust of political *antitrust legislation,* culminating in the Sherman Antitrust Act (1890), later in the Clayton Antitrust Act (1914), and in subsequent amendments designed to make mergers more difficult.

Internal growth

9. None of these laws prohibited or interfered with *internal growth.* As a result, large businesses continued to expand. A famous survey by Berle and Means in 1933 predicted that if the rate of growth of the top 200 nonfinancial corporations continued, they would soon own virtually the entire economy.

Questions

1. Describe the social and economic repercussions of the following inventions: the typewriter, the jet airplane, television, penicillin. Which do you think is greater in each case—the social or the economic impact?

2. The philosopher Karl Jaspers has claimed that modern technology brings an "immense joylessness." Do you agree? Is factory work unpleasant, to your mind? Office work in a very large organization such as an insurance company? Do you think the nature of industrial work can be basically changed?

3. Suppose that you have a business in which you hire five workers, to whom you pay $4 an hour; suppose further that you have overhead costs of $100 a day and that you pay $1 in materials cost for each item that your business manufactures. Assuming that you keep all five workers, what is your average cost per unit of output if your plant turns out 10 items per 8-hour day? 100 items? 1,000?

4. Which is more economical, a plant with a payroll of $400 a week, with $100 of overhead a week, and with an output of 100 units per week, or a plant with a payroll of $80,000 a week, an overhead of $100,000 a week, and an output of 50,000 units per week?

5. How do you explain economies of large-scale production? Why do certain businesses, such as cigarette manufacture, seem to enjoy them, whereas other businesses, such as barbering, do not?

6. Why does heavy overhead cost lead to cutthroat competition? What dangers does this competition bring?

7. Suppose Congress decided to foster a return to mid–nineteenth-century competition. What changes would have to occur in the business world? Do you think this could be achieved by legislation?

8. Compare the situations of a farmer selling his wheat crop and an auto company executive selling his car "crop." What are the major forces that bear on each, when it comes to pricing output?

TECHNOLOGY AS A SOCIAL PROCESS

We wonder how many readers felt, as we did while we were writing this chapter, a sense of sudden displacement from the past into the present. Until now, we had been observing the very slow transformation of what was, essentially, an agriculturally based society toward one based on trade and then on early industry. We saw the emergence—think of that!—of workplaces called *factories* and vehicles not pulled by animals but propelled by motors; then of wires carrying inaudible voices and invisible power. We left a setting in which we felt like tourists visiting a strange land to enter a world not exactly like our own, but nonetheless unmistakably familiar. It was the world in which our grandparents and even some of our parents had come of age.

That sense of journeying will continue as we move closer to contemporary life. However, by now another thought must have struck our readers: Is not technology the moving force of economic history? Is it not the source of pressure that has changed the insides as well as the outsides of the world in which we live? More than that, is not technological change the key to the story—we mean the all-important historical story—that constitutes the purpose of our book?

We think you already sense the answer to this question. Thinking about that answer will nonetheless throw light on why technology alone cannot constitute the history-shaping and history-making element we seek.

Now that we have challenged you to find a force behind the indisputable power of technological change, we suspect that you will know where to look. The original shaping force must lie in the developments that brought technological change (at what seems to us today a very simple level) into being in the first place. What could

that have been, other than the gradual mastery over the natural environment itself? Early caveman knew about fire, which entered his life through bolts of lightning; later caveman began to control fire after curiosity and chance taught him that flints, when struck, produced sparks that could set dry leaves afire. So too, early humankind knew that some animals could be tamed, although it was not until the Middle Ages that some imaginative person produced a U-shaped collar that did not choke the horse that was being harnessed to pull a burden.

From ancient trial and error, there gradually emerged bodies of knowledge that first opened nature to a degree of control. Not surprisingly, many of these first assertions of mastery over nature hardened into dogmatic procedures that often became obstacles to pushing the degree of control beyond some limit: The technologies of isolated tribes in Africa, or for that matter in North America, were unchanged from their original development until they were eventually preserved as exhibits in museums. Thus, technology is not inherently dynamic. It requires a social setting that encourages, rather than forbids, departures from that which is "tried and true." Technological progress emerges when society becomes less a protector of ancient ways and more a patron of new ways of doing things.

What society is that? We have watched one emerge as *economic* arrangements—the modes of producing and distributing the material needs of society—moved away from their subordination to tradition and command and toward the guidance and stimulus of the market.

It is the making of economic society that provides the incentives and guidance that vitalize discovery, experiment, and risk-taking—the kind of technology that caters to the needs of a market system, a world of business, capitalism in its youth. ⊕

CHAPTER

The Great Depression

6

In the preceding chapter, we concentrate on important aspects of the developing industrial economy—the swift rise in productivity, the impact of mass production, and the thickening texture of the market. However, we only mentioned in passing one effect of technology that, in retrospect, towers over the others. This effect was the tremendous impetus that technology gave to the process of economic growth. That question now comes to the fore.

Prior to the Industrial Revolution, a chart of the well-being of the average person in Europe would have shown a distressingly horizontal profile, rising in some years or even centuries, falling in others, perhaps tilted slightly upward as a whole, but certainly displaying nothing like a steady year-by-year increase in the output of goods and services available per capita. Even with the initial introduction of the new technology, the standard of living did not immediately improve. Starting in the third quarter of the nineteenth century, the accumulations of capital and the accretion of expertise began to display their hidden powers. In nearly every industrializing country, and most dramatically in the United States, the profile of economic well-being now began to show that steady, if irregular, improvement that has become the very hallmark of modern economic times.

THE PATH OF GROWTH

Figure 6-1 shows us the general path of this growth in the United States from the 1870s, when the process was in full swing, to 1929, when it reached a dramatic peak, to which we will shortly return. If we draw a line through the irregularly upward-moving graph to express the average rate of growth, taking good years and bad together, we find it to be about 3.5 percent (with all price changes eliminated), which means that the total volume of output was doubling about every 20 years. Because the number of people was also doubling, although more slowly, per capita shares in this mounting volume of goods obviously grew more slowly. Roughly, we can estimate that people improved their lot at a rate of about 1½ to 2 percent a year, which does not sound like much, but in fact doubles their real incomes about every 40 years.[1] There is no doubt that the period as a

---

[1]Note that Figure 6-1 shows aggregate well-being in terms of GDP, and per capita well-being as GDP per capita. GDP stands for *gross domestic product*, a term in the economist's lexicon that has entered the vocabulary (although not, perhaps, the clear understanding) of most Americans. Gross domestic product is the market value of all the final goods and services we produce over a year. The word "final" means that we do not include the market value of each item, but only of those that go into finished, or final, goods. For instance, government statisticians include in GDP the market value (the selling price) of all the automobiles made during the year, but they do not also include the value of the steel, the paint, the upholstery, rubber, and so on, that have been bought by the auto companies. The selling price of the final good—the car—includes these "intermediate" goods, and it would, therefore, be double counting to add them into GDP on top of the value of the car.

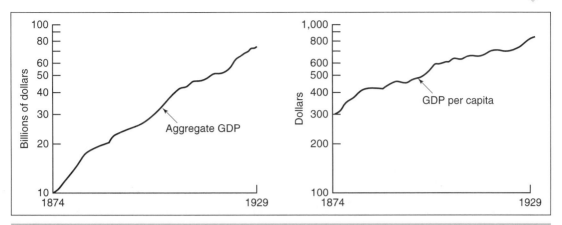

FIGURE 6-1 Real Gross Domestic Product (GDP), Aggregate and Per Capita, in 1929 Prices

whole was one of unprecedented progress and improvement. How strange, then, that it should have ended in the greatest disaster in the history of the market system—one that very nearly spelled the end of capitalism and that permanently altered the system in ways that we must now learn.

America in 1929

> We in America today are nearer to the final triumph over poverty than ever before in the history of any land. The poorhouse is vanishing from among us. We have not yet reached the goal, but, given a chance . . . we shall soon with the help of God be in sight of the day when poverty will be banished from this nation.

Thus spoke Herbert Hoover in November 1928, and indeed, by 1929, the American economy had shown extraordinary progress. Population had grown from 76 million in 1900 to more than 121 million, and 10 years had been added to the expectation of life at birth for whites and 13 for nonwhites. To hold and feed and sustain its growing numbers, the nation had witnessed the growth of two new cities to populations of over a million each, five to half a million, and nearly 1,500 from rural to urban classification. Meanwhile, there were jobs for 48 million people—all save 3.2 percent of the labor force in 1929. Furthermore, these jobs holders had seen average weekly hours of work in

---

Economists distinguish among four general kinds of final goods. One is the consumption goods and services that households buy—food, clothes, movie admissions. A second kind consists of the capital goods that business buys—their investment in plant and equipment, additional inventory, and the like. A third category consists of the goods and services bought by local, state, and federal government—police services, education, roads, the cost of defense, and so on. The last item is made up of the goods we make at home and sell abroad, minus goods made abroad and sold here—exports minus imports. These four streams of output make up our aggregate gross domestic product. Per capital GDP is the aggregate sum divided by the population. Note that we do not include in GDP the cost of "transfer payments" such as Social Security, unemployment insurance, and welfare. This is because these payments do not arise directly from production. They simply redistribute incomes that are derived from production.

One final note: Until a few years ago, the measure of our total output was called GNP, not GDP—gross national, not domestic, product. The difference in money value is small. GDP counts the value of all output that takes place within the United States, whether by a U.S. or foreign-owned company. GNP ignores the location of output and counts only its ownership: A U.S.-owned plant in France is included in GNP, but not in GDP. Nowadays, GDP is much more widely used than GNP.

manufacturing drop from nearly 60 in 1900 to 44. Average hourly earnings more than doubled, while consumer prices lagged sufficiently behind to allow a rise in real wages of some 10 to 20 percent. It was not surprising, then, that an atmosphere of optimism gripped America in 1929 and that President Hoover's official words only reflected an informal sentiment throughout the nation.

The Stock Market Boom

Certainly, few Americans suspected that a major economic calamity might be just around the corner. On the contrary, most people were concerned with quite another prospect of the American economy, and a highly attractive one. This was the great stock market boom—a boom that by 1929 had pulled perhaps 10 million people into "the market," where they had the pleasure of watching their money painlessly and effortlessly grow. As Frederick Lewis Allen, a social historian of the 1920s, described it:

> The rich man's chauffeur drove with his ears laid back to catch the news of an impending move in Bethlehem Steel; he held fifty shares himself on a twenty point margin. The window cleaner at the broker's office paused to watch the ticker, for he was thinking of converting his laboriously accumulated savings into a few shares of Simmons. Edward Lefevre (an articulate reporter on the market at this time who could claim considerable personal experience) told of a broker's valet who made nearly a quarter of a million in the market, of a trained nurse who cleaned up thirty thousand following the tips given her by her grateful patients; and of a Wyoming cattleman, thirty miles from the nearest railroad, who bought or sold a thousand shares a day.[2]

It was, of course, admittedly speculative, and yet the risks seemed eminently justified. Someone who had put $1,000 each year, from 1921 on, into a group of representative stocks would have found himself or herself worth more than $6,000 in 1925, almost $9,000 in 1926, well over $11,000 in 1927, and an incredible $20,000 in 1928—more than $100,000 in today's prices. That was just the beginning: During June and July of 1929, industrial stock averages went up nearly as much as they had during the entire year of 1928, which had been a year of unprecedented rise. By August 1929, the 3 months' summer spurt had already outdistanced the entire 1928 rise. In those 3 months alone, an investor who had bought 100 shares of Westinghouse would have almost doubled their money; even a buyer of staid AT&T would have been richer by a third. It seemed that everyone had but to beg or borrow money to buy shares in order to get rich.

The Great Crash

What pricked the bubble? No one knows exactly what final event was to blame. When the boom did break, it was as if an enormous dam had suddenly crumbled. All the frenzy that for over 2 years had sent stocks up was concentrated in a few incredible weeks in beating them down. On Tuesday, October 29, 1929, an avalanche of selling crushed the exchanges. On occasion there were *no* offers to buy stock at all—just to sell it. Goldman Sachs, a much-sought-after investment trust, lost almost half its quoted value on this single day. By the end of the trading session (the ticker, lagging behind, stretched out the agony 2½ hours longer than the actual market transactions), 16,410,000 shares of

---

[2]Frederick Lewis Allen, *Only Yesterday* (New York: Bantam, 1946), p. 349.

stock had been dumped, an unprecedented number for that time. In a single day, the rise in values of the entire preceding year had been erased. A few weeks later, $30 billion of "wealth" had vanished into thin air. Millions who had counted their paper gains and thought themselves well off discovered they were poor.

The great crash is in itself a fascinating chapter in the "madness of crowds." At first it seemed unconnected with anything bigger. In fact, the early weeks after the crash were regularly marked with expressions of confidence: The general cliché of the day was that things were "fundamentally sound." Yet things were *not* fundamentally sound. The terrifying crash ushered in the much more terrifying depression.

The Great Depression

Frederick Lewis Allen wrote:

> It was an oddly invisible phenomenon, this Great Depression. If one observed closely, one might note that there were fewer people on the streets than in former years, that there were many untenanted shops, that beggars and panhandlers were much in evidence; one might see breadlines here and there, and "Hoovervilles" in vacant lots at the edge of town (groups of tar-paper shacks inhabited by homeless people); railroad trains were shorter, with fewer Pullmans; and there were many factory chimneys out of which no smoke was coming. But otherwise there was little to see. Great numbers of people were sitting home, trying to keep warm.[3]

However invisible to the casual observer, the depression was far from being a mere figment. To begin with, gross domestic product—the measure of the nation's total output—fell by almost half from 1929 to 1933. Almost one dollar's worth of final output out of every two simply disappeared. As a result, unemployment soared. In 1929, the unemployed had numbered 1.5 million. By 1933, the number had risen eightfold until one person out of every four in the entire labor force was without a job. In the nation as a whole, residential construction fell by 90 percent; there were virtually no houses built. Nine million savings accounts were lost as banks closed their doors. Eighty-five thousand businesses failed. In Pennsylvania in 1932, it was reported by the state Department of Labor that wages had fallen to 5 cents an hour in sawmills, 6 cents in brick and tile manufacturing, and 7.5 cents in general contracting. In Tennessee, women in mills were paid as little as $2.39 for a 50-hour week. In Kentucky, miners ate the weeds that cows ate; in West Virginia, people began to rob stores for food.[4]

Causes of the Depression: Speculation

How did this tragedy come about?

An immediate, precipitating cause was, of course, the speculative fever that had engulfed the economy. The mania was not confined to Wall Street. Throughout the nation, a get-rich-quick philosophy had destroyed normal business and banking caution. Foreign bonds of the most dubious validity were eagerly (and sometimes ruthlessly) pushed by the banks into investors' hands or, worse folly, put into their own portfolios.[5] In

---

[3]Frederick Lewis Allen, *The Big Change* (New York: Harper, 1952), p. 248.
[4]Arthur Schlesinger, Jr., *The Crisis of the Old Order* (Boston: Houghton Mifflin, 1957), pp. 249–250.
[5]Many of these deals were unsavory to the point of malfeasance. The son of the president of Peru, for instance, was paid $450,000 by the securities affiliate of the National City Bank for his services in connection with a

addition, huge pyramided structures of investment trusts and holding companies erected a house of cards atop the operating base of enterprise. For instance, Georgia Power & Light Company was controlled by the Seaboard Public Service Corporation, which was controlled by the Middle West Utilities Company, which was controlled by Insull Utility Investments, Inc., which was controlled by the Corporation Securities Company of Chicago (which was controlled, in turn, by Insull Utility Investments, which presumably *it* controlled). Of these companies, only one—Georgia Power—actually produced electricity. The rest produced only profits and speculative opportunities. The Insull empire was only one of 12 holding companies that owned 75 percent of all the utility operating plants in the country.

All these manipulative activities helped to pave the way for the depression. When the stock market finally crashed, it brought down with it an immense flimsy structure of credit. Individual investors who had borrowed to the hilt to buy securities had their stock sold out from under them to meet their indebtedness to brokers. Banks and financial institutions, loaded with dubious foreign bonds, were suddenly insolvent. Meanwhile, to compound the terrible panic, the monetary authorities pursued policies that unwittingly weakened the banking system still further, greatly prolonging the length of the depression.[6]

Weakness on the Farm

In the vulnerability of an economy bound up with a rickety and speculative financial superstructure, we have located one reason for the Great Depression—or, more specifically, one reason why the Wall Street crash pulled down with it so much business activity. However, we have far from exhausted the explanations for the depression itself. For the crash, after all, might have been no worse than many previous speculative disasters. Why was it protracted into a chronic and deep-rooted ailment?

The question turns our attention away from the spectacular misfortunes of 1929 to a consideration of the state of the economy as a whole in the years preceding the collapse. We have already characterized the first quarter of the twentieth century as a time of unprecedented expansion. Could it be, however, that behind the overall figures of rising output and incomes there were concealed pockets of trouble?

There is no question that one such worrisome sector existed. This was the farm sector, especially the all-important grains. Through the 1920s, the farmer was the "sick man" of the American economy. Each year saw more farmers going into tenantry, until by 1929 four out of 10 farmers in the nation were no longer independent operators. Each year the farmer seemed to fall further behind the city dweller in terms of relative well-being. In 1910, the income per worker on the farm had been not quite 40 percent of that of the nonfarm worker; by 1930, it was just under 30 percent.

Part of this trouble on the farm, without question, stemmed from the difficult heritage of the past. Beset now by drought, now by the exploitation of powerful railroad and storage combines, now by his own penchant for land speculation, the farmer was proverbially an ailing member of the economy. In addition, American farmers had been

---

$50 million bond issue, which the bank's affiliate then floated for Peru. The president's son's "services" consisted almost entirely of an agreement not to block the deal. Eventually, of course, the bonds went into default. (J. K. Galbraith, *The Great Crash, 1929*. Boston: Houghton Mifflin, 1955, p. 186).
[6]See Milton Friedman and Anna Schwartz, *The Great Contraction* (Princeton, NJ: Princeton University Press, 1965).

traditionally careless of the earth, indifferent to the ecology of agriculture. Looking at the average individual farmer, one would have said that he was poor because he was unproductive. Between 1910 and 1930, farm productivity improved somewhat, but not nearly so fast as productivity off the farm. For the majority of the nation's agricultural producers, the trouble appeared to be that they could not grow or raise enough to make a decent living.

Inelastic Demand

If we had looked at farming as a whole, however, a very different answer would have suggested itself. Suppose that farm productivity had kept pace with that of the nation. Would farm income as a whole have risen? The answer is disconcerting. The demand for farm products was quite unlike that for manufactured products generally. In the manufacturing sector, when productivity rose and costs accordingly fell, the cheaper prices of manufactured goods attracted vast new markets, as with the Ford car. Not so with farm products, however. When food prices fell, people did not tend to increase their actual consumption very greatly. Increases in overall farm output resulted in much lower prices but not in larger cash receipts for the farmer. Faced with what is called an "inelastic" demand—a demand that does not respond in proportion to price changes—sellers are worse off before a flood of output.

That is very much what happened during the 1920s. From 1915 to 1920, farmers prospered because World War I greatly increased the demand for their product. Prices for farm output rose, and their cash receipts rose as well; in fact, they more than doubled. However, when European farms resumed their output following the war, the American farmers' crops simply glutted the market. Although prices fell precipitously (40 percent in the single year 1920–1921), the purchases of farm products did not respond in anything like equal measure. As a result, the cash receipts of farmers toppled almost as fast as prices. Meanwhile, their taxes were up by some 70 percent, and their mortgage payments and their cost of living in general had approximately doubled. Matters improved somewhat during the later 1920s, but not enough to bring the crop farmers back to substantial prosperity.

There is a lesson here in economics as well as history. Had farmers constituted an oligopolistic industry of a few sellers, like steel or autos, the decline in farm income might have been limited. A few producers, facing an inelastic demand for their products, can see the sense in mutually curtailing output. Rather than flooding a market that does not want their product, they can agree, tacitly or otherwise, to hold back production to some amount that the market will absorb at a reasonable price. The individual farmer in the 1930s, though, is about as far from an oligopolist as one can imagine. When the price for his crop falls, it gains the individual farmer nothing to decrease output. On the contrary, in this highly competitive situation, the best that the farmer can do is to rush to sell as much as possible before things get worse—thereby unwittingly making things worse.

At its core, the trouble with the farm sector was that the market mechanism in this particular case did not yield a satisfactory result.[7] That might not have been so serious

---

[7]In theory, there is a cure for situations in which the producers of one commodity are undercompensated relative to other pursuits: Producers will leave the undercompensated field for more lucrative occupations. Indeed, the American farmer tried this cure. It has been estimated that 20 farmers left the soil to seek city work

had it not been for another development: While agriculture remained static and stagnant, the manufacturing sector was growing by leaps and bounds. However, its growth was undermined because a fifth of the nation—the agricultural sector—was unable to match the growing volume of production with a growing volume of purchasing power. As the farmers' buying power lagged, it pulled down the demand for tractors, cars, gasoline and electric motors, and manufactured consumers' goods, generally. Weakness on the farm was thus symptomatic of a weakness throughout the economy, a failure of purchasing power across the whole lower stratum of the nation to keep up with the tempo of national industrial production.

Weakness in the Factory

Most economists of the 1920s would have agreed that there was a source of potential trouble on the farm. Had we suggested that there might be another potential breeding ground for trouble in the factory or the mine, however, few would have given their assent. Most people's eyes, during the 1920s, were fixed on only one aspect of the industrial sector—production—and here there was surely little reason for complaint.

Had scrutiny been closer, very serious signs might well have been spotted in this presumably most buoyant section of the economy. While production was steadily rising, employment was not. In manufacturing, for example, physical output in 1929 was up 49 percent over 1920; employment was unchanged. In mining, output was up 43 percent; employment had shrunk some 12 percent. In transportation and in the utility industry, again output was higher—slightly in transportation, spectacularly in utility's electrical output—and here, employment had actually declined.

Although employment fell in certain sectors, total employment had risen significantly in construction, trade and finance, the service industries, and government. However, all these employment-absorbing industries were characterized by one common denominator: They were all relatively devoid of technological advance. To put it another way, all the industries in which employment fell were characterized by rapid technological advance. Pressing against the overall upward tendency of the economy was an undertow of technological displacement, a negative force of technological change that was driving the system so powerfully.

Technology and Employment

In our consideration of technology, we have never stopped to inquire what its effects might be on employment. Rather, we have implicitly assumed those effects to be positive, as we dwelt on the capacity of industrial technology to increase output. However, it is not difficult to see that technology need not always be favorable for employment. When a new invention creates a new industry, such as the automobile, it is clear that its employment-creating effect can be enormous. Even in such an instance there is an undertow, albeit a small one, as the growing automobile industry crowds out the old carriage industry. When we turn to inventions that do not create new demands but merely

---

for every urban worker who came to the land. Unfortunately, the cure did not work fast enough. Although the agricultural sector steadily diminished in relative size, it could not shrink its absolute numbers significantly. From 1910 to 1930, approximately 10 million farmers remained "locked" on the farm, perhaps half of them barely contributing to national output beyond their own meager livelihoods.

make an established industry more productive, it is clear that the initial impact of technical change can generate serious unemployment.

Displaced workers may be reabsorbed eventually, particularly if the economy is growing rapidly. We will return to this problem later in the chapter, but now we want to examine still further the effect of rapid technological change in the "displacing industries" themselves during the 1920s. Here we see an interesting fact. As production soared and employment sagged, the output per person-hour rose rapidly; in fact, between 1920 and 1929, it increased more than 30 percent in transportation, more than 40 percent in mining, and more than 60 percent in manufacturing. This much larger flow of production per hour meant that wages could have been raised substantially or prices cut sharply. This is not what we find to have been the case. Only on the unionized railroads did wage rates rise (by about 5 percent). In mining, hourly earnings fell by nearly 20 percent, and in manufacturing, they remained steady. Because the hours of work per week were also declining, the average annual earnings of employees in these industries were far from keeping pace with the rise in their productivity. In mining, average yearly earnings fell from $1,700 to $1,481. In transportation and manufacturing, yearly earnings fell from 1920 through 1922 and did not regain 1920 levels until 1928 and 1929.

Thus, the gains from higher productivity were not passed along to the industrial worker in terms of higher wages. Were they passed along via lower prices? Yes, to some extent. The overall cost of living between 1920 and 1929 fell by about 15 percent. Part of this reduction, as we have seen, was due to falling food prices. Nonfood goods fell sharply in price from 1920 postwar peaks to 1921; thereafter, they declined about 15 percent up to 1929, but the fall was not enough to distribute all the gains from industrial technology. How do we know this? Because the *profits* of large manufacturing corporations soared between 1920 and 1929. From 1916 through 1925, profits for these companies had averaged around $730-odd million a year; from 1926 through 1929, they averaged $1.4 billion. Indeed, in the year 1929, profits were triple those of 1920.

Maldistribution of Income

We can generalize from what we have just discovered about the trend of wages and profits to state one further reason for the sudden weakness that overcame the economy, beginning in 1929: Income was distributed in such a way as to make the system vulnerable to economic shocks.

This does *not* mean that somehow the American economy was failing to generate enough purchasing power to buy its own output. An economy always creates enough potential buying power to purchase what it has produced.

There can, however, be a very serious maldistribution of the income payments arising from production. Not all the proceeds arising from production may be placed in the hands of people who will exercise their purchasing power. Incomes paid out to the lower-paid strata of the labor force do, indeed, return to the stream of purchasing power, for the worker tends to spend his wages quickly. However, incomes that take the form of profits, business accruals, or very high individual compensations may not quickly turn over as purchasing power. Profits or higher incomes may be saved. They may eventually return to the great stream of purchasing demand, but income that is saved does not automatically return via the route of consumption expenditure. Instead, it must find a different route—the route of investment, of capital building.

TABLE 6-1 Top Incomes		
Percentage shares of total income received by the top 1 percent and top 5 percent of total population[a]		
Year	Top 1 Percent	Top 5 Percent
1919	12.2	24.3
1923	13.1	27.1
1929	18.9	33.5

Source: Historical Statistics of the United States: Colonial Times to 1970, edited by Susan B. Carter (New York: Cambridge University Press).

[a]The table shows the "disposable income variant"; i.e., income after payment of taxes and receipt of capital gains.

Returning to the economy in 1929, we can now see what was perhaps the deepest-seated reason for its vulnerability: the fact that its income payments were not going in sufficient volume to those who would surely spend them. We have already understood why farmers and workers, who were indeed possessed of a limitless desire to consume, were pinched in their ability to buy. Now we must complete the picture by seeing how the failure to distribute the gains of productivity to the lower-income groups swelled the incomes of those who were potential *non*spenders.

What we see here is an extraordinary, and steadily worsening, concentration of incomes. By 1929, the 15,000 families or individual persons at the apex of the national pyramid, with incomes of $100,000 or more each, probably received as much income as the 5 to 6 million families at the bottom of the pyramid (see Table 6-1). More was involved here than moral equity. This extraordinary concentration of incomes meant that the prosperity of the 1920s—and for the majority of the nation, it was a prosperity of hitherto unequaled extent—in fact covered over an economic situation of grave potential weakness. For if the nation's ongoing momentum should be checked, in this lopsided distribution of purchasing power lay a serious problem. So long as the high profits and salaries and dividends continued to be returned to the income stream, all was well. But what if they should not be?

CRITICAL ROLE OF CAPITAL FORMATION

The question brings us to a critical relationship that determines the level of activity in a market society: that between the savings a society desires to make, on the one hand, and its opportunities for profitable investment, on the other. We cannot explain the main events of the Great Depression unless we have a general grasp of this central economic problem of a market society.

Actually, we have already discussed half the savings–investment relationship. In our chapter on the Industrial Revolution, we saw that saving was an indispensable prerequisite for capital formation. Now we must complete our understanding by adding the next step in the growth process. Unless we make large enough capital expenditures to absorb our saving, we will not be able to keep the economy moving forward. If saving is essential for investment, investment is essential for prosperity.

Indeed, because investment expenditure is the way we return savings to the income flow, we can see that the rate at which we add to our stock of capital equipment will have a deep effect on our overall economic well-being. When spending for investment is sluggish, bad times are upon us. When spending for capital formation quickens, good times are again at hand. In other words, the rate of capital formation is the key to prosperity or recession.

That does not yet tell us why the rate of capital expenditure should fluctuate. However, a moment's reflection makes the answer clear. Spending for consumption purposes tends to be a reliable and steady process. Most consumer goods are quickly used and must be replaced. The desire to maintain a given standard of living is not subject to sudden shifts or changes. As consumers, we are all to a considerable extent creatures of habit.

Investment and Profit Expectations

Not so with capital expenditures. Unlike consumer goods, most capital goods are durable, and their replacement can therefore easily be postponed. Again in contrast to consumer goods, capital goods are not bought out of habit or for personal enjoyment; they are bought only because they are expected to yield a profit when put to use. We commonly hear it said that a new store, a new machine, or an additional stock of inventory must "pay for itself." New investment increases output, and that additional output must have a profitable sale. If for any reason a profit is not anticipated, the investment will not be made.

This enables us to see that the expectation of profit (which may be greater or less than profits actually being realized at the moment) plays a crucial role in the rate of capital formation. But why—and this is the last and obviously the key question—should a profit *not* be expected from a new investment good?

The answers bring us back to our point of departure in the early 1930s. One answer may be that a speculative collapse, such as the great crash, destroys confidence or impairs financial integrity and leads to a period of retrenchment while financial affairs are put in order. Another reason may be that costs rise and monetary troubles impede the boom: The banks may become loaned up and money for new capital projects may suddenly become tight. Another reason may be that consumption expenditures are sluggish, owing perhaps to a maldistribution of income, such as that of the late 1920s, thereby discouraging plant expansion. The rate of population growth or of family formation may decline, bringing a slowdown in the demand for housing. Or the boom may simply die a natural death—that is, the wave of technological advance on which it rode may peter out, the great investments needed to build up a tremendous industry may be completed, and no second wave of equal capital-attracting magnitude may immediately rise to take its place.

Effects of Falling Investment

Many of these reasons, as we have seen, served to bring capital formation to a halt in the Great Depression. The crash itself, with its terrible blow to confidence and to the solvency of banks and holding companies, the weakness of the agricultural sector, the drag of technological displacement, and the maldistribution of income all combined to bring about a virtual cessation of economic growth. The figures in Table 6-2 for gross private domestic investment—the proper nomenclature for private capital formation—tell their own grim story.

Year	Residential Nonfarm Construction	Other Construction	Producers' Durable Equipment	Change in Inventories
TABLE 6-2 Gross Private Domestic Investment				
	Billions of Current Dollars			
1929	$3.8	$5.0	$5.6	$1.7
1932	.7	1.2	1.5	−2.5

Source: Historical Statistics

Therefore, the Great Depression can be characterized essentially as a tremendous and long-lasting collapse in the rate of capital formation. In housing, in manufacturing plant and equipment, in commercial building, in the accumulation of inventories, a paralysis afflicted the economy. Between 1929 and 1933, investment-goods output shrank by 88 percent in real terms—that is, after allowances for price changes. Although the capital-goods industries employed only one-tenth of the total labor force in 1929, by 1933, one-third of total unemployment had been caused by the shrinkage of these critical industries. Here is a major key to the depression.

Multiplier Effect

However, the trouble did not end there. When savings are not returned to active purchasing power because of inadequate investment, the fall in buying begins to spread. If a steelworker is laid off because of the slump in building, he will certainly pare his family's budget to the bone. This in turn will create a further loss in income for the businesses where the steelworker's family ordinarily spent its income. Others will lose their jobs or have their wages reduced. In this way, a kind of snowball effect, or to use the proper term, a *multiplier effect,* occurs.

This helps us understand the mechanism of the Great Depression. As capital expenditures fell during the early 1930s, they pulled down consumption expenditures with them—because of the multiplier effect, by an even larger amount than the fall in investment. From 1929 to 1933, consumption declined from $79 to $49 billion, nearly twice as large a drop as the absolute fall in investment. The fall of consumption, in turn, pulled down still further the flow of capital expenditures.

To be sure, the process works the other way around, as well. When capital expenditures again begin to mount, consumption expenditures typically climb by an even larger amount. For example, in 1949 President Truman pointed out in a radio address that $1 billion of new public expenditures, which gave initial income to some 315,000 people, also added to the incomes of some 700,000 more. In expansion as well as in contraction, there is a typical cumulative pattern to economic activity, as success breeds further success, and failure breeds further failure.

Our brief excursion into theory of economic fluctuations comes to an end at this point. However, the understanding we have gained enables us to see the Great Depression not only as a historical phenomenon, but also as an instance of a more endemic problem of a market society. We have seen how that society paved the way for the Great

Depression by its malfunctions in the 1920s. Now let us follow the struggles of the economy in the 1930s as it sought to escape from the deepest and most destructive depression it had ever known.

Key Concepts and Key Words

Growth   1. The outstanding economic fact of the 100 years prior to 1929 was the long trend of *economic growth*—a trend that doubled per capita incomes in the United States roughly every 40 years and that brought U.S. prosperity in 1929 to unprecedented heights.

Depression   2. The long trend of growth came to a disastrous stop—for nearly a decade—with the advent of the *Great Depression*. The causes of the depression were many:

Credit structure
- A *speculative and shaky credit structure* that was demolished by the *stock market crash* of 1929, and by *inept monetary policy*.

Technological unemployment
- A *steady deterioration of farm purchasing power* aggravated by the inelastic demand for farm products.

- A considerable undertow of *technological unemployment*.

Distribution of income
- A bad and *worsening distribution of income*.

Capital formation   3. The joint effect of these causes was a tremendous *collapse in capital formation*. Between 1929 and 1933, investment (in real terms) declined by 88 percent.

National income   4. *A fall in investment is a prime cause of a fall in national income,* because investment is the route over which savings return to the flow of national spending. When investment fails to return savings, recession begins.

Investment spending   5. Investment is thus a critical element in determining the level of prosperity. It is, however, a highly volatile element, because *investment spending depends on expected profits*. When expectations are not optimistic, new capital will not be built.

Multiplier effect   6. A relatively small decline in investment spending can spread through the economy. This is called the *multiplier effect*.

Questions

1. Discuss the causes of the Great Depression in terms of what you know about the economy today. Do you think another Great Depression is possible?
2. Among the families you know, how many work for companies that provide goods or services for capital formation—that is, for investment purposes rather than for consumption?
3. Suppose that you were in business and intended to build a plant to turn out a promising new item—say, a pencil that would last twice as long as the kinds available now. What sorts of developments might discourage you from making this investment? How much would your final decision hinge on what you anticipated for the future, compared with what you knew to be the situation today?
4. How can the money you put into a bank get back into someone's hands as his or her income? The money you put into a newly formed business? The money you put into insurance?
5. If your income (or your parents') were suddenly reduced to half, by how much would your expenditures fall? What sorts of businesses would be hit by your reduced spending? Would they, in turn, curtail their expenditures?
6. Why is investment so critical in determining the level of prosperity?

Thinking Back, Looking Ahead

LESSONS FROM THE GREAT DEPRESSION

We have gone from a chapter dominated by technological change, in which we had to search out the role of economics, to one in which we have to search out the role of—what? Our suggestion: economics of another kind. Until now, *economics* has referred to the social arrangements by which humanity has brought order into the most important activity of human existence—the assurance of its collective survival. In that context, economics has referred to the very different ways in which tradition, command, and the market mechanism brought about different outcomes, with different degrees of success and failure over the passage of time.

What is striking about the preceding chapter is that its economics does not fit into this succession of different modes of seeking social sufficiency. Instead, during the depression years, economics focuses on processes of social disintegration rather than order, on decline rather than advance.

Once again, the centerpiece of our chapter on the depression, like that of the previous one on technology, may actually distract attention from an understanding of the dynamics of economic history, our larger goal. The focus of an examination of technology was not the inventions themselves, but the change in social attitudes and ambitions that led to their discovery and improvement. In the same way, the crucial task for us, as students of economic history during the age of depression, will not be an examination of the damage it brought, but an understanding of the processes that brought about deep and persistent underutilization of human and machine capacity where not so long before there had been deep and persistent expansion. As we shall see in our next chapter, economics would find a new and immensely important focus in a search for the causes of economic failure in the workings of the very system that had performed so remarkably for two centuries before the great crash.

What constructive outcome could possibly have arisen from the tragedy of unprecedented economic collapse? The answer is the gradual attainment of a new understanding of how a capitalist economy worked—and sometimes did *not* work. This is a theme to which we will turn in our next chapters.

CHAPTER 7

The Rise of the Public Sector

"This nation asks for action, and action now. . . . We must act and act quickly."

The words are from the inaugural address of the incoming President, Franklin Delano Roosevelt. It is hard today to reconstruct the urgency, the sense of desperation, against which the words were addressed on March 4, 1933. A few hours before the actual inauguration ceremony, every bank in America had locked its doors. The monetary system was at the point of collapse. Nearly 13 million Americans were without work. A veterans' march on Washington, 15,000 strong, in the previous year had been dispersed with tear gas, tanks, and bayonets. On the farms, mortgage-lifting parties, at which a noose was tactfully displayed, served as powerful deterrents to any representatives of insurance companies or banks who might be thinking of bidding on foreclosed land. Meanwhile, a parade of business leaders before the Senate Finance Committee had produced a depressing sense of impotence. Said the president of a great railroad, "The only way to beat the depression is to hit the bottom and then slowly build up." "I have no solution," said the president of one of New York's biggest banks. "I have no remedy in mind," testified the president of US Steel. "Above all we must balance the budget," urged a long string of experts.[1] The crisis was a deep and genuine one; it is doubtful if the United States has ever stood closer to economic collapse and social violence.

THE NEW DEAL

The new President's response was immediate and vigorous: In the 3 months after Roosevelt's inauguration, writes Arthur Schlesinger, "Congress and the country were subjected to a presidential barrage of ideas and programs unlike anything known to American history." This was the famous Hundred Days of the New Deal—the days in which, half by design, half by accident, the foundation was laid for a new pattern of government relationship to the private economy, a pattern that was to spell a major change in the organization of American capitalism.

The change was the appearance of the public sector as a major force within the economy, a change marked by an unprecedented enlargement of the range and reach of governmental powers within the market system. In this chapter, we follow that enlargement from early New Deal days until the 1970s and 1980s; in our next chapter, we trace a similar course of affairs in Europe. Thereafter, we turn to more recent aspects of the problems at home, along with new challenges, that demand chapters of their own. However, we cannot consider these contemporary issues until we have learned something about the great change that marks capitalism in all advanced nations in the mid-twentieth century from its earlier appearance.

---

[1]Arthur Schlesinger, Jr., *The Crisis of the Old Order* (Boston: Houghton Mifflin, 1957), pp. 457–458.

We begin to trace its general outline in the main measures of the Hundred Days. In all, some 15 major bills were passed: the Emergency Banking Act, which reopened the banks under what amounted to government supervision;[2] the establishment of the Civilian Conservation Corps to absorb at least some of the young unemployed; the Federal Emergency Relief Act to supplement the exhausted relief facilities of states and cities; the Emergency Farm Mortgage Act, which loaned four times as much to farmers in 7 months as all federal loans in the previous 4 years; the Tennessee Valley Authority Act, setting up TVA, a wholly new venture into government enterprise; the Glass-Steagall Banking Act, divorcing commercial banks from their stock- and bond-floating activities and guaranteeing bank deposits; and the first of the Securities Acts, aimed at curbing stock speculation and reckless corporate pyramiding.

The Hundred Days only inaugurated the New Deal; it did not by any means complete it. Social Security, housing legislation, the National Recovery Act, the dissolution of public-utility holding companies, and the establishment of a Federal Housing Authority were yet to come. So was the Wagner Act, which protected the rights of labor unions. Indeed, it would not be until 1938 that the New Deal would be completed with the passage of the Fair Labor Standard Acts, establishing minimum wages and maximum hours and banning child employment for interstate commerce.

It would take us beyond the boundaries of our survey of general economic history to investigate the content of each of these important pieces of legislation, but we can gain an overall view of the New Deal by summarizing its achievements against the backdrop of the problems and issues of economic history that we have already encountered. We will see that the New Deal marked a genuine change in the development of the market economy itself. With its advent, we begin to trace the evolution of a new kind of capitalism, different in significant ways from that which we have already studied. We must understand the nature of this evolution if we are to bring our survey of general economic history to its contemporary terminus in our own society.

Intervening in Markets

In industry as in agriculture, during the first years of acute economic distress, intervention mainly took the form of an attempt to limit supply. Under the provisions of the National Industrial Recovery Act (NIRA), passed in 1933, business was permitted to make sweeping price-and-production agreements (in return for wage agreements designed to better the incomes of the poorest paid). In other words, recovery was attempted by legalizing the partial oligopolization of business. *Oligopoly* refers to the concentration of power in a few hands, rather than one hand, as in the case of monopoly.

The NIRA was greeted with great enthusiasm, and nearly 800 industrial codes were elaborated under it. However, as the demoralized markets of the early 1930s regained some degree of orderliness, a new source of complaint arose. Smaller producers within many industries claimed that the codes favored the large producer. By the time the experiment was declared unconstitutional by the Supreme Court in 1935, it had already become apparent that the problem was not too much competition, but too little.

---

[2]Some idea of the desperation of the times can be gained from the fact that the act was passed by the House of Representatives *sight unseen!*

There arose a radical shift in policy signaled by the vigorous prosecution of the antitrust laws, a development we trace in Chapter 5. Although the angle of attack had changed completely, the objective was much the same: to make the market work.

To what extent can a government make markets work? The answer is far from clear. Against the powerful forces of oligopoly on the one hand and the self-defeating effects of atomistic competition, such as farming, on the other, the market-shaping powers of government may well prove to be inadequate. However, the aim of deliberately trying to use governmental powers to make markets work better marked a new chapter in the evolution of capitalist philosophy.

In this new philosophy, laissez-faire no longer necessarily constituted the best relation between government and the economy. Rather, there arose a recognition that different kinds of markets would benefit from different relationships with government, ranging from laissez-faire, which indeed continued to be the general rule, to rules and regulations of one kind or another.

New Interventions

We had, in fact, already seen an early recognition of this latter view in the late nineteenth century, when trust-busting was approved as a form of government intervention whose rationale was to make the market work better. This recognition was broadened under the New Deal philosophy. For instance, there appeared an acknowledged need for government to intervene in markets that generated negative externalities—bad side-effects, such as poisonous wastes or air pollution in certain manufacturing operations, like steel. There arose as well a consensus that companies should be required fully to inform their customers about the products they sold, whether these were medicines or stocks and bonds, and the Fair Trade Commission and the Securities and Exchange Commission were established to achieve those purposes. Later, in the years after World War II, there was general agreement that government should enforce standards of safety in markets such as air travel and in products whose failure could inflict severe damage, such as automobiles and tires, as well as agreement that the government should ensure minimum standards of health and safety for men and women exposed to hazardous work processes.

The questions of how much intervention and what kind of intervention remained— and still remain—disputed matters. There is more than one way to make a market work better, and well-meant attempts to remedy market shortcomings can end up as cumbersome bureaucratic interferences. Therefore, the heritage of the New Deal is not a blank check for the government to regulate whatever it wishes however it wishes. It is, rather, a recognition that markets do not always work for the public interest when they are left alone, and that government is the only means by which a democratic polity can resolve the inescapable tensions between its economic activities and its noneconomic values.

A Historical Detour into Banking

Redefining the relation between government and markets was the first way in which the structure of capitalism began to change during the New Deal. A second way was a new conception of how government should exercise its powers over the quantity of money. To do this we must look briefly into the past.

Governments have always possessed a unique prerogative within their borders: They alone were entitled to create money, originally by minting coins from the precious metals kept in the royal treasuries. From early times on, however, this monopoly was infringed on by rich merchant bankers who loaned their own money to other merchants—and on occasions to monarchies themselves. It was not only this lending that threatened the monopoly rights of government. It was that the merchants did not themselves always possess the funds they loaned, delivering instead written promises to hand over the coins or the precious metal on call. Because their wealth was so great and their reputations so high, the promissory notes of these merchant-bankers were "as good as gold." They became, in fact, nongovernmental money.

Actual banking, as we know it, did not become widespread until the eighteenth century. It was, in fact, sufficiently ill-understood that Adam Smith thought it useful to include an explanation as to how banks worked in *The Wealth of Nations*, published in 1776:

> When the people of any particular country have such confidence in the fortune, probity, and prudence of a particular banker, as to believe that he is always ready to pay on demand such of his promissory notes as are likely to be at any time presented to him; these notes come to have the same currency as gold and silver money, from the confidence that such money can at any time be had for them.[3]

RISE OF NATIONAL BANKS

Not surprisingly, the growth of private banking eroded the previous exclusive rights of governments to establish the quantity of money in their lands; also not surprisingly, this sovereign right was gradually reinstituted during the nineteenth century as governments established national banks in which private banks were required to place their own reserves. In this way, national banks were able to exercise a degree of control over the ability of private banks to issue their promissory notes, now called *bank-notes*. The notes themselves differed from one bank to the next, so that nothing like uniform dollar bills or other paper currencies yet existed.[4]

In the United States, efforts to create such a national bank were for a long time unsuccessful, largely owing to the reluctance of the states to have such a centralized power over money. Not until 1913 did United States banking take on its current form with the creation of a Federal Reserve system, with a national Board of Governors and 12 Federal Reserve Banks around the nation. All important banks were required to keep their own reserves in the Reserve bank of their district.

As a result, the Federal Reserve was able to control the quantity of money in the banking system as a whole. By increasing or decreasing the percentage of its customers' deposits that member banks had to keep at their local Fed as reserves, the new system was able to increase or decrease the ability of its member banks to make loans. By raising or lowering the interest that the Fed charged its member banks, who often needed to borrow from *their* Fed to cover temporary overdrafts, they also expanded or contracted the ability of private banks to lend to customers at large. Thus, the Fed-

---

[3]Adam Smith, *The Wealth of Nations* (New York: The Modern Library, 1937), p. 277.
[4]If you look at a dollar bill, you will see that it says "This note is legal tender for all debts, public and private." No private bank could possibly make such a claim.

eral Reserve system became the U.S. "monarch" in charge of the amount of money in circulation.

MONETARY POLICY

Our brief look at banking history now enables us to see how monetary policy emerged as another new instrument of public sector capitalism not only in this country but in all advanced economies throughout the world.

Prior to the Great Depression, national attempts to regulate the money supply were largely limited to matching the lending capabilities of banks with the borrowing needs of their customers. At Christmastime, for example, money was always in demand by the banks' customers, and so the Federal Reserve usually lowered interest rates to help supply match demand. During crises, such as slumps or speculative binges, the Fed likewise tried to make money "easy" or "tight," depending on the judgments of the Board of Governors as to which policy would best tide the banking system as a whole over the crisis.

There was, however, one objective of monetary policy that was not tried out in these early days of what we now call central banking. The Federal Reserve did not try to use its ability to swell or shrink the lending power of the banking system as a means of accelerating or diminishing the overall pace of economic growth. The rhythms of the increasingly discussed cycles of business were regarded with much interest, but with no thought of using banking policy as a counterforce over these natural workings of the economy.

The New Deal's New Policy

That was the daring departure that took place during the years of the New Deal.[5] There was never any dramatic announcement of such a change from a passive to an active standard of monetary policy. Rather, under the pressure of the Great Depression, a new objective began to be enunciated by the governors of the Federal Reserve and by many leaders of the Roosevelt administration: It was that *a central objective of monetary policy was to help restore the growth of the economy itself.*

That may not sound like a particularly daring policy, but compare it with the view that prevailed in pre–New Deal days. During the early 1930s, for example, while the economy plummeted and unemployment rose alarmingly, the Board of Governors of the Fed slowed down the increase in the supply of money by *raising* interest rates! Again, in 1931 when the Board feared that there might be a flight of U.S. capital abroad, it raised the rate of interest more sharply than ever before in its history to keep money here.[6] Measured against that psychology of passivity, the new policy of trying to turn around the "natural" course of events was daring indeed.

---

[5]We might note that one of the major reforms introduced by the New Deal was to issue federal insurance for bank deposits. The familiar sign we see in all banks—*Insured by FDIC* (Federal Deposit Insurance Corporation)—has probably been the single most stabilizing force in modern capitalism, assuring private individual persons that they would not lose their money if their bank went broke.

[6]We might note that unlike national banks in other countries, which are explicitly under the guidance of their governments, the Federal Reserve system was created to be an independent body. Its Board of Governors is selected by the President, but there is no Presidential or Congressional right to establish or change Federal Reserve policy. The result, not surprisingly, is a considerable amount of friction when the Fed's view of economic prospects differs from that of the executive or legislative branch.

Public Spending as a New Force

Last, we turn to the third and, by all odds, most important of the changes we are studying. It is the rise of public expenditure from a small and essentially passive part of national spending to a larger, and on occasion strategic, flow intended to serve as an economic stimulus, not unlike private investment spending.

It is curious that the Roosevelt administration had no such idea when it first took office. Neither, as we have seen, did the business community. Indeed, for nearly everyone, economists included, the only "remedy" for the depression was thought to be a balanced budget for the government.

However, there were emergencies to be faced that could not be deferred, even if they unbalanced the budget. Many of the unemployed were literally at the brink of starvation, and the resources of private, state, and local charities were in most instances exhausted. President Roosevelt, unlike his predecessor, did not believe that the receipt of federal relief would "demoralize" the unemployed any more than the receipt of federal loans from the Reconstruction Finance Corporation had "demoralized" business. By May of the inaugural year, a relief organization had been established; and a year later, *nearly one out of every seven* Americans was receiving relief. In nine states, one out of five families—in one state one out of three families—was dependent on public support. Not that relief did much more than keep these unfortunate families from starvation— the average grant per family was less than $25 per month—but it did provide an economic floor, no matter how rickety.

The immediate aims of relief were humanitarian. Shortly, however, they were followed by thoughts of the useful possibilities of relief expenditures. Soon the great bulk of relief spending was being paid for public works of various sorts: schools, roads, parks, hospitals, slum clearance—and even federal art, theater, and writing projects.

As the public-works program grew, however, the finances of the federal government took a turn for the worse, until, by the mid-1930s, it was clear that something like a chronic deficit of $2 billion to $3 billion a year had been achieved. The word *deficit* means borrowing. Thus, as the government spent more than it took in through taxes— not only for relief, but for conservation, farm subsidies, veterans' bonuses, public housing, and aid to the states, as well—it borrowed the necessary money from the public through the sale of government bonds to individual people, corporations, and to commercial banks. Obviously, as the total amount of bonds outstanding grew each year, so did the total debt of the nation. In 1929, the national debt totaled $16.9 billion. By 1935, it had risen to $28.7 billion, and each year it steadily rose: to $36 billion in 1937, to $40 billion in 1939, to $42 billion in 1940.

The Economy Fails to Respond

At first, the heavy spending of the federal government was greeted with wary acceptance by the business and banking communities as a necessary temporary expedient. Before long, however, even within the administration itself, the mounting deficit was regarded with considerable misgivings. The recurrent excess of government expenditure over tax receipts was thereupon apologized for as "pump priming"—as an injection of government fuel which would, so to speak, start the stalled motor of private expenditures, making further injections unnecessary. Thus, a few billions of government spending, it was hoped, would set into motion an upward spiral of spending and job expansion by the business sector.

The upward spiral did not materialize. After 1933, helped by government spending, consumption expenditures began to rise, but private capital expenditures lagged behind. Although they, too, improved after 1933, by 1938, they were still 40 percent below the level attained in 1929.

Why did private investment fail to rise? The answer lies partly in the fact that the very government deficits that were supposed to cure the depression only frightened business into a condition of economic paralysis that prolonged it. Coupled with the reform legislation of the New Deal, the new presence of government's large-scale economic activity caused business to lose its former confidence. The business executive felt ill at ease in a changing economic and political climate and was in no mood to plan boldly for the future. The general outlook stressed caution rather than promise; cycles rather than growth; safety rather than gain. Too, behind the psychological factors, real forces were also at work. A much slower rate of population growth in the 1930s depressed the important housing market. Even more serious, no major industry-creating technological breakthrough, comparable to the railway or the automobile, held sufficient promise of profitable growth to tempt private capital into a major capital-building boom of its own.

Therefore, for many reasons, the new federal expenditures failed to prime the pump. Private investment did not spontaneously rise to take over its traditional propulsive function, now temporarily carried out by the government. This did not mean, however, that the economic influence of government was therefore relegated to a minor role. On the contrary, the failure of pump priming—conceived as an emergency measure—caused a widening in the conception of the government's role. Government now began to be envisioned as a permanent stabilizing and growth-promoting agency for the market economy as a whole.

Compensatory Government Spending

The idea was slow in taking form and did not, in fact, receive its full-dress theoretical exposition until the middle 1930s. The most influential book setting forth the concept—albeit in highly technical terms—was John Maynard Keynes's *General Theory of Employment, Interest and Money,* published in 1936. Few books have roused such controversy or left so permanent a mark. As is often the case with new ideas, the book seemed at first complicated and difficult, and even among professional economists its basic concepts were the subject of murky discussion for several years. In retrospect, it appears as a very simple argument—the stuff of freshman economics courses!

The key to prosperity or depression, it had become increasingly evident, lay in the total volume of expenditure that a market society laid out for its goods and services. When that volume was high, employment and incomes were high; when it declined, output and employment declined as well. What determined the volume of expenditure? Consumption spending tended to be a passive factor, rising when individual persons' incomes rose and diminishing when they fell. The volatile item, as both history and theory made clear, was the stream of investment expenditure.

From this starting point, it is not difficult to take the next step. If lagging private capital expenditures were responsible for lagging employment and output, why could the government not step in to make up whatever deficiencies arose from private expenditure? There had always been, after all, a fairly regular flow of public expenditure, much of it for capital-creating purposes, such as roads or dams. Why could not this flow of public spending be deliberately enlarged when the occasion demanded? True, this required the government to borrow and spend and thereby increase its debt, but did not much private capital spending also require corporate borrowing? Why could not the debt itself be handled like corporate debts, which were never "paid off" in the aggregate but refunded, with new bond issues being sold to take the place of those coming due?

To the economists of the Roosevelt administration, the answers to these questions seemed clear. The government not only could, but should, use its spending powers as an economic instrument for securing full employment. By this, they did not have in mind a radical revision of capitalism. Rather, they envisaged the evolution of a new form of *guided* capitalism—a market society in which the all-important levels of employment and output would no longer be left to the vagaries of the market but would be protected against decline and stimulated toward growth by public action.

Fears of Government Intervention

This was not how matters appeared to many members of the nation, however, and especially to the business community. They saw government spending as inherently wasteful, and the mounting debt as evidence that we would spend ourselves into bankruptcy. Beneath these arguments there lurked a deeper suspicion, a suspicion that government spending, whatever the protestations to the contrary, was the entering wedge for socialism or worse.

The controversy raged through 1940, and as we shall see still smolders today. However, in a sense, it was an empty debate in the New Deal years. At its peak, the annual deficit never touched $4 billion, and federal government purchases never contributed more than 6 percent to gross national product. Judged by the importance of government in the economy, probably no industrial nation in the world was *less* socialist than the United States. Yet, if the fears of the conservatives were hardly realistic, neither were the hopes of the liberals. In the prevailing atmosphere of distrust, the remedy of government spending could never be more than halfheartedly applied. Deficit spending in the 1930s was a holding operation and not an operation of growth. By 1939, although conditions had improved considerably over the levels of 1932, there were still 9.5 million people—17 percent of the labor force—without work.

Impact of the War

In the end, it was not theory that settled the history of compensatory government spending, but history that settled the theory. With the outbreak of World War II came a tremendous forced expansion in government outlays. Year by year, spending for war purposes rose, until in 1944 federal expenditures totaled just over $100 billion, and with this unprecedented rise in expenditure came an equally swift rise in GDP. By 1945, our gross domestic product had risen by 70 percent in real terms over 1939, and unemployment had dwindled to the vanishing point. The demonstration that public spending could impel the economy forward—indeed, could lift it beyond all previously imagined bounds—was unmistakable. So was the fact that a government could easily carry an enormously larger debt, a debt that now towered more than $250 billion, provided that its gross domestic product was also much larger.

With the war had come a marked change in attitude both toward the government and toward the economy in general. After 4 years of unprecedented effort, the American people looked to a strong public sector with a more accustomed eye; so, too, after 4 years of record output, they looked back upon the days of mass unemployment with a new feeling of shame. Perhaps most important of all, they looked ahead to the postwar period with considerable trepidation. Virtually every economist, contemplating the huge cutback in spending consequent upon a termination of hostilities, feared the rise of a vast new army of the unemployed. Even the most conservative opinion was uneasy at the political possibilities of such a return to the 1930s.

The upshot of the change in attitude was the passage of the Employment Act of 1946, which declared that it was "the continuing policy and responsibility of the Federal Government . . . to provide maximum employment, production, and purchasing power." It was, as we shall see, one thing to write such an act and another thing to implement it; but without question, the act marked the end of an era. The idea that the best thing the government could do to promote recovery was to do nothing at all and, beyond that, the trust in the blind forces of the market as inherently conducive to prosperity—these once firmly held convictions now seemed old-fashioned. The debate within capitalism was no longer whether government should undertake responsibility for the overall functioning of the market system. Now only the specific means were questioned: how best to achieve that end.

Aftermath of the War

The war ended in 1945; within a year, federal spending dropped by almost three quarters, and the nation waited tensely for the expected fall in employment, incomes, and prices.

Instead, it found itself confronting the least anticipated of all eventualities: a rousing boom. It is true that unemployment doubled, rising to 2 million, but this was still less than 4 percent of the labor force. Meanwhile, the number of people at work showed a steady rise: 54 million jobs in 1945; 57 million in 1946; 60 million in 1947; 63 million in 1950. Industrial production, after a brief postwar dip, was buoyant.

We can see this in Table 7-1, which shows the trend in current dollars that remove the effect of rising prices from just before the Great Depression down to the threshold of our own era. The magnitude of the postwar boom is evident from the first column on the left: Gross national product in 1969 was more than three times larger in real terms—that is, with inflation eliminated—than it was at the peak of the 1929 boom.

TABLE 7-1   Gross National Product, 1929–1969

	Billions of Current (1958) Dollars[a]			
Year	*Gross National Product*	*Private Investment*	*Federal Purchases*	*State & Local Purchases*
1929	203.6	40.4	3.5	18.5
1939	209.4	24.7	12.5	22.7
1949	324.1	48.0	27.6	25.7
1959	475.9	68.8	52.5	42.2
1969	725.6	110.5	73.5	72.4

Source: Historical Statistics. Pt. 1, Series F, pp. 32, 53, 66, 70.

[a]This means that the figures are adjusted for changes in the price level over the period.

What was the source of this extraordinary growth? Private investment almost tripled during the period, a huge increase. But look at state and local expenditures, almost quadrupling, and then consider the explosive growth of federal spending, up more than twentyfold. Clearly, the public sector played a strategic role in the economic transformation of those crucial years.

FISCAL POLICY ENTERS THE SCENE

Our brief excursion into the impact of government spending gives us additional understanding of the change that is the focus of our chapter. The change involves the use of fiscal policy, that is, expenditure, as a new means of economic control, using government spending to push the entire economy forward or taxation to hold it back. Together, fiscal and monetary policy constitute the means by which every modern capitalist economy manages its affairs.

Unlike monetary policy, fiscal policy cannot trace its origins back to the nineteenth or even eighteenth centuries. In Adam Smith's day, there was no conception that government either could or should seek to interfere with the workings of the economic system, other than to promote the freest possible play of the forces of competition. The sole moving force of which Smith was aware was lodged in the "desire of bettering our condition," a force he believed "comes with us from the womb, and never leaves us until we go into the grave."[7]

Surprisingly, however, Smith sees an important economic role for government:

> the duty of erecting and maintaining certain public works and certain public institutions, which it can never be to the interest of any individual . . . to erect and maintain because the profit could never repay the expenses . . . , though it may frequently do much more than repay it to a great society.[8]

LOOKING AT THE PUBLIC SECTOR

Therefore, Smith saw a need for the provision of public investment—the roads and dams and schools and other such projects we call *infrastructure*. This governmental "duty" was not, however, fiscal policy because it was not intended to sustain, or accelerate, economic growth, but to promote national well-being. To put it differently, Smith did not have a conception of the government's expenditures as a "sector" of the economy.

Such a notion would not even be explicitly spelled out in Keynes's book that did so much to clarify our understanding of what we today call *macroeconomics*—the study of the large flows of expenditure that determine the size of our gross domestic product. Even today, some people feel there is something inherently wrong in using the government as an economic as well as a political entity of society. They forget that under capitalism there is always a relationship between government and the economy insofar as government is expected to help a market society overcome obstacles that it encounters or generates. Like monetary policy, fiscal policy is ultimately aimed at making a business society work. As the Great Depression showed all too vividly, without a central

---

[7]*The Wealth of Nations,* op. cit., pp. 324–325.
[8]*Wealth,* op. cit, p. 65.

banking system and a responsive fiscal policy the very continuance of a capitalist order can be placed in serious jeopardy.

A last word: What we describe here is nothing less than the appearance of a new stage of capitalism, now equipped for the first time with a means to limit or even overcome depressions, and perhaps to ensure a smoother course into the future. As we shall see, the rosy visions that attended the birth of fiscal policy were much too simple, as is always the case with economic cure-alls. Nonetheless, a corner had been turned. In the remaining chapters of this book, as we investigate the modernization of Europe and then the rise of new and disconcerting problems in the United States, fiscal policy will continue as an important means by which we will be seeking to master the challenges of the twenty-first century.

Key Concepts and Key Words

New Deal

1. The *New Deal* emerged from the inability of the laissez-faire capitalism of the late nineteenth and early twentieth century to deal with its self-generated problems. Among these were serious market failures, both in the corporate and the agricultural world. Three policy departures marked the lasting impact of the New Deal.

Market policy

2. First, the New Deal interfered with the structure of malfunctioning markets to a previously unknown extent. Both agricultural and industrial markets were reorganized (as with the Agricultural Adjustment Act [AAA] and the National Industrial Recovery Act [NIRA]) to help minimize the damage inflicted by market forces. Although most of these efforts failed, they left behind a heritage of government responsibility and an end to the philosophy of laissez-faire.

Monetary policy

3. A second major policy innovation involved the government's view toward regulating the supply of money. The pre–New Deal view had sought little more than to ensure an orderly condition in the market for credit. The new policy was the use of power of the Federal Reserve System to impart an expansionary impetus by lowering interest rates, thereby encouraging bank lending in bad times, and raising rates to discourage lending in inflation-prone periods.

Fiscal policy

4. Third, and most important of the new policy departures, was the deliberate use of the government's powers of taxation and expenditure to impart momentum to a stagnant economy. The policy began as *pump-priming,* in the hope that a burst of public spending would quickly generate a resumption of private investment. When this failed— partly owing to its small scale, partly to business uneasiness—*fiscal policy* turned in a new direction, in which government spending was viewed as a normal adjunct to private spending, especially in periods of unemployment. The new policy was based to a considerable degree on the ideas of the English economist John Maynard Keynes. It was a departure that appeared in capitalist economies around the world.

Questions

1. How do you explain the change in political philosophy between the Hoover and the Roosevelt administrations? Does it suggest that economic policies reflect political pressures as much as economic ideas? Or does it show that without new ideas, policy changes are hard to bring about?

2. Why are market structures so important? What policies make sense to you with regard to the U.S. wheat or corn markets? What about the automobile or airplane markets? Why do you (we hope!) choose different policies for each? What about new

inventions, such as computers, antibiotics, or toothpastes? Is some sort of regulation needed here too? If not, why not?

3. Do you think that government spending is inherently waste-prone, if not necessarily wasteful? Can wasteful spending also be stimulative? Do the same considerations—and the same responses—apply to corporate spending? How does one measure "waste"?

4. What would invalidate the idea that government spending is a proper and useful policy for a capitalist economy? What would validate it? Does the impact of World War II on the economy provide such a test? Why or why not?

Thinking Back, Looking Ahead

EXPENDITURE FLOWS AND THE BIRTH OF MACROECONOMICS

Chapter 7 is a climax—although not, as we shall see, *the* climax—in our history of the evolution of capitalism and of economics. Of course, an immediate aspect of that climax is announced in our title: What we economists call the *public sector* suddenly appears as a strategic—even crucial—element in determining the performance of capitalism. Not only is the dramatic appearance of government a turning point in the making of economic society, but it is also a climactic development in something else. As you have undoubtedly already grasped, this is the entrance of a new understanding of economics itself. What is this dramatic new perception? It is a change from x to y as the most important element in economics as a system of social clarifications.

We have left it to you—for a moment, anyway—to fill in the words for which *x* and *y* stand. Think back to what was the all-important variable in the economic models and scenarios of all the great economists from Smith through Marx. What single undramatic term was indispensable in designing their models as to how market systems worked?

The answer is *price*—a word so familiar that it hardly seems worth mentioning. However, was it not the prices of things that determined what buyers and sellers would do, even though the same price evoked different, and even opposite, actions between the two? When we say *price,* we mean that prices in a market system serve as both the magnets and the repelling forces that transform what would seem like a recipe for chaos into a means of establishing economic order.

Price, we remember, determines what both buyers and sellers would do. We know that at any given price each side wants to do different things. Buyers of good *A* cut back their demand for it when its price goes up; sellers increase their willingness to buy *A* when the price of that same good goes higher. Someone unfamiliar with economics might expect such a situation to lead to disaster and incoherence, but economists see that it leads toward stability, balance, and equilibrium. To understand price is to get one's first grasp of economics.

Now something changes: A new term, virtually unknown before the Great Depression, becomes the key word in the language of economics. What is this word? Though we have encountered it only in our most recent chapter, it may not leap to the fore as did its predecessor. However, when we think about the preceding chapter, we can see that *expenditure* was now to become the strategic word in economics. To be sure, the price at which things are offered or bought will always be important in a market system, but the total spending that flows from buyers to sellers—the volume of expenditure—now becomes the crucial term for those who want to understand how our economic system works.

As we know, it is not the expenditure of a single buyer that now interests us, but of all buyers, a vast river of spending that drives society itself. Total spending had, of course, always constituted the moving force of all market systems, but as long as the focal point was on how individual prices could bring order to what must have appeared as a setting for disorder, the role of expenditure in determining the vitality of economic life was not yet recognized.

What is expenditure? In the preceding chapter, we have seen that it consists of two categories. One is the flow of private spending, familiar to us all as the entries in every family's checkbook. In addition are the expenditures made by business firms; these include outlays for raw materials, machines, wages, and executive salaries.

Thus, the great river of private expenditure is, in fact, two rivers. One we call *consumption expenditure*—the outlays that enable households and businesses to get on with the ordinary business of life. The second flow we call *investment expenditure*—the not-so-regular spending used to buy a new home or, on the business side, to establish a new line of output, build a new factory, or buy another business.

Why has the concept of expenditure taken on new significance in our understanding of the making of economic society? There are two reasons: One was the drama of the Great Depression, a violent turnaround of economic life that could not be explained by changes in prices—the result, not the cause, of the national collapse. The depression brought to the fore the vital importance of flows of spending, especially for investment purposes, a main source of economic growth.

No less important was the role played by government expenditure in dealing with the depression. Here the all-important discovery was that government spending—for arms, for transportation, for the relief of poverty—was a way to increase expenditure to dramatically change the economic future of a nation. Thus, the importance of price as the key means of bringing order to a market system has been nudged aside by the vital contribution of expenditure, public as well as private, for investment and for consumption. Today, expenditure—private and government—has taken its place as our key economic concept. In fact, expenditure is the basis for what economists call *macroeconomics,* the study of the overall economic system (including output, employment, and productivity). We will follow the trail of expenditure in the chapter to come.

CHAPTER 8

Modern Capitalism Emerges in Europe

W e have focused our narrative of economic history on the rise of modern capitalism in the United States, but our initial narrative is not yet complete. The central subject of our earlier chapters was not just the rise of American capitalism, but also the emergence of the market system itself; in describing its development in the United States, we have by no means described it everywhere. Let us turn to Europe, for there are lessons to be learned in comparing the course of capitalism there and in the United States. We concentrate on *institutional changes,* rather than trying to follow Europe's ups and downs in any detail.

THE FEUDAL HERITAGE

Capitalism in Europe evolved from a very different social and political framework than was the case in the United States. There, a market system came into being in a society that had, to a large degree, shed the feudal encumbrances of the Old World. In that Old World, many of the social outlooks and habits of the past lingered. An awareness of class position—and more than that, an explicit recognition of class hostility—was as conspicuous by its presence in Europe as by its absence in the United States. In Vienna in 1847, writes one social historian:

> At the top were the nobles who considered themselves the only group worth noticing. The human race starts with barons, said one of them. Then there were the big businessmen who wanted to buy their way into the human race; the little businessmen; the proud but poor intellectuals; the students who were still poorer and still prouder; and the workers who were poor and had always been very, very humble.[1]

The result was a totally different climate for the development of an economic society. Capitalism in the United States, building on a new and vigorous foundation, was, from the beginning, a system of social consensus. Capitalism in Europe, building on a feudal base, was deeply tinged with class conflict. It was without effort that American capitalism obtained the loyal support of its "lower orders"; in Europe, by the time of the revolutions of 1848, those lower orders had already turned their backs on capitalism as a vehicle for their hopes and beliefs.

National Rivalries

Second, and no less important in explaining the divergence of American and European economic evolution, was the profound difference between the political complexion of the two continents. In the United States, except for the terrible crisis of the Civil War, a

---

[1]Priscilla Robertson, *Revolutions of 1848* (New York: Harper, Torchbooks, 1960), p. 194.

single national purpose fused the continent; in Europe, a historic division of languages, customs, and mutually suspicious nationalities prevented just such a fusion.

Accordingly, American capitalism came of age in an environment in which political unity permitted the unhindered growth of an enormous unobstructed market. In Europe, a jigsaw puzzle of national boundaries forced industrial growth to take place in cramped quarters and in an atmosphere of continued national rivalry. It is curious to note that whereas Europe was considered "wealthier" than the United States all through the nineteenth century, American productivity in many fields began to outstrip that of Europe from at least the 1850s, and perhaps much earlier. For instance, at the Paris Exposition of 1854, an American threshing machine was twice as productive as its nearest (English) rival and eleven times as productive as its least (Belgian) competitive model.[2]

These advantages of geographic space, richness of resources, and political unity were widened by subsequent developments in European industry. Not surprisingly, European producers, like those in the United States, sought to limit the destructive impact of industrial competition, and for this purpose they turned to *cartels*—contractual (rather than merely voluntary) agreements to share markets or fix prices. Unlike the United States, where we have seen the illegal emergence of trusts that were cartel-like in purpose, this self-protective movement received the blessing, overt or tacit, of European governments. Although "anticartel" laws existed in many European countries, these laws were almost never enforced; by 1914, there were more than 100 international cartels, representing the most varied industries, in which most European nations participated.[3]

Cartelization was undoubtedly good for the profit statements of the cartelized firms, but it was hardly conducive to growth—either for those firms or for new ones. By establishing carefully delineated and protected "preserves," the cartel system rewarded unaggressive behavior rather than economic daring; together with the ever-present problem of cramping national frontiers, it drove European producers into a typical high-cost, high–profit-margin, low-volume pattern rather than into the American pattern of very large plants with very high efficiencies. The difference in economic scale is dramatically illustrated by steel. In 1885, Great Britain led the world in the production of steel; 14 years later, her entire output was less than that of the Carnegie Steel Company alone.

The Lag in Productivity

As a result, by the early twentieth century, European productivity lagged very seriously behind American. A study in 1918 showed that the daily output of coal per underground worker was 4.68 tons in the United States, as contrasted with 1.9 tons in Great Britain, 1.4 tons in Prussia, and 0.91 tons in France. In 1905, the output of bricks per person employed was 141,000 in the United States and 40,000 in Germany; U.S. pig-iron production was 84.5 tons per worker in 1909, compared with only 39 tons in Great Britain in 1907.[4] Part of these differences was attributable to geological differentials, but these,

---

[2]Thomas Cochran and William Miller, *The Age of Enterprise,* rev. ed. (New York: Harper, Torchbooks, 1961), p. 58.

[3]In 1939, an estimated 109 cartels also had American participation, because American companies were not prohibited by antitrust laws from joining international restrictive agreements.

[4]Heinrich E. Friedlaender and Jacob Oser, *Economic History of Modern Europe* (Upper Saddle River, NJ: Prentice Hall, 1953), p. 224.

too, were made worse by restrictive business practices. The result was a steady falling behind in Europe as the twentieth century continued.

The divergence was strikingly noticeable in per capita incomes. In 1911, for example, when per capita income in the United States was $368, the corresponding figure for Great Britain was $250; for Germany, $178; for France, $161; and for Italy, $108. By 1928, American per capita incomes had increased by almost half; British, German, and French incomes by less than a tenth; and Italian incomes had actually declined.

Crucial Role of European Trade

Still another consequence followed from the division of European industry and agriculture into national compartments. To a far greater extent than in the United States, it made the development of European capitalism subject to the expansion of international trade.

The division of the European continent into many national units made international trade a continuous and critical preoccupation of economic life abroad. For instance, a study shows that in 1913, when manufactured imports provided but 3.6 percent of United States consumption of manufactured goods, they provided 9 percent of Germany's, 14 percent of England's, and 21 percent of Sweden's. Perhaps even more striking is the degree to which some nations in Europe depended on international trade for the foodstuffs on which they lived: In the 5 years preceding World War I, for instance, England produced less than 20 percent of the wheat she consumed and barely more than 55 percent of the meat.[5] We find the same dependence on foreign trade in the export side of the picture. Whereas the United States in 1913 exported a mere fifteenth of its national product, France and Germany exported a fifth, and Britain nearly a quarter.

Therefore, to a far greater degree than the United States, Europe lived by foreign trade. Here we see clearly the advantage to the United States of its enormous unbroken market over the fragmented national markets of Europe. Many of the economies of scale realized in the swift rise of American productivity were denied to Europe. To put it differently, in the United States, the division of labor was permitted to attain whatever degree of efficiency technology made possible, for in the end, virtually all products entered into a single vast market where they could be exchanged against one another.[6]

Obviously, there are lessons for our time in this story. But let us hold back until we finish our thumbnail history of European capitalism. In Europe, international trade struggled against the retarding hand of national suspicions, rivalries, and distrust—and lost. A striking example was provided in the early 1950s by the great cluster of European steel and coal industry near the German–Belgian–Luxembourg orders. Here, in a triangle 250 miles on a side, was gathered 90 percent of European steelmaking capacity, but this natural geographic division of labor had to contend with political barriers that largely vitiated its physical productivity. Typically, German coal mines in the Ruhr sold their output to French steelmakers at prices 30 percent higher than to German plants; in turn, French iron-ore producers charged far higher prices in Germany than at home. As a result, although American steel production soared 300 percent between

---

[5]*Der Deutsche Aussenhandel* (Berlin: 1932), II, 23. Friedlaender and Oser, op. cit., p. 206.
[6]For a fascinating analysis of different national "styles" of coping with technology, see Alfred Chandler, *Scale and Scope: The Dynamics of Industrial Capitalism* (Cambridge, MA: Harvard University Press, 1990).

1913 and 1950, the output of Europe's steel triangle rose but 3 percent during the same period.

Breakdown of International Trade

Our example itself poses a question, however. Prior to 1913, something like a great international division of labor did, in fact, characterize the European market, although nothing like the extent seen in the United States. By 1913 a very considerable flow of international trade was enhancing European productivity, despite the hindrances of cartels and national divisiveness. It was only the beginning of a truly free and unhampered international market, but at least it *was* a beginning.

What brought this promising achievement to an end? Initially, it was the shock of World War I, with its violent sundering of European trade channels and its no less destructive aftermath of punitive reparations, war debts, and monetary troubles. In a sense, Europe never recovered from its World War I experience. The slow drift toward national economic separatism, at the expense of international economic cooperation, now accelerated fatefully. Tariffs and quotas multiplied to place new handicaps before the growth of international trade.

The final blow was the Great Depression of 1929 that began in the United States. As the depression spread contagiously, nation after nation sought to quarantine itself by erecting still further barriers against economic contacts with other countries. Starting in 1929, an ever-tightening contraction of trade began to strangle economic life around the world. For 53 grim months following January 1929, the volume of world trade was lower each month than in the preceding one. Between the late 1920s and the mid-1930s, manufactured imports (in constant prices) fell by a third in Germany, by nearly 40 percent in Italy, and by almost 50 percent in France. As international trade collapsed, so did Europe's chance for economic growth. For two long decades, there followed a period of stagnation that earned for Europe the name of the "tired continent."

European Socialism

Against this background of economic malfunction, it is easier to understand the growing insecurity that afflicted European capitalism. During the 1930s, serious rumblings were already being heard. In England, the Socialist Labour Party had clearly displaced the middle-class Liberals as the Opposition. In France, a mildly socialist "Popular Front" government came to the fore, although insecurely. Even in Italy and Germany, the fascist dictators repeatedly declared their sympathy with "socialist" objectives—and whereas their declarations may have been no more than a sop to the masses, they were certainly indicative of the sentiments the masses wanted to hear.

Note that the socialist movements were not communist—that is, they were pledged strongly to democratic political principles and envisaged a "takeover" through education and persuasion rather than by revolution and coercion. In addition, the socialists sought to convert only the strategic centers of production into public enterprises, not to "socialize" all of industry and agriculture. Thus, socialism was always a much more evolutionary program than communism. Nevertheless, to the European conservatives of the 1930s, the socialist leaders appeared every bit as dangerous as the socialists' bitterest enemies, the communists.

By the end of World War II, socialist ideas were clearly ascendant throughout most of Europe. Even before the war was concluded, the Labour Party swept into office in

England and rapidly nationalized the Bank of England (previously a private bank), the coal and electricity industries, much of the transportation and communications industries, and finally steel. As the first postwar governments were formed, it was evident that a socialist spectrum extended across Europe from Scandinavia through the Lowlands and France to Italy (where the communists came very close to gaining power). To many observers, it seemed as if capitalism in Europe had ended.

RECOVERY OF EUROPEAN CAPITALISM

Welfare Capitalism

However, European capitalism did not come to an end. Instead, after the war, it embarked on a period of unprecedented economic growth. As we can see in Table 8-1, from 1948 to 1962, the nations of Europe not only doubled or tripled (and in the case of Italy octupled) their pre–World War I rates of per capita growth, but widely outstripped the contemporary performance of the United States' economy.

   To bring about such results, important changes must have taken place in these economic societies. One of them, it is hardly surprising to learn, was political. The postwar socialist governments quickly showed that they were not revolutionary but reform-minded administrations. When in power, they instituted several welfare and social-planning measures, such as public health insurance, family benefits and allowances, and improved social security; but, they did not engage in fundamental institutional changes. Despite its socialistic rhetoric during the 1960s and 1970s, Europe was still unmistakably capitalist.

   When many of the socialist governments, facing the exigencies of the postwar period, were voted out again, they bequeathed to the conservatives the framework of a welfare state, which the conservatives by and large accepted. Returning to one of the traditional weaknesses of European capitalism, we can say that this represented a conservative attempt to create a social-service state that would mend the historic antagonism of the working class—a European-style New Deal. As a result, we find today that in most European states, welfare expenditures form a considerably higher proportion of government spending than in the United States. For example, Social Security expenditures in most European Community countries run 50 to 100 percent higher than in our own and include such things as mandated prenatal care, generous vacations, and universal child care, none of which are provided by the United States government.

TABLE 8-1 Comparative Growth Rates					
Average Annual Growth Rates of Per Capita Income					
	France	*Germany*	*Italy*	*U.K.*	*U.S.*
Pre–World War I (1870–1913)	1.4	1.8	0.7	1.3	2.2
Post–World War II (1948–1962)	3.4	6.8	5.6	2.4	1.8 (1950–1964)

Source: M. M. Postan, *An Economic History of Western Europe* (London: Methuen, 1967), p. 17.

The second reason for the survival of European capitalism was even more important. This was the rise of a movement within the conservative ranks to overcome a still more dangerous heritage of the past—the national division of markets. This great step toward creating a full-scale continental market for European producers is called the European Economic Community—or more familiarly, the Common Market.

The Common Market

To some extent, the Common Market was born out of the vital impetus given to postwar European production by the so-called Marshall Plan, under which Europe received some $12 billion in direct grants and loans from the United States to rebuild its war-shattered industry. Despite Marshall Plan aid, it soon became apparent that Europe's upward climb would necessarily be limited if production were once again restrained by cartels and national protectionism. To forestall a return to the stagnation of the prewar period, a few farsighted and courageous statesmen, primary among them Jean Monnet and Robert Schumann, proposed a truly daring plan for the abolition of Europe's traditional economic barriers.

As it took shape, the plan called for the creation of a supranational (not merely an international) organization to integrate the steel and coal production of France, Germany, Italy, Belgium, Luxembourg, and the Netherlands. The new Coal and Steel Community was to have a High Authority with power to eliminate all customs duties on coal and steel products among members of the Community, to outlaw all discriminatory pricing and trade practices, to approve all major corporate mergers, to order the dissolution of cartels, and provide social and welfare services for all Community miners and steelworkers. By the fall of 1952 the Coal and Steel Community was a reality, and more than 40 percent more coal and steel was being shipped across national boundaries than was shipped prior to the establishment of the Community.

This was followed in 1957 by the creation of Euratom, a trans-European center for nuclear research and atomic power, and in 1968 by the establishment of the European Economic Community (EEC)—a true Common Market with no internal trade barriers and a single "external" tariff vis-à-vis the world. Ten years earlier, a similar organization (although with much less unified internal "government") had already linked the Scandinavian trio plus Austria, Portugal, England, and Switzerland (joined later by Finland and Iceland) into EFTA, the European Free Trade Association.

By the year 2000, a truly pan-European economy existed, capped by the creation of a common European currency—the euro—and a European Central Bank. Several European countries, most notably the United Kingdom, have not yet adopted the monetary agreement out of a concern with losing control of an important arm of government: monetary policy. However, in the hopes of the supporters of the common currency arrangement, the euro will someday rival the U.S. dollar and Japanese yen as an international currency, raising the power and improving the performance of Europe's economy.

CORPORATISM

We present an overview of Europe's institutional transformation, but we need to look more closely at one specific aspect of it: the attempt to create a more cooperative relationship both between the public and the private sectors and between labor and management. This development, begun in the 1980s, was called *corporatism,* which does not mean that business corporations now openly dominated the system; the term referred, rather, to a genuine effort to concert, as far as possible, the aims and policies of business, government, and labor.

Corporatism varied from one nation to the next, but it usually featured two institutional changes. The first of these took the form of "social contracts" between management and labor. These usually aimed at giving as much security of employment as possible to wage-earners, in exchange for getting as acceptable a wage outlook as possible for management. In Germany, for example, trade union representatives sit on many corporation boards, thereby becoming privy to crucial strategies of these firms. In turn, they agreed not to press for wage settlements that would exert unmanageable pressures on the enterprise.

A second aspect of corporatism was agreements that sought to strengthen the nation's place in world production. For example, with labor and government sanction, the steel producers of the Ruhr agreed to pool skilled labor forces and specialized capital equipment in the production of highly specialized antipollution equipment, thereby avoiding the prohibitive expense that would result if each producer tried to seize the market for itself. Another form of public–private cooperation was a combination of government finance and business management to produce high-tech, high-finance products that would hold their own in the world market. An outstanding success was the creation of the Airbus, which became a formidable competitor of the Boeing Company. By the 1980s, some form of corporatism was visible in Austria, Denmark, Finland, Germany, the Netherlands, Norway, Sweden, and Switzerland, and aspects of it were recognizable in France and Italy, as well. Meanwhile, halfway around the world, Japan had worked out a form of corporatism in which a close working relationship among government agencies, banks, and large enterprises earned it the name of Japan Incorporated.

EUROPE SLOWS DOWN

In our focus on the evolution of institutional change in Europe, we have lost sight of its economic trajectory. We can catch up in a few strokes. Recall that the Marshall Plan helped set into motion the extraordinary recovery of the European economy, which by the 1960s was unquestionably reestablished as a powerful and well-functioning entity. That postwar boom continued through into the 1980s. Then growth began to slow, mirroring a similar slackening in the United States (to which we turn in our next chapter). As is often the case when the pace of advance quickens or slows for a period of time, the reasons for the slowdown are not clear. There was much talk of "Eurosclerosis," with its vague implications of overly protected workers and a weakening of economic energies, but this really masked the fact that observers did not clearly understand why the great postwar boom had run out of steam—a phenomenon we also look into in the chapter ahead.

Whatever its causes, there is no doubt that the slowdown had negative effects on the further development of corporatism. As unemployment in Europe rose to levels that were more than double those of the United States—higher than 10 percent in much of the Continent, compared with 5 and 6 percent in the United States—the atmosphere needed to support corporatism came under considerable strain. The amity between management and trade unions began to fade. Not surprisingly, many conservative voices in Europe called for a scaling down of welfare programs that threatened to overstrain national budgets when economic growth was no longer as vigorous as it had been a decade ago. Not less interesting, several European countries began to decouple government and private enterprise, most immediately visible in the privatization of formerly nationalized airlines such as the British BOAC and the German Lufthansa. The argument was that private enterprises were bound to be more efficiently run than state-run companies, regardless of any social benefits a public company might be able to provide.

At this writing we seem to be in a period of uncertainty with respect to the future of corporatism. Europe still has a considerably more integrated public and private economic life than does the United States, but it may well seek to return to a more "American" pattern if economic growth does not return to satisfactory levels.

What deeper interest does this unfinished story have for the United States? We see its relevance in Americans' belief that the twenty-first century is likely to be a time when all nations, rich and poor, will have to make changes in their economic institutions. The United States will not be exempt from this worldwide process, imposed by a globe visibly shrinking under the pressures of technology, ecology, and ever more intense international competition.

From this viewpoint, Europe is a kind of laboratory in which we can observe what programs seem to work best for societies that are more like ourselves than those anywhere else on earth. The adaptations and endeavors of advanced capitalisms in Europe thus constitute the rarest of opportunities in which it may be possible to learn from others' experience—and, need we add, to suffer the consequences of having failed to learn.

Key Concepts and Key Words

Breakdown of trade

1. The development of European capitalism was severely hampered by a *feudal heritage* that brought serious political problems and *severe national rivalries* that crippled international trade. Therefore productivity lagged far behind the United States.

Socialist opposition
Conservative reformism

2. European capitalism was also threatened by a widespread *socialist opposition.* However, after World War II, conservative parties generally accepted the reformist programs of socialism, including generous programs of social welfare.

Common Market

3. Among many attempts to overcome Europe's economic backwardness, the most important was the creation of a *Common Market* without tariff barriers, a breakthrough in modernizing and unifying Europe. Together these measures brought about a remarkable revival of growth and well-being in Europe.

"Social contracts"
Joint ventures

4. Capitalism in Europe has moved in a "corporatist" direction since the collapse of the Soviet Union. It has attempted to build management-labor accords (*social contracts*) with labor and has also tried to encourage joint ventures between business and government, such as the Airbus and other public–private ventures.

Corporatist outlook

5. These measures were initially very successful, but are now in some question. Social contracts are hard to create when the economy worsens, and several state enterprises are now being privatized. The corporatist movement's future is uncertain.

Questions

1. Do you think there are lessons for American capitalism in Europe's experience? Is it the other way around? Might both have things to learn?

2. Do you think that the general acceptance of the market framework by Europe's socialist parties signals an end to the historic confrontation between capitalism and socialism?
3. Why is it so difficult to create a single currency for the Common Market when we have no such problem with the American 50 states?
4. Can we draw any conclusions regarding the limits of the public sector from the European experience? Do you think the same limits would apply to the United States?

Thinking Back, Looking Ahead

VARIETIES OF CAPITALISM

There is a hidden point of interest in this brief, but many-faceted chapter. It is not, as we might think, the future shape of capitalism if, as seems possible, the system spreads to such places as the Balkans or the Near East or parts of Africa. When we study the prospects for a "globalized" capitalism in chapter 12 that will certainly be an important question; but, in the chapter we have just finished, there is a still broader and deeper question.

The question takes us back to chapter 1, when we traced the immense structural changes through which human society had to pass before capitalism came into being. The first of these, we remember, was to develop a system of discipline to provide guidance for prehistoric societies that lived by hunting and gathering. The solution was tradition, often embodied in kinship relations as the guide for these activities, thereby creating a kind of insurance for the future by following the road that had led to the present.

Eventually, as we also know, a new system for organizing economic life made its appearance, as political command began to play a central role in organizing production and distribution—the building of the Egyptian pyramids and the creation of the Biblical empire. A thousand years later came the next great step in bringing about the system of economic guidance that we know—the market. In chapter 6, we watched as the Great Depression forced the recognition that capitalism—the word was now entering the public vocabulary—required a well-organized public sector as both a supplement to, and a counterbalance for, the private sector.

Why should we mention this at the conclusion of a chapter on European capitalism?

The spread of capitalism makes us rethink our description of its structural elements. Are they still found in today's capitalisms? Tradition is still a respected guide for many activities—for instance, the relations of newcomers into any field and their experienced elders—although the place of tradition is much less than in the world of corporations and the government. Needless to say, the market is everywhere and, of course, we find two sectors—a workable capitalism requires a strong public sector as well as a dynamic private one.

Now we raise a new question: Do these structural elements give us a blueprint of capitalism today? Not many years ago, our answer would have been "yes." Today, we are not so sure. A look at the capitalisms in Europe makes us aware of an aspect of our system that seems to require us to speak of capitalisms more and more in plural.

What is new is the striking degree to which capitalist societies, all of which share the same *economic* institutions, manifest different social and political cultures. Thus, there is a strong orientation toward a socially oriented capitalism in Scandinavian countries and a much more hesitant one in the United States. So, too, there is a quite conservative English, and a quite liberal German, capitalism. On a smaller scale, there is the modern capitalism of Northern Italy and the very unmodern capitalism of Southern Italy. Compare the capitalisms we find in New York and Maryland, in Texas and Maine, in North Carolina and South Carolina. Is it a difference in basic economic institutions that accounts for these differences? We suspect, rather, that it is differences in their local histories, social customs, and cultures.

Why do we bring up this intriguing matter now? As capitalism(s) arise in many countries during the coming decades, they will all no doubt have tradition, command, market mechanisms, and public and private sectors that will identify these new economic systems as capitalist. We suspect, however, that we will find a widening spectrum of capitalisms as its basic structures arise in the very different cultures of Asia, Latin America, and Africa. We will keep our eye on this problem in the chapters to come; you will have to see if we are correct in the decades ahead of us.

CHAPTER

The Golden Age of Capitalism

9

POSTWAR POSSIBILITIES

World War II brought the deaths of more than 10 million people. It altered the geography of Europe and redefined world politics. The infrastructure and industrial capacity of Europe and Japan were devastated. In contrast, the productive capacity of the U.S. economy greatly expanded in response to the demands of the war effort. Not only did American output rise steadily during the war years, but the technological requirements of wartime production—including motor vehicles, airplanes, weaponry, communications equipment, and even clothing—brought a rise in the efficiency of mass production and an improvement in product quality.

But with the end of the war and the stimulus to manufacturing that it brought came fears of a sharp drop in demand, and the possibility that the U.S. economy would fall back into the depressed state of the 1930s. To the surprise of some of the best economic analysts of the day, this gloomy prospect never occurred. On the contrary, the period 1945–1973 was one of fast economic growth—indeed, among the fastest of any in the history of the world. As a result, the period has become known as the "Golden Age" of capitalism. Not only did the U.S. economy grow at a very rapid pace, but so did Europe and Japan as they rebuilt their economies. Colonial rule largely came to an end, and some developing countries grew even more rapidly than the industrialized ones, as demand in the advanced countries spurred a commodities boom that benefited natural resource-rich countries such as the oil producers of the Middle East, and that made possible a few centers of industrialization, such as the "tigers"—South Korea, Singapore, Malaysia, and Taiwan—of East Asia. The Golden Age was, therefore, a period of rapid economic growth in both the United States and a wide range of countries elsewhere. It was, indeed, as close to a worldwide boom as the world has ever known.

What brought about such a Golden Age? How were the economic minefields of the postwar era avoided? There is no single answer. Instead, we must look at the evolution of the central institutions of modern capitalism—large firms, labor unions, the state—and at the influences on these institutions of international forces, social pressures, and technological change.

International Forces

We begin with the first of these developments. As the only country whose productive capacities were greater after the war than before, the United States took the lead in designing the postwar institutions that would mold international economic relations. At the Bretton Woods Conference in 1946 (named for the New Hampshire resort town where the conference was held), the United States and its European allies established a new international financial system and a framework to aid the rebuilding of Europe.

132

Under the charismatic leadership of John Maynard Keynes, the conference brought into being three institutions that played a major role in the Golden Age, two of which continue to play important international roles today. The first was the International Monetary Fund, established to help struggling nations by lending them "hard" currencies, such as the dollar, with which to buy goods needed to develop their economies. Second was another international bank, the International Bank for Reconstruction and Development—also called the World Bank—established to provide financing for major investment projects, such as roads, bridges, and so on, especially in Western Europe.[1] These two institutions are still in existence and have played an important role in financing economic development and easing international financial relations.

The third newly created institution was perhaps the most important: This was the set of rules for the international monetary system itself. The Bretton Woods Agreement established that the value of the U.S. dollar in terms of gold would be fixed at $35 per ounce and other currencies would be valued at a fixed rate in relation to the dollar— and thus, indirectly, to gold. Therefore, if one British pound was to be worth $5, its gold price would be fixed at £7 per ounce (35 ÷ 5).

Two other institutions served to further international cooperation, again with the United States at the helm of both. The General Agreement on Trade and Tariffs (GATT) signed by 23 countries in 1947, promoted tariff reductions and the principle of nondiscrimination in trade policy—that is, agreement that no signatory country would impose higher tariffs on one country than another. This is the principle behind the "most-favored nation" clause of the GATT, according to which any country achieving "most favored" status automatically received the lowest tariff rates offered by signatory countries for the same category of goods. The United States, for example, could not impose 10 percent tariffs on German wine while it levied a 3 percent tariff on French wine.

Finally, we turn to the international initiative that had the most immediate impact of all those mentioned so far. This was the Marshall Plan, named after General George Marshall, who had been U.S. Army Chief of Staff during World War II and then served as President Truman's Secretary of State. The plan was a $12 billion aid package by the United States to be used for rebuilding war-torn economies. Marshall funds were not only vitally important in providing Europe with desperately needed purchasing power, but served other purposes as well. Because the funds were administered by an international board, the Marshall Plan promoted a coordination of policies in Europe that eventually led toward a European common market. In addition, the plan had benefits for the United States. Insofar as it was the main industrial power after the war, the purchasing power gained by Europe would be largely spent in the United States. Thus, the Marshall Plan provided aid to Europe, but conveniently also gave a big push to U.S. exports.

Geopolitics Enters the Picture

These major initiatives in international economic policy went a long way in shaping and providing ground rules for the postwar world economy. However, they functioned within a very different political world than what existed before the war. The first feature of this postwar world was a new war, the so-called Cold War between the two

---

[1]The Bank was also intended to lend money for ambitious projects in the underdeveloped world, but there, unfortunately, it was unsuccessful, perhaps because of excessive reliance on free market policies. See Catherine Caufield, *Masters of Illusion: The World Bank and the Poverty of Nations* (New York: Henry Holt, 1997).

superpowers, the United States and the Soviet Union. Allied during World War II, the two countries became immediately suspicious of each other after the war. Germany was the first locus of conflict and was divided into two sovereign countries: a communist-led East and a capitalist, western-oriented West. In addition, for the next 30 years, the two superpowers would indirectly face off with each other in countries as diverse as Korea, Cuba, Angola, Vietnam, Chile, and Afghanistan.

The Cold War was of overriding importance in defining the post–World War II global economy. Both superpowers designed their international economic policies with the aim of maintaining strong alliances with other countries in opposition to the other superpower. For example, U.S. efforts to promote European unification were in part aimed at securing West Germany's place as a partner in capitalist Europe. More directly, both superpowers devoted considerable energy and resources to the military. Production of arms and war-related equipment became major sectors of the economies of both countries, as the two engaged in an arms race, scurrying around the world to secure alliances with other nations, especially developing countries. This emphasis on military also affected the direction of economic change in the United States. Much of the technology that energizes our economy today—computers (both hardware and software), radar, and aircraft design—had their origins in military research connected with World War II and the Cold War.

How can we sum up the complex changes in the international scene, some directed at repairing war damage, some at trying to help the developing nations, some at securing the United States' place as the hegemon—the leader—of the Free World? The very variety of its component elements makes any summary incomplete. Nonetheless, one central theme must be acknowledged: The Golden Age was both propelled and guided by military–political considerations. Had the Soviet Union collapsed 20 years before it did, a considerable impetus for economic growth would have been lacking. As we demonstrate, the Golden Age itself must be considered as one of the most constructive eras in Western history, but there is no denying that it was in part fueled by military considerations that provided a deep and lasting economic impetus to the Western world generally and to the United States in particular.

Meanwhile, Back at Home

We move now from the world of geopolitics to that of the domestic economy. Although the Bretton Woods institutions laid the foundation for international cooperation as opposed to rivalry and retaliation, still, even with the infusion of Marshall Plan aid, a war-torn Europe could not be expected to provide much demand for U.S. products. A growing U.S. economy would have to rely on domestic demand. The question was, Where would it come from? With the war over, government spending seemed sure to shrink. Private investment, although no doubt eager to make up for 4 years of war-enforced neglect, hardly seemed capable of rising to the extent needed to make up for the end of the armaments boom. That left the burden on the shoulders of the consumption sector, but where would households get the necessary billions, in the face of the decline in employment that everyone expected?

Here is where social pressures enter the picture. The surprising fact was that consumer demand grew vigorously in the immediate postwar years—indeed, between 1945 and 1955 it grew at an unprecedented rate. Where did the demand come from? The immediate source was the social effect of 4 years of "going without." During those years, gasoline was rationed, along with foodstuffs needed for the armed forces; automobiles were no longer produced, as the great assembly lines switched to making airplanes; new housing slowed to a standstill; uniforms took priority over ordinary clothing. When the war effort finally came to an end, Americans not only celebrated victory and peace, but also the possibility of satisfying long-denied consumer demands with savings accounts that had become swollen because there had been no place to spend four years of high wages!

Just as the mass consumption of standardized goods had spurred economic growth in the United States during the nineteenth century, the mass consumption of consumer durable goods acted as a powerful force for growth in the early postwar years. Levittown, Long Island, in New York state, is a good example. Levittown was a cluster of closely grouped, virtually identical houses designed to be priced within the range of middle and even lower-middle incomes. They sold like hotcakes. Of course, each house required one or more cars, televisions, refrigerators, telephones, washers, dryers, and other appliances. Consumption of these goods became part of the American dream—the popular belief that the attainment of middle-class status was made manifest in a particular consumption bundle.

STRUCTURAL CHANGES IN AMERICAN CAPITALISM

Technology Lends a Hand

Finally, we must take technical progress into account. Household pent-up demand could not have been satisfied without the ability of firms to produce affordable goods on a mass scale. New production techniques developed during the war, including the beginnings of automated—that is, machine-guided—new production processes, lent a hand.

One particularly dramatic example was the rise of a new industry—tourism—on the wings of 4-engine prop planes adapted from wartime bombers, and then the new jet planes. Transatlantic jet service began in October 1958, with scheduled New York–London flights. Within a few years, tourism had become the fastest growing industry in the United States. Americans who once felt that taking a trip to Florida was a great adventure now found themselves sitting, knee to knee, with families just like themselves off to London (where they spoke English) and soon thereafter to Paris and Rome, where it was soon discovered they also spoke English, at least to visiting Americans.

New technologies stimulated growth in many areas, besides tourism; for example, in 1950 there were just more than 1 million television receivers in use in the United States; 10 years later, 10 million; by 1960, more than 50 million. Automatic dishwashers, laundry machines, and new kinds of ovens and toasters remade the (ideal) American kitchen; automatic shifts made driving easier for many people. These and endless other technical advances, large and small, helped realize the unexpected, and therefore all the more welcome, prosperity. The new technologies did not yield their growth-bestowing benefits indefinitely; no advances do. In particular, as we see in our next chapter, the technology that substituted machines for human labor was soon to raise questions, but in the years of the Golden Age, these problems had not yet appeared.

The Capital-Labor Accord

If the postwar economic boom was initially spurred by household consumption demand, it substantially required a response by business in the form of new investment. However, private sector investment depends on the expected profitability of such investment, and this very dependency seemed to doom any possibility of a long-lasting boom. Would not such a boom increase the demand for labor, and would not such an increase result in higher wages? Would they not, in turn, bring the boom to an end?

Here, of all places, we come to the role played by labor unions in making possible the Golden Age. More surprising, the crucial element did not lie in an agreement to forego wage increases. It lay, rather, in an agreement to key them into increases in productivity. As productivity rose, so would workers' remuneration. Far from bringing the boom to a halt, such an arrangement prolonged it.

Now, for the first time, workers shared an interest with management in raising productivity. According to labor historian Jerome Rosow, the labor contract signed in 1948 between General Motors and the United Auto Workers was the first to "work out a system for wage increases which committed the union to seek to improve productivity and to support rapid technological change." This had a twofold effect: Workers now had a direct stake in the performance of the firm and therefore supported, rather than opposed, technological advances that raised productivity.

Second, because labor unions felt more secure, they were more content to leave issues of workplace organization and control in the hands of managers. Managers, in turn, became an increasingly distinct and powerful social group, closely consulted with respect to long-run investment decisions and detailed questions of shop-floor organization. Business administration itself became increasingly "scientific" and professional. This separation of management from ownership became standard practice, at least in the nation's large corporations. Economists even developed a "managerial" theory of the firm, according to which firms were seen as following the long-run strategies of managers rather than the short-sighted tactics of the owners. Undoubtedly, there was some truth in this, which gives us yet another ingredient in the answer to why the Golden Age lasted so long.

Finally, we should note that under this new arrangement, the share of total national income going to wages tended to remain constant, rather than falling, as it would have, had wages declined, and that the share going to profits also tended to remain constant, rather than falling, as would have been the case had workers not agreed to a productivity standard for wages. This built-in stability in turn provided a boost to firms' confidence in the future, therefore reinforcing the willingness to invest that brought that future into being.

The Government Finds Its Place

Last, but certainly not least, government played a central role in directing the postwar economy. During the war, government spending as a share of total output shot up to unprecedented levels—from 9 percent in 1940 to almost 45 percent in 1945, and individual consumer goods markets were regulated to an extent never before seen. However, when the war ended, it was not at all obvious what the role of the public sector in the economy would be.

The New Deal of the 1930s had established certain "entitlements," including social security, unemployment benefits, and agricultural price supports. There was no question that these enormously popular programs would continue after the war. Indeed, a new GI bill, greeted with wide approval, extended the government's entitlement program by providing a free education to every veteran who sought one. The result was that millions of men and women were able to benefit from a college education that would otherwise have been beyond their means.

Second, the nation clearly perceived a need to continue its military predominance, especially in light of its new position as leader of the world's efforts to contain Soviet communism. As mentioned previously, the Cold War justified massive spending by the federal government, ranging from conventional arms to space exploration, perhaps the most expensive scientific endeavor ever undertaken by any government.

The third objective was to use the government's enlarged productive capacity for civilian purposes. The most important effort in this regard was the planning and construction of a national network of highways. Under Republican President Eisenhower, the federal government undertook a multimillion dollar effort to connect all the major cities, from New York to Los Angeles, Miami to Chicago, with "superhighways"—a wholly novel kind of highway network that we take for granted today. The project immediately boosted interstate commerce and was crucial in making American society into a "car culture" and the premier producer of commercial motor vehicles. Similarly, government funding for airport construction provided a great boon to the aircraft business, which, even more than automobile production, was heavily supported by the demands of the military during the war.

As the postwar economy showed unexpected strength, the government could expand its role beyond that of providing entitlements and public goods, into the stabilization of the macroeconomy. In spite of the strong upward trend of growth, the economy still experienced cycles of upturns and downturns. Now, for the first time, the government began experimenting with fiscal policies to minimize these cycles. In 1961, President Kennedy began deliberately cutting taxes to stimulate the economy, and economists began speaking of "stabilization policy" as an important task for government. We come back to this question later, but it is interesting to note that a collection of essays published in the mid-1960s by well-known economists was titled *The End of the Business Cycle*. As we see, they were somewhat over-optimistic.

While Keynesian economists were promoting stabilization, another ambitious battle began in earnest, again with government resources as the main weapon of attack. This was President Johnson's "Great Society," a vision of a rich society in which the elimination of poverty was a central objective. The vision was transformed into a "war on poverty"—a wide set of programs aimed at aiding the poor through grants for community development, housing, and education. Poverty did in fact decline in the late 1960s and 1970s, only to rise again in the 1980s as these programs were dismantled. As we see in our next chapter, it remains a great, and unsolved, challenge.

WORLD PROSPERITY AND CONVERGENCE

Our analysis of the new, expanded role of government in the Golden Age has focused exclusively on the United States. Similar patterns developed abroad, albeit with differences that reflected the particular cultures. In France, the state continued its "dirigiste" (literally, *directive*) role, using a national economic plan to determine spending and subsidy decisions. England sought to cope with its crippling loss of empire, vacillating between an ambitious attempt to install a far-reaching welfare state and a more modest effort to reinvigorate British industry—neither entirely successful. In Germany, the memory of horrendous hyperinflation after World War I—largely the result of draconian terms imposed by the Allies in the Treaty of Versailles—led to macroeconomic policy that stressed strict control over the money supply but that also encouraged extensive labor–management cooperation, including the placement of union members on corporate boards. In the Scandinavian countries, a remarkably successful marriage was arranged between the extremely egalitarian Labor Party and highly sophisticated corporate elites. In Italy, stagnation persisted in the south, but prosperity bloomed in the north.

Thus, policies varied from one country to the next, reflecting past experience, current political unity and vision, and persisting traits of national culture. However, one overarching generalization can be applied to all these varied economic experiences. The period 1960–1980 was perhaps the most prosperous the capitalist world has ever known. The Golden Age is not an exaggerated title for these decades. As can be seen in Table 9-1, other than the brief boom of the 1920s, the period from 1950 to 1970 was one of significantly higher growth in per capita income than any other since the early nineteenth century, in both developed and developing countries.

Tarnish Begins to Show

The postwar era is often described as unique in world history. Rapid economic growth occurred along with major technological change at the same time that gains in civil rights from women and minorities—especially African-Americans—were making themselves felt domestically. A hopeful new geopolitical order seemed to be on the international horizon. These last prospects would soon be disappointed, as the underdeveloped world proved to be a massive and unbudgeable weight, save for islands of success. Meanwhile, at home the remarkable amalgam of economic and political components of the Golden Age began to erode before the assault of an ever-growing pressure of globalization and a general turn of political sentiment away from government involvement in the economy. A tarnish begins to appear, as we see in our next chapter.

TABLE 9-1 Trends in Economic Growth, 1830–1990			
Annual Growth Rates of the Volume of GNP Per Capita, Based on 3-Year Averages			
	Developed Countries	*Developing Countries*	*World*
1830–1870	0.6	−0.2	0.1
1870–1890	1.0	0.1	0.7
1890–1913	1.7	0.6	1.4
1913–1920	−1.3	0.2	−0.8
1920–1929	3.1	0.1	2.4
1929–1950	1.3	0.4	0.8
1950–1970	4.0	1.7	3.0
1970–1990	2.2	0.9	1.5

Source: Paul Bairoch, *Economics and World History: Myths and Paradoxes* (London: Harvester, 1993).

Key Concepts and Key Words

Forces behind the Golden Age
1. With this chapter, we try to answer a very important question. What made possible the postwar boom that took everyone by surprise? We identify the complex assortment of factors that explains it.

International causes GATT and Marshall Plan
2. Part of the answer lies in favorable developments on the international front. The first was the establishment of unprecedented efforts to coordinate intereconomic efforts. Here we find the establishment of the International Monetary Fund, the World Bank, and the Bretton Woods Agreement—the first aiding war-torn European nations, the second helping developing countries, and the third establishing stable rates of currency exchange. Together with GATT and the Marshall Plan these policy initiatives imparted a strong military–political impetus to the Golden Age.

Domestic causes Pent-up demand New products
3. The Golden Age was certainly given a strong impetus by the Cold War, but at its core it was a domestically generated and sustained boom. Here three elements played key roles: The first was the vast latent demand for goods in an American nation that had earned high incomes during the war and now hungered to spend them on cars, homes, or the new television. A second propulsive element was provided by new technologies and products that emerged from World War II, including aviation as a new means of mass transportation and a new tourism industry.

New labor relations "Managerial capitalism"
4. At least as important was the development of a new labor wage contract that tied wages to productivity. This gave workers a direct stake in effective management; helped managers attend to long-run strategies; and helped maintain a stable ratio of wages to national product.

Government's larger role
5. Important among the forces behind the Golden Age boom was the enlarged role of government. In part, this was a continuation of New Deal policies; in part, new, much larger military-related Cold War expenditures; and in part the first deliberate use of fiscal policy as a stabilizing force.

A unique boom
6. With all its complexities and differences from country to country, the Golden Age was a remarkable period of the history of capitalism, a time without precedent. What remains to be seen will be whether it can be repeated in the future.

Questions

1. Has war always been a propulsive force for economies? How about World War I? How about winners versus losers? How about England, which was on the winning side in World War II?

2. If postwar demand was so important in getting the boom going, why isn't there a similar kind of pressure after every period of hard times?

3. *Managerial capitalism* is a phrase we hear less today than in the Golden Age. Why do you suppose it has dropped out of fashion? What changes do you think might bring it back?

4. The three preceding questions are very difficult to answer. However, they serve a purpose in making us think. Here is a fourth equally difficult—and thought-provoking—question: What do you think is different about today's economic situation and that described in this chapter?

Thinking Back, Looking Ahead

TURNING THE PAGE ON THE PAST

We cannot imagine anyone who has read this far and not looked ahead to the chapter titles that follow—above all, chapter 14, "Problems and Possibilities." These two words summarize the reason why economics can be at once a fascinating, and yet baffling, subject. Does not our own time hold extraordinary prospects for change, both good and bad? Do we not all imagine a capitalism that will have recaptured the spirit of the Golden Age and hope to assure its continuance in a manner that escaped its pioneers?

All this is to emphasize that we have just finished a truly heartrending period of history—full of hope and achievement, ending in a feeling of helplessness as the rate of global growth was cut in half in the 20 years from 1970 to 1990. We do not want to anticipate the findings of the chapters to follow, where these matters will be the focus of our interest. Instead, we end with a simple injunction: We have obviously reached a major turning point in the large theme of the making of economic society. Now is the time for our readers to broaden their views: They—and we—are no longer just students and teachers, but participants in, beneficiaries, and victims of the problems we will be considering. The following chapter examines the making of an economic society that is going on around us, on whose outcome much will depend.

CHAPTER
10
The Golden Age Comes To An End

MACROECONOMIC DILEMMAS

Like all good things, the Golden Age came to an end. The near quarter century of growth and stability, which was all the more welcome because it was unexpected, gave way to a quarter century of semistagnation, disruption, and uncertainty, which were all the more disquieting because they, too, had not been expected. Not of least significance in considering this period is that it leads us into the chapter of economic history in which we live. Therefore, we are leaving the study of "history" as an effort to discover how we came to be what we are and entering a study of history in which we try to understand what we may become.

All that is by way of introduction the final chapters that lie ahead. A very important task must be undertaken before we can hazard projections about the future: to investigate the changes that brought us from the Golden Age to the very different time in which we now live. That in itself is a daunting project. How can a few chapters adequately cover a period during which the political and economic maps changed out of all recognition in a mere 25 years?

Obviously, we cannot begin to do justice to the complexity of those forces of change. We hope, however, that we can illuminate the processes that seem most likely to affect our own prospects. We shall do so as follows: In this chapter, we largely confine ourselves to identifying "internal" economic developments that have changed the workings of the advanced capitalist economies. In chapter 11, we look at the past and future of the former communist countries of Eastern Europe. In chapter 12, our focus is almost exclusively directed to the powerful "external"—that is, international— changes that led to the present. In chapter 13, we take up the issue of economic development and ask why some nations remain poor. That done, we fasten our safety belts and in chapter 14 try to speak about what prospects seem likely to determine the character of the age through which we will be journeying in the years ahead.

Inflation Enters the Scene

There was no single moment in which the postwar boom turned into what economist Wallace Peterson calls a "silent depression."[1] If any single phenomenon can be said to mark the end of the Golden Age, it was the appearance of a new, persistent, and eventually alarming reality on the American scene—inflation. What was its cause? Many commentators have remarked that a nation's economic policies generally reflect its political aims. Certainly this has relevance to the American case, for if there is any single event that marked the beginning of the inflationary trend it was the United States'

---

[1]Wallace Peterson, *Silent Depression* (New York: W. W. Norton, 1994), p. 20.

full-scale entrance in the Vietnam War in 1965. Until 1964, the price index for consumer goods had risen each year by just more than 1 percent. As an example of the policy response to inflation at the time, in 1962 President Kennedy actually made a public appeal for the U.S. Steel Corporation to rescind an announced price increase on steel products. The company concurred, but in 1966, consumer prices rose by 1.6 percent, and the next year by 2.9 percent. Three years later, it was rising at a rate of 5.7 percent, and by 1974 it had leaped to 11.0 percent!

Was the increasingly expensive effort to win the war the sole cause of this alarming jump? Most historians would say, rather, that Vietnam was more important as the first of many serious misjudgments by the United States as to its ability to control events than as the sole—or even central—cause of an inflation that seriously undermined its power and prestige. We follow this story later in this chapter when we observe the inflationary consequences of the American attempt to maintain the dollar as the central currency of the world—a failure distinct from its inability to impose its will in Vietnam, but also reflecting a serious overestimation of its capacity to control events.

Oil Shock

Meanwhile, let us trace the next step in the inflationary scenario. This time the villain was oil. We tend to forget that during the Golden Age (and long before that) the United States dominated world oil production. All through the 1950s and 1960s, huge new oil fields were discovered in Texas and Oklahoma, with the consequence that American oil was by far the cheapest source of energy on the globe. American tourists who rented cars in France or England were always astonished at how expensive gas was abroad and how many miles they got to the gallon in cars built to economize on it.

No such economy was practiced at home, and as the number of automobiles increased by leaps and bounds during the Golden Age, U.S. oil production began to fall short of U.S. consumption. This set the stage for the rise of a Middle East–centered cartel called OPEC—the Organization of Petroleum Exporting Countries—that was soon able to determine the availability of oil to Europe, and to the United States as well. In 1973, in response to the pro-Israel foreign policy of most industrialized nations, OPEC suddenly imposed an embargo on its overseas shipments of oil, cutting off the supply of oil to its foreign customers. Lines began to form behind gas pumps all over Europe and the United States, and given the price-inelastic nature of the demand for oil—"fill up the tank, never mind the price"—fuel prices soared, tripling in the United States from $3 to $10 per barrel. In Europe and Japan, the rise was even more alarming.

More than just inconveniencing motorists, the price shock forced up production costs in almost every sector in the economy. Any industry that required energy, from the running of a steel furnace to the heating of a travel agency office, saw its cost of doing business rise rapidly and unexpectedly. The price of goods generally went up as well. Firms had little choice but to lower profit margins or to raise prices to cover the cost increase. Most did a combination of the two, and the result was upward pressure on prices and a slowdown in the rate of investment.

A second shock soon followed. At the end of 1979, as the mounting inflation rate reduced the real value of the cartel's earnings, OPEC again curtailed production, this time with the effect of boosting the oil price to more than $35 per barrel. This produced a second, and much more powerful, wave of inflationary pressure: In 1980, consumer prices in the United States rose by 13.5 percent.

Once again, the jump in fuel prices affected a wide range of goods. The oil shock was quickly translated into a rising index of consumer prices. As we have seen, already during the 1960s, the inflation rate had begun to move toward 4 and 5 percent per year, probably as a result of the rising level of wages in a high-employment economy. As we have seen, by 1974 the consumer price index rose by more than 10 percent. Now something really alarming happened. In 1980, following the second shock, it actually rose by 13.5 percent, one of the largest jumps in American history.

The oil price shock presented a clear and difficult question: What to do about this new inflationary threat? With our historical perspective, we might pose the question differently: Why was the rise in oil prices so "contagious" in the late 1970s? One very important part of the answer lay in the fact that the capitalism of the times was not that of 50 years before. If we can imagine something like an oil shock having raised prices of, say, coal in the 1920s or 1930s, it is very doubtful that it would have produced anything like a national inflationary threat. Rather, faced with unchanged personal incomes, households would have had no alternative to pulling in their belts and consuming less coal.

By the 1970s, deep institutional changes greatly lessened such an inflation-resistive response. New income support systems—Social Security, unemployment insurance, insurance of bank accounts, and cost-of-living adjustments built into wage contracts—limited the fall in consumer spending that a sudden price increase would likely have produced in those earlier days. Thus, the movement from the recession-prone capitalism of the 1930s to the recession-resistive capitalism of the Golden Age had the unexpected effect of increasing our inflationary susceptibilities.

Stagflation and the Policy Dilemma

The combination of strong inflation and weak investment created a fragile economic environment. Postwar economic policy had been premised on the existence of a trade-off between inflation and unemployment. When prices rose, it was assumed that the reason was a "tight" labor market—that is, a low level of unemployment that resulted in wage increases, which in turn raised costs and, therefore, prices. When inflation fell, the reason was assumed to be a rise in unemployment, which tended to lower wages and, therefore, prices. Prices and unemployment were pictured as opposite ends of a seesaw. There was a reassuring aspect to this. No one wanted higher unemployment, but at least it was seen as bringing about lower prices, which everyone wanted. No one wanted inflation, but rising prices were seen as the consequence of higher employment, which everyone did want.

All this served to cement the acceptance of the economic theories of John Maynard Keynes, which we have already encountered in learning about the responses to the Great Depression. By the 1960s, Keynesian economics, with its strong endorsement of government spending as a counterforce against slumps, was widely accepted not only by economists but by politicians: In the early 1970s President Nixon made the famous remark that "We are all Keynesians now."

However, the Keynesian consensus among politicians and economists began to unravel quickly in the face of the new challenge—the simultaneous experience of price inflation and a downturn in growth and employment. Through the 1970s, inflation steadily moved toward double-digit levels while real output actually *fell* in 1970, 1974, 1975, and 1980. *Stagflation,* as this new environment became known, could not be handled with the traditional tools of Keynesianism. The Keynesian response to rising inflation would be to reduce government spending and to ease pressures on the economy. The response to slow or negative growth would be to raise public spending and thereby stimulate the economy. Therefore, the new state of affairs put Keynesianism in a bind: With prices rising and output tending to fall, whatever you did was bad as well as good. That was no basis from which to conduct a convincing, much less effective, policy. In this impasse, the reins of power passed to another branch of government—the Fed, that is, the Federal Reserve system that was responsible for conducting the monetary policy of the government.

The Fed lost no time in rising to the challenge because it was a bank, and because inflation, to bankers, was clearly a monetary problem: "Too much money chasing too few goods," as the old adage went. Therefore, the overriding necessity of the Fed was to reduce the supply of money in the economy. This meant making it much more difficult for persons or businesses to borrow, for borrowing and spending was undoubtedly the main source of the inflationary pressure.

How to cut down on this expenditure? The answer was to raise the rate charged by the Fed to its member banks, who regularly borrowed from it to make loans to their customers. Starting in late 1979, under the leadership of Paul Volcker, the Fed ruthlessly tightened the rate until it reached almost 18 percent in 1981—a rate that translated into more than 20 percent on bank loans to customers. No one, even the largest corporations, could afford to borrow at such prices. Loans fell, and with them, expenditures, and as a consequence, the rate of inflation.[2]

It was a draconian, but effective, policy. By 1982 the national inflation rate was running at what now seemed like the quite moderate rates of 5 to 6 percent. Meanwhile, because expenditures were falling, unemployment rose—to 11 percent—but this was welcomed by the Fed because it kept the inflation menace in check. Indeed, it was frequently referred to as the Volcker recession—a term of praise as well as blame.

Not surprisingly, the whole episode left a scar. Preventing inflation, not encouraging all-out growth, now became the central preoccupation of the monetary authorities. Even as the economic situation worsened during the 1980s, the concern of the Federal Reserve was more to nip the inflationary tendencies in the bud than to encourage more investment and consumption.

The scar left by the oil shock has been a specter of inflation that has haunted all advanced economies since that time. In chapter 14, we talk about what counter steps may be possible to escape from the damned-if-we-do, damned-if-we-don't heritage of this period.

---

[2]What exactly is the mechanism the Fed used so powerfully? The two main targets of Federal Reserve policy are the growth of the money supply and the level of interest rates. Although the Fed is responsible for distributing cash to banks for the use by its customers, bills and coins make up only a small fraction of the overall money supply. Money is mainly made up of checking accounts, money market accounts, and even (by some definitions) lines of credit. Accordingly, banks create money when they make a loan by opening a checking account in the name of the borrower. Thus, the Fed controls the money supply by raising the price of borrowing. When loans cost more, fewer new accounts are opened, and banks must charge more for whatever loans they make.

The Uneven Recovery

The stagflation crisis, if not its specter, finally came to an end, only to open the way for a second, and in some ways more troubling because less easily cured, condition: the onset of stagnant living standards for the working class. In the United States, the new problem was most clearly evident as a fall in the rate of growth of productivity—that is, in the rate of increase in the value of output per worker. Productivity is of vital importance because, in the end, workers' wages are primarily determined, or at least limited, by the value of what they produce. From 1959 to 1973, output per worker grew at an annual rate of 2.9 percent, a rate consistent with a comfortable potential rise in the standard of living of the workforce. But from 1973 to 1994, that rate of productivity growth fell by almost two-thirds, to a mere 1 percent average increase.

Happily, in the late 1980s and early 1990s productivity growth in manufacturing increased nearly to its earlier level, but by then manufacturing accounted for a much smaller share of total output, so that on a national level the potential for a comfortable upward movement in workers' living standards was still seriously below that of earlier times. In all, real wages (wages corrected for inflation) rose by less than one-third of 1 percent from 1973 to 1993. Between 1979 and 1994, real wages of production workers actually *fell* by about 8 percent.[3]

Following another recession in the early 1990s, U.S. economic growth increased and continued at a steady pace through the 1990s. This was at first driven by a precarious rise in consumer spending—precarious because it required historically unprecedented levels of consumer debt. In the last 3 years of the century, investment spending also picked up, as did productivity growth. The rate of unemployment fell to its historic low of 4.2 percent in 1999, and real wages rose for the first time in decades (see Figure 10-1).

In Europe generally, it should be noted, real wages had fared much better than in the United States, with most countries enjoying wage growth of between 1.5 percent and 3 percent. However, Europe suffered from a second problem of the silent depression that followed the inflationary danger: a disturbing rise in unemployment. France, Italy, Belgium, and others have had double-digit rates of unemployment in almost every year since 1982, roughly twice that of the United States. In the late 1990s, Germany, which historically had a very low rate of unemployment, saw its unemployment rate rise to almost 10 percent. (see Figure 10-1)

Perhaps more important, the United States, which has been widely supposed to have escaped the unemployment problem, may also be suffering from something like the European ailment. In the fall of 1995, says economist Lester Thurow, the number of America's officially "unemployed" came to 7.5 million workers. "But like an iceberg that is most invisible below the waterline," writes Thurow, "those officially unemployed are just a small part of the total number of workers looking for work." Thurow adds 5 to 6 million citizens without work who say they want it, but do not officially qualify as "unemployed" because they do not meet one or another of the official prerequisites, plus another 4.5 million who do not count as unemployed because they have accepted part-time employment although they want full time. In all, this yields an unemployment rate of 14 percent.[4]

---

[3]Figures are from David Gordon, *Fat and Mean* (New York: The Free Press, 1996), chap. 1.
[4]Lester Thurow, *The Future of Capitalism* (New York: William Morrow, 1996), p. 165.

FIGURE 10-1 The Rate of Unemployment in the Main Industrialized Countries, 1970–1999 (in percent)

	1970–1974	1975–1979	1980–1984	1985–1989	1990–1994	1995	1996	1997	1998	1999
United States	5.3	7.0	8.3	6.2	6.6	5.6	5.4	4.9	4.5	4.2
Japan	1.2	2.0	2.4	2.6	2.4	3.1	3.4	3.4	4.1	4.7
Canada	5.8	7.6	9.9	8.8	10.3	9.5	9.7	9.2	8.3	7.8
France	2.7	4.9	7.9	10.1	10.5	11.6	12.3	12.5	11.8	11.1
Germany	1.1	3.7	5.0	7.8	6.6	8.3	8.1	8.8	9.8	9.3
Italy	4.3	5.1	7.0	9.9	9.6	11.7	11.7	11.8	11.9	11.6
United Kingdom	2.6	4.6	9.6	9.5	8.8	8.6	8.0	6.9	6.2	6.1

Source: Organization of Economic Cooperation and Development, *Economic Outlook* Data Base (n66) (Paris: OECD, 2000).

EXPLAINING ECONOMIC DECLINE

Behind the Numbers: The Shift to Services

How can we explain these figures? Let us start with the disturbing fall in productivity in the United States. Here there is one explanation that attracts widespread agreement. It is the fact that employment in service occupations has grown much more rapidly than in manufacturing and that productivity in services is generally much lower than in manufactures. Manufacturing employment in 1970 accounted for 26 percent of total employment; in 1990, it was 16 percent. Meanwhile, employment in services (including government) grew from 62 percent in 1975 to 69 percent of total employment in 1990. With the growth of such sectors as finance, insurance, real estate, retailing, and fast food, the American economy appeared to be entering a postindustrial phase. Moreover, this structural shift toward a service economy corresponded with the increasing entry of women into the labor force. Because on average women leaving the home to go to work had less training than those already in the workforce, their entry into the labor market also lowered average productivity.

The Slow Pace of Investment

Keynes identified investment in plant and equipment as the key variable for the understanding of the income and wealth-generating capacity of capitalist economies. Investment may play an even more important role today, because it is the carrier of new technologies into the production process. It is not surprising that slow growth in private sector investment also lowered productivity growth. Investment is driven by the expectations of profits. When oil prices soared in the 1970s, expectations plummeted, and private investment growth also slowed. In the 1980s, interest rates on financial assets such as Treasury bonds rose to new highs. This too dampened investment growth: Potential investors asked themselves why they should invest in a risky, long-term venture, when a no-risk investment yielded almost the same return. Again in the 1980s, investment growth was inadequate to return the American economy to anything like the Golden Age.

The gloomy investment picture had long-run implications for productivity as well. When firms delay in introducing new technology, they eventually lose markets and sales to rival firms. These losses can be cumulative: Once a technological laggard, the firm will find it doubly difficult to catch up. For example, as the innovativeness of American firms diminished, the Japanese began to dominate the consumer electronics markets. The videocassette recorder (VCR), by then practically a standard household item, was developed by Japanese firms, and U.S. firms were largely left out of this extraordinary boom market. From a failure to stay abreast in technology, the United States saw its share of world sales of high-technology goods drop in the 1980s and 1990s. Because they tend to be high-productivity and high-wage sectors, their decline was felt throughout the U.S. economy.

Downsizing

Partly in response to the productivity growth slowdown, U.S. corporations began to reorganize themselves, in particular by laying off workers in large numbers. The phenomenon of mass layoffs at the large corporations became known as "downsizing"—mass terminations of employment by which firms sought to reduce labor costs and raise productivity and profit margins. Successive waves of downsizing began in the late 1980s. Some of the largest U.S. corporations participated, including IBM, AT&T, and General Electric. In 1990, for example, 300,000 workers were laid off; in 1991, the number surged to 550,000. Two years later, this time with the economy out of its recession, 600,000 workers were laid off. In January 1994 alone, firms laid off more than 100,000 people, and the figure for all of 1994 was 516,000. In total, from 1990 to 1994, corporations laid off 2.5 million people.[5]

This dramatic restructuring of corporations had a direct effect on firms' productivity and profits, but its most important implication was for wages. Economists traditionally view slowdowns in the growth of output and wages as the result of the productivity slowdowns. However, the link between wages and productivity is never airtight, because wages are often the result of a bargaining process between corporate managers and labor unions, and the relative strength of the two sides will vary depending on economic and political conditions and the degree to which workers are organized into unions.

The impact of downsizing on wages was both direct and indirect. As workers were laid off, they joined the pool of people already looking for jobs. This allowed companies to offer lower wages to any new employees they took on, because there was more competition for those jobs. Those who were not caught in the net of massive layoffs were also affected, because they faced an environment of rising job insecurity. With each successive layoff announcement, a collective chill could be felt among those still on the job. This had a dampening effect on union wage demands. Many unions abandoned hope of increasing wages, focusing instead on attaining guarantees of job security.

As the numbers make clear, downsizing quickly became a popular corporate strategy. It is not surprising, then, that it also caught on in Europe. German firms announced layoffs of 180,000 in the first quarter of 1994. Italian firms cut about 200,000 jobs in the early 1990s, and France's largest tire producer announced plans to cut its workforce in half.[6]

FROM SLOWER GROWTH TO GREATER INEQUALITY

Now we change our focus but not our question. While the policy dilemmas of the post–Golden Age era continued to mount, something else was happening—not nearly so dramatic as an oil shock and not nearly so easy to explain. It was a change in the manner in which the system was distributing income and wealth. The Golden Age was not only a time when the aggregate incomes of Americans grew steadily and satisfactorily, but also a time when the distance between rich and poor steadily, if slowly, diminished. In the 20-odd years in which we are now interested, these healthy tendencies came to a halt. Indeed, they reversed themselves.

Let us begin with wealth—or more precisely with financial assets owned by families—in order to concentrate on the form of wealth most quickly subject to change, upward or downward. In the booming 1920s, the top 1 percent of all families owned 42 percent of the financial wealth in the nation, an unprecedentedly large share. Not surprisingly, this percentage fell dramatically after the market crash of 1929, and then still

[5]Thurow, op. cit., 1996, p. 26.
[6]*Ibid.*, p. 28.

further with the long period of low stock prices of the 1930s and the impact of the tax policies of the New Deal. As a consequence, by 1940, the share of financial wealth in the hands of the top 1 percent had been approximately cut in half.

Thereafter, as the nation regained its stride, and as the Golden Age took hold, national wealth increased rapidly, its shares going to rich and poor in more or less the same proportion as their existing wealth holding in 1962: From that date to 1983, the top 1 percent of families received 34 percent of the increase in wealth, the next 19 percent received 48 percent, and the bottom 80 percent got 18 percent. Now compare this result with the period from 1983 to 1989: In this mere 6-year span, the top 1 percent of wealth holders received 62 percent of the total gain in wealth; the next 19 percent received only 37 percent, and the lowest 80 percent received a minuscule 1 percent.[7] In the words of Edward Wolff, whose research has produced these figures:

> The increase in wealth inequality recorded over [this] period in the United States is almost unprecedented. The only other period in the twentieth century during which concentration of household wealth rose comparably was from 1922 to 1929. Then inequality was buoyed primarily by the excessive increase in stock values, which eventually crashed in 1929, leading to the Great Depression of the 1930s.[8]

What of the trend in the distribution of income, the measurement we ordinarily think of when we consider the problem of inequality? Perhaps the most effective way to depict the trend is to compare the ratio of the wages of an average male worker with that of a top chief executive officer (CEO). If we take an estimated figure of $25,000 as the average wage of such a worker in 1970, the income of his company's highest paid executive was around $1 million. If we now turn to 1990, the average wage has risen to $35,000, but the top CEO pay now approached $8 million. The ratio has jumped from 40 to 1 to more than 225 to 1. Although less dramatic, the trend toward inequality was also clearly visible in the widening disparity between wages of low-skilled and high-skilled workers, and in particular between workers who enjoy college, or higher-than-college, educations and those who do not.

These comparisons give a dramatic picture of the worsening pattern of income distribution in the United States, but even broader measures of income distribution reveal a similar pattern. During the Golden Age, *all* income groups experienced a growth of income at an annual rate of about 2.5 percent. Since 1973, income growth has been negatively correlated with relative income level. That is, the richest 20 percent of the population experienced the most rapid income growth, the next richest 20 percent had less income growth over the period, and so on down the income pyramid. The poorest fifth of the population actually saw its incomes fall in the period 1973–1989. Professor Paul Krugman has compared the two eras as going "from picket fence to staircase," the former referring to a tall flat graph of income growth across the population in the early period and the latter to the step-like growth of income as we move up the income ladder.[9] To make matters worse, income inequality has also been associated in the post–Golden Age with rising rates of poverty. The number of persons whose income was

[7]Edward N. Wolff, *Top Heavy* (New York: Twentieth Century Fund, 1996), pp. 12–13.
[8]Op. cit., p. 13.
[9]Paul Krugman, *Peddling Prosperity* (New York: W. W. Norton, 1994), p. 131.

below the poverty line in the United States jumped from 11 percent during the 1970s to between 14 and 15 percent in the 1980s and 1990s.

Therefore, there is little doubt that income distribution patterns have changed, and changed for the worse if one believes, as we do, that growing inequality presents serious moral and economic problems. That leaves unanswered the question of how we can explain this phenomenon, which we find to a much lesser degree in almost all capitalist nations than in the United States.

Behind the Inequality Problem

The disconcerting answer is that there is no single answer. In a brilliant discussion of the issue, economist Barry Bluestone discusses nine "suspects." In brief, they are as follows: (1) Technological changes are placing a premium on skilled labor and reducing the demand for the less skilled; (2) Employment is concentrated in low-wage service industries such as McDonald's, rather than high-wage sectors like commercial aircraft production; (3) Deregulation of many industries, like trucking, brings in nonunion, low-wage employers; (4) Unionization itself is way down: The proportion of workers in manufacturing industry having fallen from more than 35 percent to less than half of that; (5) Corporate personnel policy has replaced long-term employees with short-term part-timers; (6) Modern means of publicity creates "winner-take-all" markets in which a few big performers—executives as well as entertainment and sports stars—walk off with the lion's share of earnings; (7) Foreign producers are capturing markets for goods that were previously produced with relatively well-paid domestic workers—a matter we look into in chapter 12; (8) International capital mobility, the crux of the globalization phenomenon, does much the same thing; and (9) Immigration raises the supply of workers competing for low-wage jobs.

How does Bluestone assess this impressive list? He concludes that very likely the answer is the same as that given in Agatha Christie's *Murder on the Orient Express:* "They all did it." "Every major economic trend in the U.S.," writes Bluestone, "contributes to growing inequality." He adds, "None of these trends shows the least sign of weakening."[10]

The Government Retreats

We must add one important factor to Bluestone's otherwise exhaustive list: the retreat of the government as an active source of income support for the poor. First in the United States and the United Kingdom, and now increasingly in continental Europe, we find a curtailment of income support to combat poverty. The stage may well have been set for such a move by the failure of Keynesian policy to solve the stagflation problem in the 1970s. By the 1980s, skepticism with regard to the ability of the government to spur demand attained the level of popular ideology. The landslide election of Ronald Reagan in 1980 signaled this change in the United States. Similar views swept Margaret Thatcher and the Conservatives into power in England. An increasingly popular view was that the government was part of the problem, not the solution, because Keynesian policy had not succeeded in reducing inflation or eliminating poverty.

In addition to this shift in ideology, governments faced growing constraints and pressure to dismantle the welfare state that had flourished in the 1960s. With slower

---

[10]Barry Bluestone, "The Inequality Express," in *Ticking Time Bombs* (New York: The New Press, 1996), p. 66.

economic growth came a slower rise in tax revenues. At the same time, demographic changes were slowly putting more pressure on state coffers, especially the problem of how to care for the income and health needs of an aging population. Finally, growing international competition and the increased mobility of corporations put increasing pressure on all national governments to reduce the tax burden on corporations to induce them not to move abroad.

This has not been an easy chapter to read or write. It is not pleasant to trace the trajectory of the Golden Age into the discouraging conclusion of a silent depression. Worse is yet to come. One last aspect of the problem of inequality still requires our attention: The United States, once upon a time the country with the most equitable distribution of wealth in the Western world, is now the country with the least equitable distribution.

Here we have the findings of a recent survey of the shares of the rich and the poor in the most affluent modern nations of the world. At the top in terms of equality of distribution stands Finland, whose topmost 10 percent of income receivers attained 2.7 times as much income as the poorest 10 percent. Next was Norway, only slightly less egalitarian than Finland, the rich top 10 percent enjoying 2.79 as much income as the poorest 10 percent. Holland was third in order, with the top decile enjoying 2.9 times the income of the lowest tenth; then Canada, 2.84 to 1. Last was the United States: The income of its top tenth was 5.67 larger than that of its bottom tenth.[11]

How do we explain this disturbing state of affairs? How do we account for the extraordinary share of income accruing to American CEOs, compared with that of any other advanced capitalist nation? The question is of great importance—but it will have to wait before we can consider it. Unpleasant or not, we must have the clearest possible view of our problems and difficulties before we go about trying to explain, much less suggest remedies for them. So we must brace ourselves for one more chapter of difficulties before we try to put the United States' problems into some more constructive perspective.

Key Concepts and Key Words

The end of an age
1. This is a long chapter about a lengthy process. The Golden Age came to an end in the 1970s, not for any single reason but as the outcome of many changes, some interconnected, some not.

Inflation
"Oil shock"
The entire economy becomes inflationary
2. There is no question as to the first of these destructive developments. It was the gradual appearance, then the dramatic explosion, of inflation. In 1967, the cost of living rose by 2.9 percent. Seven years later, it leaped by 11 percent. The cause of the initial gradual appearance was probably the pressure of military spending on the economy in the Vietnam period. Thereafter, the explosion occurred when "oil shock" from the OPEC cartel twice imposed embargos that tripled the price of gasoline in 1973 and again in 1979. In Europe, the effect was even more drastic. Everywhere, the rise in the price of oil affected prices generally. Consumer prices in the United States, for example, rose by 13.5 percent as a result of the second shock.

Stagflation and the Keynesian breakdown
3. The combination of rising prices and a weakening economy brought stagflation in place of vigorous growth. Equally important, it threw doubt on the relevance of Keynesian economy and thrust monetary power to the fore as the main weapon against inflation.

---

[11]See Surenda Kushlik, "India's Democratic Economic Transformation," *Challenge* (September/October 1996), p. 54. See also Timothy Smeeding, "America's Income Inequality: Where Do We Stand?" *Challenge* (September/October 1996), pp. 45–53.

Inflation ends, a slump begins, a specter remains

4. Monetary power was exercised by the Federal Reserve, which raised the interest it charged for loans to member banks. In turn, member banks raised their interest charges on loans to business. As a consequence, the boom turned into a slump, but runaway inflation came to an end. Although the Fed's policy worked, it has left a fear of inflation as a specter haunting the economy.

A silent depression appears

5. The painful end to inflation brought what has been called a silent depression. Economic growth slowed, productivity fell, and real wages declined, not just in the United States but abroad. The new age has many disconcerting features. Manufacturing declined in importance and services grew, both adding to the slowdown in the productivity of the labor force.

Inequality increased Division of wealth deepens

6. Of greater consequence was an unprecedented shift of income away from poorer and middle-income families to those at the peak of the income pyramid. The causes for the shift are not clear, but there is no doubt that one of the most striking changes of the new period was the widening of the gap between working and top managerial incomes.

The end of the Golden Age

7. The change in economic fortunes resulted in a change in political attitudes. Government's powers were curtailed and the private sector was regarded as a natural source of economic momentum, needing only the encouragement of lower taxes. Thus, the end of the Golden Age signaled a turnaround in the relations of government and the economy.

Questions

1. Why was the inflation at the end of the Golden Age so disruptive? Do you think that even without the two oil shocks it would have become so powerful a force? Without the Vietnam War? Was it "in the cards," or was it the product of these two political events?
2. How would you describe "stagflation" as opposed to "inflation"? Does it refer to the presence or absence of economic growth? What, in turn, determines how strong growth will be?
3. The Federal Reserve has the power to change the rate of interest that it charges its member banks when they borrow reserves (government bonds) from the Fed. Why would a member bank want more reserves? Why would a higher rate of interest change the interest rate that a bank charges a company seeking a loan?
4. Inequality has been a growing concern for Americans. Do you think there is some "right" distribution of income? How would it be determined? Why is a growing percentage of income going to high-income families and a declining percentage going to low-income families regarded as an unwelcome phenomenon? Is the reason moral, economic, or both?

Thinking Back, Looking Ahead

KEYNES'S LEGACY

With the end of the Golden Age, Keynesianism went into decline, both in practice and in the way economists understood the economy. However, many economists today believe that Keynes's broad economic vision and the lessons he taught in his famous 1936 book *The General Theory of Employment, Interest and Money* continue to be important in the twenty-first century. As we will see in the following chapters, the global economy now has productive capacity that far exceeds the demand for goods and services. This global excess capacity would not be a problem if it automatically created demand for all the potential output. However, as Keynes wrote in 1936, capitalism has no automatic mechanism in place to create this additional demand, which would generally come from higher wages and more jobs. The result is a world in which, despite this enormous productive capacity, leaves many people in poverty, without work, and even marginalized in terms of the formal economy.

Keynes's insights about the possibility of an economy (in this case, the world economy) remaining in a condition of high unemployment were drawn from his observations about the Great Depression. The idea, however, was rooted in a general concept of capitalism that continues to be relevant today. For Keynes, capitalism was first and foremost a money-based system in which wages are paid by entrepreneurs in advance of their receipt of income from sales. As a result, entrepreneurs' hiring decisions are based heavily on their expectations of future sales. If these expectations are not realized because of low demand, then entrepreneurs might scale back their hiring and their purchases of machinery and equipment. In this world, the existence of a lot of productive capacity is no guarantee of the level of demand adequate to spur entrepreneurs to expand their workforce; in fact, a lack of demand may be a signal for them to reduce production (and, thus, employment). Keynes identified in capitalism an inherent tendency not to generate full employment. As we will see, today's globalized economy, for all its free-market policies, continues to suffer from the problems that Keynes identified in the first part of the last century.

C H A P T E R

11

The Rise and Fall of Socialism

SOCIALISM VERSUS CAPITALISM?

We would expect that, with the mixed performance of capitalism since the end of the Golden Age, there would come some questioning of the value of the system itself and perhaps some consideration of an alternative. Instead, capitalism's mediocre performance over the past 20 years coincided with the collapse of capitalism's historic opposite: the systems of communism and socialism that had governed economic society in many parts of the globe since the early part of the twentieth century. This unexpected spread of capitalism to former socialist countries spurred an extraordinary turnabout in the way we perceive economic history itself. These days, one could read the newspapers for months on end without seeing a word about communism or the rivalry between the capitalist and socialist systems. However, not 15 years ago, the world was fixed in a Cold War—a political confrontation that molded much foreign and international economic policy in the two superpower nations, the United States and its rival, the Soviet Union.

If we go back even further, say, to the late 1930s, a mere blink of the eye as historic chronologies unfold, the direction of world economic change seemed even more dramatically different than it does today: World capitalism then appeared to be on its way out, socialism of one kind or another on its way in. Without a single exception, the Western capitalist nations had gone through, or were still embroiled in, the most devastating economic depression in history. Ahead lay a world war whose outcome, most observers quite correctly foresaw, would be the destruction of capitalist colonial empires abroad and the emplacement of "socialistic" welfare schemes at home. Who could entertain optimistic expectations for capitalism in the face of such events and prospects?

Meanwhile, the fortunes of socialism were rising as dramatically as those of capitalism seemed to be fading. The Russian Revolution had seized the imagination of much of the world, especially in the old colonial regions, where socialist parties and leaders were already preparing to reorganize the lands of Asia and Africa under the banner of national planning, whose galvanizing force had been made evident by the Soviet example. The coming war seemed to the Third World a great turning point, signaling the end of the old order. With such expectations, who would not have painted the socialist future in bright colors?

Need we say that things have not turned out that way? Capitalism is very much alive today, even though it is not in perfect health. More striking, socialism has collapsed, most dramatically in the Soviet Union and the Soviet block of countries in Eastern Europe, all of which are rapidly introducing capitalistic reforms. Perhaps equally surprising, South Korea, Mexico, and other Third World countries generally have not left the fold of the capitalist system but have actually become more enmeshed in it. Some of that entanglement is the result of their financial indebtedness to their former political and military masters. Perhaps more significant, the entanglement also proceeds from the emergence of new centers of industrial production in many countries that were certainly not capitalist 50 years ago—Hong Kong, Singapore, Taiwan, and South Korea, along with strong signs of further capitalist development elsewhere—Brazil, Mexico, and India. In the face of these events, who could today declare that capitalism is dying or that socialism is the wave of the future?

EXPLAINING THE HISTORIC SHIFT

Can we explain this astonishing change of historic course? Two generalizations will help us think about what has happened.

1. *Capitalism has changed.*

Capitalism is very much a vital economic force in modern history, but it is not the same capitalism as that to which the gloomy predictions of the past applied. The nature of that change has been spelled out in this book and does not need to be examined in detail. At its core is that overall capitalist performance, including policies of socialization such as old-age retirement, have proved more effective in generating economic patriotism than their counterparts in contemporary socialism.

As every reader of this book must know, that certainly does not mean that capitalism is today free of serious problems. Nonetheless, it helps explain the profound change that marks off capitalism's current self-assessment from that of the not-so-distant past. The outlook for the future, at least in the main capitalist nations, no longer appears to be a choice between capitalism and socialism. Rather, it concerns the kind of capitalism most likely to work well. The debates we have followed in our text—debates over Keynesian policies, welfare, government deficits, protectionism, industrial regulation, and the recognized need for "socialization"—are taking place within a general consensus about the viability of capitalism, an outlook very different from that of 50 years ago.

2. *Socialism revealed unexpected economic and political difficulties.*

By and large, the early enthusiasts for socialism laid their bets on two aspects of a planned economic system. One was its capacity to move a backward, moribund economy off dead center. The other was the elimination of the inefficiencies and wastefulness of capitalism. One of those bets paid off, at least in part. The other did not.

The bet that paid off was the ability of central planning to bring backward nations into the modern world. This was most dramatically evidenced in the Soviet Union (into whose history we shall shortly look) and in China. No one can compare the old tsarist empire or the hopelessly inefficient Chinese landlord system with the societies created by the Soviet or the Chinese communists and not recognize that an unprecedented transformation has taken place, however horrendous the cost.

Getting a society off dead center is one thing; however, keeping it going is another. This is the bet that socialism lost. Without exception, the impressive socialist "takeoffs" were followed by increasingly disappointing, and finally disastrous, economic performance. Moreover, the reason for the failure was the same in every case—the vitality of the early stage of mobilization was followed by the inertia and then the downright disorganization of bureaucratization. The unexpected lesson of socialism was that planning was an easy word to spell, but a hard one to spell out.

Planning was intended to be the remedy for the ills of capitalism. In many cases, it became a remedy worse than the disease.

THE SOVIET SYSTEM

Let us begin by looking into the history of the Soviet system. We must start by realizing that the Russian system did not evolve gradually over time, as did capitalism. It was created, forcibly, after the Revolution of 1917. A semifeudal society dotted with a few large capitalist enterprises was taken over by revolutionaries who had read deeply in Marx but who knew nothing about how to administer, much less organize, a "socialist" economy.

Marx was of little use to the revolutionaries because *Capital,* his great opus, was entirely about capitalism, not socialism. In those few essays in which Marx looked to the future, his gaze rarely traveled beyond the watershed of the revolutionary act itself. With the achievement of the revolution, Marx thought, a temporary regime known as the "dictatorship of the proletariat" would take over the transition from capitalism to socialism. Thereafter, a "planned socialist economy" would emerge as the first step toward a still less specified "communism." In the latter state—the final stage of economic revolution, according to Marx—there were hints that the humdrum tasks of production and distribution would take place by the voluntary cooperation of all citizens and that society would run its serious attention to matters of cultural and humanistic importance.

In reality, the revolution presented Lenin, Trotsky, and the other leaders of the new Soviet Union with problems far more complex than this utopian long-term design. Shortly after the initial success of the revolution, Lenin nationalized the banks, the major factories, the railways, and the canals. In the meantime, the peasants themselves had taken over the large landed estates on which they had been tenants and had carved them up into individual holdings. The central authorities then attempted for several years to run the economy by requisitioning food from the farms and allocating it to factory workers, while controlling the flow of output from the factories by a system of direct controls from the government.

This initial attempt to run the economy was a disastrous failure. Under inept management, industrial output declined precipitously; by 1920, it had fallen to a mere 14 percent of prewar levels! As goods available to the peasants became scarcer, the peasants themselves were less and less willing to acquiesce in giving up food to the cities. The result was wild inflation, followed by a degeneration into an economy of semibarter. Toward the end of 1920, the system threatened to break down completely. To forestall the impending collapse, in 1921 Lenin instituted a New Economic Policy, the so-called NEP. This was a return toward a market system and a partial reconstitution of actual capitalism. Retail trade, for instance, was again opened to private ownership and operation. Small-scale industry also reverted to private direction. Most important, the farms were no longer requisitioned but operated as profit-making units. Only the "commanding heights" of industry and finance were retained in government hands.

A bitter debate ensued for several years about what course of action to follow next. Though the basic aim of the Soviet government was still to replace the private ownership of the means of production with state ownership, the question was how fast to move ahead—and, indeed, *how* to do so. The pace of industrialization hinged critically on one highly uncertain factor: the willingness of the large peasant sector to deliver food that city workers needed to be sustained in their tasks. Every student of Russian history will find this a fascinating story.[1] We need note only how it was ultimately resolved. In 1927, Stalin took command and made the decision not to appease unwilling peasants but to "collectivize"—that is, to seize—their holdings in the name of the state. The result was a ghastly period of Russian history in which an estimated 5 million kulaks (well-off peasants) were executed or put into labor camps; in the cities, workers were ordered to perform their tasks, forbidden to strike, and subjected to brutal speedups.

The history of this forced industrialization has left an abiding scar on socialism as a form of economic organization. It is helpful, nonetheless, to view it with some objectivity. If the extremes to which the Stanlinist authorities went were extraordinary, and perhaps self-defeating, we must bear in mind that industrialization on the grand scale has always been a wrenching process. We have already seen what happened in the West at the time of the Industrial Revolution, with its heavy-handed exploitation of labor; without excusing these acts, we have seen their function in paving the way for capital accumulation.

Indeed, without seeking to justify the Russian effort, it is worth pondering whether rapid industrialization, with its inescapable price of low consumption, could ever be a "popular" policy. Will poor people willingly vote for an economic transformation that will not pay out for 20 or 40 years? We might note that universal male suffrage was not gained in England until the late 1860s and 1870s. One historian has written, "It is highly doubtful whether the achievements of the Industrial Revolution would have been permitted if the franchise had been universal. It is very doubtful because a great deal of the capital aggregations that we are at present enjoying are the results of the wages that our fathers went without."[2]

Market Versus Plan

A massive industrialization drive requires a determined effort to hold consumption to a minimum and to transfer resources to capital-building—an effort greatly facilitated by a totalitarian political apparatus. There is still another question to be considered: How will the freed resources find their proper destination in an integrated and poorly working industrial sector?

Let us remind ourselves of how this is done in a market economy. There, the signal of profitability serves as the magnet for the allocation of resources and labor. Entrepreneurs, anticipating or following demand, risk private funds in the construction of the facilities they hope the future will require. Meanwhile, as these industrial salients expand, smaller satellite industries grow along with them to cater to their needs. The flow of materials is thus regulated in every sector by the force of private demand, making itself known by the signal of rising or falling prices. At every moment, a magnetic pull of demand emanates from the growing industries to secondary industries, while, in turn, the growth salients themselves are guided, spurred, or slowed down by the pressure of demand from the ultimate buying public. All the while, counterposed to these pulls of demand, are the obduracies of supply—the cost schedules of the producers. In this crossfire of demand and supply exists a sensitive social instrument for the integration of the overall economic effort of expansion.

---

[1]See Alexander Erlich, *The Soviet Industrialization Debate: 1924–1928* (Cambridge, MA: Harvard University Press, 1960).
[2]Aneurin Beval, cited in Gunnar Myrdal, *Rich Lands and Poor* (New York: Harper, 1957), p. 46.

In the absence of a market, the mechanism must be supplied by the direct orders of a central controlling and planning agency. The planning agency must provide a substitute for the forward-looking operations of the corporate management structure in a market economy. In the place of an IBM or a General Motors building their plants in anticipation of, or in response to, a demand for their products, the planning body must itself set overall goals and objectives for economic growth. Not the consumer, but the planners' own judgments and desires determine the force of demand.

Establishing the overall objectives is, however, only the first and perhaps the easiest part of the planning mechanism. It is not enough to set broad goals. We must remember that planning in a totalitarian economy does not allow for individuals who will take care of the details of production according to the incentives of price and profit. In a totally planned economy, each and every item that goes into the final plan must also be planned. Schedules of production are needed for steel, coal, coke, and lumber, on down to nails and paperclips, for there is no automatic device by which these items will be forthcoming without a planning directive. Supplies of labor must also be planned; if labor is free to move where it wishes, wage rates must be planned in order to draw labor where it is needed.

Therefore, supplementing and completing the master objective of the overall plan must be a hierarchy of subplans, the aggregate of which must bring about the necessary final result. Here is a genuine difficulty. An error in planning, small in itself, can seriously distort—or even render impossible—the fulfillment of the total plan, if it affects a strategic link in the chain of production.

With all its difficulties, central planning worked in the years following World War II, when the ravaged Russian economy was rebuilt in a storm of energy resembling that of the early 1930s. Thereafter, however, the problems of socialism began to change. Once the essential work of rebuilding had been accomplished, the main task of planning shifted from construction to coordination. The challenge facing the planners was no longer to bring into being the basic framework of a modern industrial state, but to make such a framework function effectively.

That proved to be much more difficult than the earlier effort. Under Stalin's successors, especially Nikita Khrushchev and Leonid Brezhnev, the system began to show alarming signs of failure. According to U.S. government estimates, real Soviet gross national product grew at an average annual rate of about 6.5 percent from 1965 to 1980 but by only 1.8 percent per year from 1980 to 1985. In a few parts of the economy, where no expense was spared and where the bureaucracy was subordinated to the highly demanding requirement of special "consumers," the system had its triumphs—the Soviets launched the first space shot, built impressive military planes and tanks, and created whole new cities in strategic regions.

However in other areas, where the special interests were not in a position to dominate the bureaucracy, very different results followed. Consumer goods were produced in quantity, but of such poor quality that warehouses bulged with unusable shoes and shoddy cloth. Although the USSR produced twice as much steel per capita as the United States, there was a chronic steel shortage because the material was used so wastefully. Lumber was in short supply because only some 30 percent of the Soviet timber harvest was utilized, compared with 95 percent in the United States and Canada.

Why was Russian planning an increasingly evident failure? Let us answer the question by learning how planning actually worked. Soviet planning was carried out in successive stages. It began at the center, where the Gosplan, the official state planning agency, laid out the basic guidelines for a 5-year effort. This 5-year plan dictated such crucial decisions as the rates at which consumption and investment would grow, the foreign trade balance with the Soviet Union's satellite states, and the priorities for basic research.

The overall plan was then broken down into shorter 1-year plans. These 1-year plans, specifying the output of major sectors of industry, were then transmitted to various government ministries concerned with, for example, steel production, rail transportation, or lumbering. In turn, the ministries referred the 1-year plans further down the line to the heads of large industrial plants, to experts and advisers, and so forth. Thus, the overall design was unraveled into its constituent parts, until finally the threads were traced back as far as possible along the productive process to the officials in charge of factory operations.

In this way, the factory manager of a plant—say, a coking operation—would be given a set of instructions to make operations dovetail with those of the industries to which output would presumably flow and from which inputs would presumably arrive. The manager would then confer with production engineers and plant supervisors and would transmit requirements for meeting "targets"—perhaps an authorization to hire more workers or to order additional machines. In this way, demand requirements flowed down the chain of command and constraints of supply flowed back up, all coming together in a giant production blueprint (a vast series of computer printouts) in the Gosplan offices.

Inefficiencies of Planning

As we can imagine, the coordination and integration of these plans was a fantastically complicated task. Even with the most sophisticated planning techniques, the process was slow, cumbersome, and mistake-prone. To get around the constant shortages that brought things to a grinding halt, factory managers were given strong financial incentives to surpass their planned output.

This only introduced yet another problem. The success indicators by which plan achievement was measured invariably produced their own bottlenecks and distortions. If the target for a textile mill was specified in yards of cloth, there was obviously a strong temptation to weave the cloth as loosely as possible to maximize the yardage from a given input of thread. If the success indicator was a measure of weight, the temptation was to skimp on quality or design. A cartoon in the satiric magazine *Krokodil* showed a nail factory proudly displaying its "record output"—one gigantic nail suspended by an immense gantry crane. The economic system was, in fact, soon heavily dependent on so-called *tolkachi*—wheelers and dealers who arranged for shipments to be rerouted, shortages to be filled, and excess inventories to be disposed of, either behind the authorities' backs or with their tacit permission.

It was to remove these suffocating inefficiencies that Mikhail Gorbachev began to speak in 1985 of *glasnost*—openness—and of *perestroika*—the fundamental restructuring of the economic system. But Gorbachev's plan for a very gradual easing of political controls and the introduction of some market-based mechanisms was quickly overtaken by a rush of events that rapidly brought the Soviet Union to the brink of economic and political chaos, the consequence of the increasing disorganization of the economy. The chaos took everyone by surprise and is still not clearly understood. In all likelihood, sclerosis simply mounted to crisis proportions. It became increasingly difficult to assure shipments from one factory or region to another, so production began to fall precipitously. We speak of a serious recession in the United States when GNP drops by a percent or two; in the Soviet Union during the first years of the 1990s, production may well have dropped by 25 percent, perhaps even more. As food shortages began to occur in the major cities, *tolkachi* "fixers" gave way to hucksters. The black market was probably the only growth sector in the Russian economy. From there, it was a short step to political disorganization as the Soviet Union itself began to come apart at the seams.

THE TRANSITION TO CAPITALISM

Although the dissolution of the Soviet Union occurred for internal economic and political reasons, the end of the Soviet regime was sparked by events outside the borders of the USSR. In 1989, in the face of economic decline and the decline of political legitimacy of the USSR, the "satellite" countries that formed the Soviet political and economic block, most significantly Poland, Hungary, and Czechoslovakia, repudiated their Soviet-socialist ties with a series of "velvet"—that is, relatively peaceful—revolutions. Two years later, with its power having disintegrated and its reforms internally viewed as too little too late, the Soviet Union was dissolved, recreating the nation of Russia and 15 small independent nations, some of which would be unviable economically, but all of which resounded with nationalist fervor and relief at the end of Soviet domination.

Meanwhile, the transition to capitalism in most countries has not been a smooth one. For all their problems, the socialist countries had provided people with jobs, health care, housing—in sum, a social safety net. With the move to a more market-based economy, countries subjected themselves to the vicissitudes of the market. As seen in Table 11-1, in most countries the rate of unemployment reached double-digit levels. Price inflation appeared for the first time in a generation, with Russia experiencing nearly hyperinflation rates of price increase. Unable to compete internationally, many countries ran significant deficits in trade, severely weakening the value of their curren-

TABLE 11-1   Main Economic Indicators in Selected European Transition Economies

	GDP Growth 1990–1999	*Unemployment Rate 1998*	*Inflation (Rate of Change, 1999)*	*Current Account Balance, 1998[a]*
Czech Republic	0.9	6.5	2.1	−1392
Hungary	1.0	8.0	10.0	−2304
Poland	4.7	10.6	7.3	−6901
Romania	−1.2	10.3	45.8	−2918
Russian Federation	−6.1	13.3	85.9	1241
Slovakia	1.9	15.6	10.7	−2126

Source: IMF World Economic Outlook, 2000 (Inflation), Washington, D.C.: IMF; *World Bank Report 2000 (GDP and current account deficit),* Washington, D.C.: World Bank; *Human Development Report 2000 (unemployment),* New York: United Nations.
[a]Millions of dollars

cies on world markets. Perhaps even more of a surprise was the level of corruption and criminality aimed at the control of markets and resources. Behind these economic and legal problems lie political and social questions that affected not only the Russians but all the former socialist countries of Eastern Europe struggling to find freedom and prosperity in the transition to capitalism.

Let's summarize the difficulties in the transition to capitalism:

1. It is one thing to introduce "the market" and another to accept the changes it brings. Moving from a planned to a market society means making a political, not just an economic, shift, in which power is transferred from government officials to a new class of capitalist entrepreneurs. That has occurred only once before in history, in the commercial revolution whose bloody and difficult course we witnessed in chapter 3. That transformation took several centuries. Today's reformers want to accomplish it in a decade or two.

2. The promoters of capitalist rejuvenation stress the improvements that a market society will bring. They do not mention the unemployment, inflation, and intense domestic and foreign competition it will also bring. These unavoidable side effects of a transition to capitalism are likely to make their unwelcome presence felt long before economic growth and well-being arrive. Political pressures on a huge scale are virtually certain to plague the ex-communist countries for a very long time, not only delaying the advent of economic growth, but perhaps setting the stage for a retreat from the democracy that is an even more important goal than their economic progress.

3. Finally, there is a grab bag of knotty institutional and legal problems. How will the institutions of capitalism be introduced? Who will write the laws that establish and define private property? How with the property of the state—above all, its potentially profitable enterprises—be transferred into private hands? Whose hands will they be? Just as small stumbling blocks: How will a workable economy be established when there are no private banks, no commercial lawyers or accountants, virtually no checking accounts (all payments made in cash or in book entries between ministries and their factories), no "Yellow Pages" in the phone books, and very few phone books?

It remains to be seen how, and even if, these problems will be overcome. One thing is clear, however: The problems we have presented as economic are ultimately political in nature. Thus, much hinges on the type of political culture. In some cases, Hungary and Poland for example, vigorous working-class and middle-class groups have entered the political life in those countries, establishing more politically legitimate political systems. Elsewhere, for example in Russia itself, there has been little progress in the building of civil society and the democratic processes to which this can give rise.

THE FUTURE OF SOCIALISM

This raises a question of central importance for ourselves, who are less interested in the analysis of the Soviet downfall than in the repercussions of this epochal event on the major theme of our book. That theme has been the trajectory of capitalism as the principal form of economic society in Western civilization. For a time, it seemed as if centrally planned socialism would be a powerful contestant with capitalism, and very possibly its successor. In the aftermath of the debacle of central planning, is there anything left of "socialism" at all?

One part of that question can be disposed of with some degree of certainty. Socialism as a society built around a core of strong central planning is a form of economic society whose prospects appear very dim, at least for the advanced industrial nations. It is possible, however, that in underdeveloped countries, seeking to change backward peasant societies into modern industrial ones, central planning may prove to be as successful as it was, for a while, in the Soviet Union. Some kind of "military socialism" may well continue for a time as the framework of China or of impoverished societies elsewhere that seek to make the painful ascent into industrial sufficiency.

If the experience of the West is any lesson, this kind of socialism will not yield its hoped-for results, once the initial industrial undertakings have been completed. Again judging by this same experience, the creation of smooth-functioning complex economies geared to the fulfillment of consumers' needs will prove to be very difficult, perhaps impossible, under central planning. The inertia of bureaucracy and the stultifying atmosphere of political uniformity are deadly obstacles to economic dynamism. Dictatorial societies are not good breeding grounds for the entrepreneurial spirit. A successful centrally planned socialism does not seem a likely possibility over the foreseeable future.

There is, however, another way of thinking about the future of socialism. Imagine a country that comprised the most desirable features of existing capitalist nations. It might (for example) combine the culture enjoyed by France, the school system of Sweden, the public health achievement of Canada, the income distribution patterns of Norway, the labor-management accords of Germany, the civil liberties of the Netherlands—or whatever other combination of national institutions pleases the reader. The question of socialism could then be posed as follows: What changes would be required to make this imaginary but unmistakably capitalist country into a "socialized" one—that is, neither capitalist nor socialist, with active market and state sectors and a culture of social concern?

The question helps put into historical context the problem of what could come next, for it poses the question as a matter of institutional realities, not ideological visions. Take, for example, whether the economic future might not be "market socialism," using markets instead of central planning, while retaining some of the other institutions of socialism. The questions we now ask are: How do we decide which institutions to keep? What kinds of planning, and in what areas? A more egalitarian income distribution? How equal, and how attained? Worker participation? In what decisions, and how structured?

These difficult questions force us to confront the discomfiting fact that the institutional form of advanced capitalism is not easy to draw. They ask us to consider how far we wish to press for "socialist" ideals within the general institutional forms of capitalism, and whether and where we want to breach those boundaries.

Is there a final judgment? Perhaps it is to say that the adaptive capabilities of capitalism appear quite large within the near-term future, so that something resembling a socialized capitalism might well be achieved in some nations, within a framework of private property and market relations. Over the longer term, however, there are likely to be limits to that adaptive capability. For example, it is uncertain whether capitalism would be able to retain its vitality if the ecological vise really closed in, or if the relationship between the developed and developing worlds continue, along its present antagonistic course. If these challenges arrive, they will usher in historic changes whose general nature we cannot predict with accuracy.

Key Concepts and Key Words

Transition to Capitalism

1. A striking change has occurred in our time. Socialism, the longtime challenger of capitalism, has suffered a tremendous setback. Socialist systems everywhere in the world are moving toward the market mechanism—the central mechanism of capitalism. In this chapter, we trace the causes of, and prospects for, that change.

Soviet Union

2. The Soviet economy was created by fiat, rather than freely evolving, as did our own. Following the Russian Revolution, the partly peasant and partly capitalist framework of tsarist Russia was first organized into a halfhearted command system, then ruthlessly forced into a totalitarian structure.

3. The early command system worked because it was able to mobilize resources for the relatively simple task of "forcing" industrialization atop a preindustrial base. In retrospect, we can see that some degree of political command seems always to accompany the wrenching transformation of industrialization, although Stalin's use of power was hideously excessive.

4. After World War II's reconstruction was completed, the command system began to display serious difficulties. Command economies are good for mobilizing, but not for flexibility and adaptation. The old planning system no longer worked because its success indicators failed to generate the responses that the system needed to avoid shortages and mismatches.

5. In 1985, Mikhail Gorbachev announced a basic restructuring for the Soviet system— a restructuring that would have gone a long way, but not all the way, to introducing the fundamental institutions of capitalism. That plan was never actually instituted, and in 1991 the government dismantled the Soviet Union and established a newly elected Russian government and other new independent nations that had been part of the Soviet Union.

6. Similar kinds of economic disorganization and political upheaval took place in virtually all the centrally planned socialisms of Europe. One by one, they have rejected communist political rule and sought to introduce a capitalistic economy. The difficulties of such transformations are very great, and their success is uncertain.

7. Is capitalism thereby assured of its future? It is not likely to be challenged by any centrally planned economy. However, it will certainly be characterized by the dynamic tendencies that have marked its history—above all, the strains and stresses of an expansive drive working within the encouragements and discouragements of a competitive market. In all likelihood, this will drive capitalism in the direction of socialization—not socialism—by using various means such as financial market regulations or corporate codes of conduct to lessen its instabilities and correct its market-driven inequities.

Questions

1. What were the strengths and weakness of the system of central planning in the Soviet Union?
2. Was the decline of socialism in Eastern Europe the result of purely economic factors? What role was played by politics and culture?

3. Why do you think the ideas of Marxism were mostly not realized in the actual experiences of socialist countries?
4. Why do you think capitalism has not been a great success in the formerly communist countries of Eastern Europe?
5. A few countries—notably China, Cuba and North Korea—have remained socialist in spite of the shift to capitalism in Eastern Europe. What obstacles do you think these countries face and what do you imagine their future will be?

Thinking Back, Looking Ahead

COMMUNISM AS A UTOPIAN IDEAL

The collapse of the Soviet Block ended the decades-long divide between communism and capitalism. Capitalism today extends into more corners of the globe than ever in history: In fact, this expansion of capitalism is one way of defining the globalization that will be the focus of the next chapter. The end of communism was a great relief to many people in the former Soviet Block countries, especially those who had suffered under its excruciating political oppression, rigid controls, and poor standards of living. In this chapter, we described the difficulties experienced by many of these countries in their efforts to shift rapidly from communism to capitalism. In retrospect, it was naïve to think that the transition would be simple or that living standards would quickly rise.

If there is one lesson from this book, it is that the creation of economic society is not a natural phenomenon, but is created by people, their ideas, and their actions. Today's economy is created by us, and how well that society functions depends in large part on our imagination of its potential. The idea of communism has, for generations, played a central role in forming that imagination, broadening our sense of society's possibilities and warning us of its pitfalls. Thus, while we celebrate the gain of individual freedoms that came with the end of Soviet rule, we should also not lose sight of the utopian dimension embodied in the idea of communism. Communism in theory is a system based on notions of equality, fairness, and cooperation. Karl Marx, the nineteenth-century philosopher and economist who created a theory of communism, believed that the system would work on the principle "from each according to ability, to each according to need."[a] It is this vision of distributive justice that risks being lost as the idea of communism fades with our memory of the Soviet Union. The challenge for future generations is to keep alive the sense of equality, fairness, and cooperation imagined in Marxism without the oppression that has been part of its ill-constructed reality. 🌐

---

[a]Karl Marx, *Critique of the Gotha Program* (New York: International Publishers, 1938).

CHAPTER

The Globalization of Economic Life

12

THE RESHAPING OF THE WORLD ECONOMY

A new word has entered today's economics: *globalization.* As it suggests, globalization puts the whole world in a new and very important economic focus. In part, that focus is on the problem of global poverty: Globalization makes us rethink the causes of and possible cures for the miseries of Africa or Asia that we glimpse on television or read about in the papers.

A second aspect of globalization makes us reconsider our own economic destiny; globalization is obviously about increasing economic connectedness. Given that the United States is the richest single economy in the world, the global impacts of poverty obviously bear on our own future prospects. Globalization also brings into focus a matter we have not previously considered. It concerns how money makes its way from one country to the next, and how the globalization of production may affect our financial well-being. These are the issues we will examine in this chapter.

The Collapse of Bretton Woods

As capitalism moved beyond its Golden Age, a central question emerged: What policies could bring about a return to the prosperity of that earlier era? The difficulty was that, in at least one important aspect, a return to the earlier era was impossible. The difficulty lay in the decision to abandon the 1944 Bretton Woods Agreement on fixed exchange rates. That agreement, we recall, was built on the ability and willingness of the United States to play the role of international financial leader. The Bretton Woods Agreement guaranteed a fixed rate of exchange between the dollar and gold, and sought to inject sufficient dollars into the financial structure of the participants to encourage growth in the volume of economic activity and international trade. As long as the U.S. promise to maintain a fixed price of gold remained beyond a shadow of doubt, the holding of dollars by foreigners was as good as holding gold. In fact, it was better because dollars were used in many international transactions, and the cost of keeping a stock of gold was not cheap. This agreement was one of the most important foundations on which the Golden Age rested.

In the early years of the Bretton Woods system, there were few transactions at the U.S. gold "window"—that is, few purchases of U.S. gold by foreign governments in exchange for dollars. Indeed, in the early postwar years, the system suffered from a dollar shortage, a scarcity of dollar reserves in the hands of foreigners. Given the role of the dollar as international reserve currency and the dominance of the United States in the postwar world economy, the dollar was used not just in trade with the United States but also to pay for trade between other countries, especially for major commodities such as wheat and oil. As a result of the foreign demand for dollars and the associated desire to hold foreign reserves in dollars, a shortage of dollars was soon apparent.

However, by the mid-1960s, cracks had begun to appear in this system. In 1968, the United States imported more than it exported; that is, the United States paid more dollars to foreigners for their goods and services than foreigners paid to the United States for its goods. As these trade deficits continued and grew, the dollars that the United States paid for its imports began to flood world markets. That problem became exacerbated when U.S. needs for foreign goods and services increased as a consequence of the Vietnam War. As a result, what had been since 1944 a chronic shortage of dollars now turned into a dollar glut—more dollars in the hands of foreign banks or traders than they needed.

The danger posed by this glut was the threat of a run on the U.S. gold stock. Under the rules of the Bretton Woods Agreement, $35 could always buy an ounce of gold. It now appeared that there were already more dollars in foreign hands than were needed. The risks were now two: First, it was feared that a cheapening of the dollar could cause their holders to get rid of them before they fell. In that case, the United States would find its dollars no longer regarded as being "as good as gold." However, a much larger risk also loomed. It was that a world monetary system with reasonably steady exchange rates would give way to a free-for-all.

Increasingly alarmed at this prospect, the U.S. government made numerous efforts in the late 1960s to ease the pressure against the dollar, but none were sufficient to stem the wave of speculation against the dollar. In August 1973, President Nixon officially closed the gold window, ending the Bretton Woods system and tacitly announcing that the American dollar was no longer the most reliable currency in the world.

The Era of Flexible Exchange Rates

The closing of the gold window ended an era of international monetary cooperation that has never again been achieved. The breakdown of the Bretton Woods system occurred for internal reasons, not as the result of some external shock. The system, whose rules were designed largely by the United States, collapsed because of the inability or unwillingness of the United States to abide by those same rules—in particular, to control its foreign deficits and to avoid a run on the dollar. According to social historian Fred Block, "The breakdown of the postwar monetary order was rooted in the inability of the United States both to pursue its global aims and to live within the rule of international monetary behavior it had earlier devised."[1]

What system would replace the fixed exchange rates that were the lynchpin of the Bretton Woods Agreement? It soon became apparent that only one system was possible—a system in which all currencies floated—that is, exchanged with other currencies—depending on the supply and demand of buyers and sellers. What this meant was that all governments, including the United States, had entered a new era of economic coexistence in which not even the most powerful nation could guarantee its currency's value. More importantly, private firms and individuals, who used foreign exchange for business and travel, were forced to accept the risks of currency price fluctuations that are inevitable in any free market.

The collapse of the Bretton Woods system signaled the end of the Golden Age of capitalism. As we saw in chapter 10, the experience in most industrialized countries since 1973 has been one of considerably slower growth in output and real wages, higher

---

[1]Fred Block, *The Origins of International Economic Disorder* (Berkeley, CA: University of California Press, 1977), p. 215.

rates of unemployment, and rising income inequality. However, if slow growth is one feature of the post–Golden Age world, another is the increased internationalization of economic activity. We take up the question of the connection between these two phenomena later in this chapter, but first we must try to understand the dramatic and complex process that has come to be known as *globalization.*

THE GLOBALIZATION OF PRODUCTION AND FINANCE

Capital Moves Around the World

The term *globalization* has been used to describe a variety of phenomena, from the spread of popular music, movies, and fashions around the globe to the increasing ease of global communication and transportation; to the rapid international diffusion of new technologies and the increasingly international scope of large corporations. Essentially, however, globalization refers to the increased interconnectedness of markets in different countries. This process is reflected in the growth in international trade and foreign investment and especially in the rise in international financial flows. In sum, this means the vastly increased mobility of capital.

The increased mobility of capital affects both production and finance. On the side of production, markets become interconnected internationally as firms increasingly engage in overseas operations. For example, the shipment to the United States of cars manufactured by Ford in Mexico is counted as a Mexican export and U.S. import. Foreign investment includes expenditure abroad on productive assets, regardless of nationality, such as when PepsiCo builds a foreign bottling plant in the Philippines, or when Sony invests in the United States by buying an already existing motion picture company in Hollywood.

In contrast, the globalization of finance involves international bank lending and portfolio investments, which are purchases by foreigners of stocks, bonds, and bank accounts. In summary, the globalization of finance relates purely to monetary flows, whereas the globalization of production involves both foreign direct investment as well as international trade.

The Extent of Globalization

Only the era of the pre–World War I gold standard, from 1870 to 1913, is comparable to the current period in terms of the amount of international economic activity. More importantly, there has been a rise in international trade and investment as a share of world economic activity since 1960, and especially since 1980. Figure 12-1 shows that after 1982 the volume of world trade grew much more rapidly than world output as measured by gross domestic product. Today, merchandise exports as a share of total output are now about twice their 1950 level and have achieved levels never before attained in recorded history, as Table 12-1 shows. Note also that even today the United States is a much less open—that is, foreign trade oriented—economy than most of the world. This is because of its enormous domestic market and its geographic isolation in relation to other large, wealthy markets. Still, the United States is heavily entwined in the international economy, with exports in 1999 of $956 billion and imports of $1,221 billion. The United States is the number-one country in the world in terms of foreign investment. Its entry into the

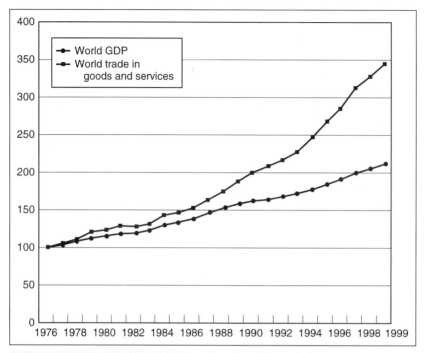

FIGURE 12-1 World Trade and GDP, 1976–1999 (1976 = 100)

Source: World Economic Outlook (Washington, D.C.: IMF, 2000).

North American Free Trade Agreement (NAFTA) with Canada and Mexico in 1994 and the signing of the Uruguay Round Agreement of the General Agreement on Trade and Tariffs in the same year served to further the process of integrating the United States into the world economy.

However, the rise in international trade and investment is only one indicator of globalization. A more dramatic indicator is the rise in the number and range of transnational corporations—that is, corporations with operations in more than one country. By 1995, there were more than 38,000 such corporations with more than a quarter of a million branches or affiliates operating in foreign countries. The total sales of these transnationals was estimated to be $5.2 trillion, more than the total value of world exports and over double what sales of transnational corporations had been only 10 years previous. Today, transnationals dominate sales in industries as diverse as petroleum refining, motor vehicles, food, electronics, and chemicals. For many companies, foreign sales are as important as domestic sales. General Motors employs 270,000 people out-

TABLE 12-1 Merchandise Exports as a Percentage of GDP

	1870	*1913*	*1950*	*1973*	*1985*	*1993*
World	5.1	11.9	7.1	11.7	14.5	17.1
United States	5.4	6.4	3.8	5.2	5.2	7.0

Source: Milberg, W. "Globalization and International Competitiveness," in *Improving the Global Economy* (Aldershot, UK: Edward Elgar, 1997).

side of its home country, the United States. The Swiss food company, Nestle, has more than 200,000 employees outside of Switzerland. Companies have increasingly met their need to compete in markets around the globe through mergers with and acquisitions of foreign companies.

The third and most stunning dimension of the globalization process is international finance. In the market for foreign exchange, daily transactions are now $1.3 trillion. This is more than the value of all world trade in one year! Purchases and sales of foreign currencies today are more than five times what they were 20 years ago. Their speed and volume have become one of the defining characteristics of this era. Whether for the purpose of buying a building or a factory abroad or for buying or selling foreign currency for purely speculative reasons, international capital movements are driven by the search for profits. One would think that this competition among currencies would raise the efficiency of enterprise globally. However, the sheer volume of international financial movements and the occasional surges of capital flow in and out of countries have also been disruptive. Indeed, the Wall Street stock market crash of 1987 is attributed by some to a threat by Japanese investors to sell their holdings of U.S. financial assets. The Mexican peso crisis of 1994, which almost bankrupted the Mexican banking system, was the result of rapid capital flight from that country brought on by international speculators trying to get their assets out of Mexico before it was too late. The financial crisis of 1997 that rolled through Thailand, South Korea, Brazil, and Russia is widely attributed to the herd behavior of investors that dominate international financial markets. Today, even the most powerful countries in the world run their monetary policy with a close eye on the international financial markets.

THE CAUSES OF GLOBALIZATION

Technology Shrinks the Globe

What drives the globalization process? One factor is the steady decline in transportation costs. According to the World Bank, shipping costs today are less than half their 1950 level. Airfreight costs have dropped even more. Today, it is profitable to ship fresh-cut flowers from Amsterdam and apples from South Africa for sale in New York—an impossibility 20 years ago.

A similar drop in communication costs has made it possible to design clothing in New York for production in Hong Kong and sale back in New York, all in a matter of days. The possibility of transmitting enormous amounts of data at minimal cost has enabled firms to locate different parts of the production process in different countries without losing control of the overall operation.

However, simply lowering the cost of international shipping and communicating was not enough to make possible the new globalization. An equally important element lay in an altogether new degree of technological standardization that made it possible to use low-wage, but adequately skilled, labor in different countries, and to integrate these separated subproduction operations in a single global production flow. A dramatic example of this new capability was the making and merchandising of Ford Motor Company's "world car" in 1993. The car was designed in Belgium; built with basic materials and equipped with an engine, transmission, and other components manufactured in locations throughout Europe, East Asia, Canada, Mexico, and the United States; and finally assembled both in the United States and abroad. Moreover, because there existed a strong convergence of tastes in cars—formed mainly by coordinated advertising—the world car was then sold in 15 countries with only minor variations to suit local tastes. The key was the ability to capture hitherto unknown economies of scale by coordinating the worldwide manufacture of materials and parts to produce what was essentially the same car to be sold all over the world. Nothing like this had ever been possible. Since then, other car companies—notably Honda, Toyota, BMW, and DaimlerChrysler—have moved toward the Ford approach.

The globalization of production—breaking up of the production process into parts and performing those functions in different countries—has spread well beyond the automotive sector and is now widely used in manufacturing and even services. Consider the case of a seemingly simple product like the Barbie Doll:

> The raw materials for the doll (plastic and hair) are obtained from Taiwan and Japan. Assembly used to be done in those countries, as well as the Philippines, but it has now migrated to lower-cost locations in Indonesia, Malaysia, and China. The molds themselves come from the United States, as do additional paints used in decorating the dolls. Other than labor, China supplies only the cotton cloth used for dresses. Of the $2 export value for the dolls when they leave Hong Kong for the United States, about 35 cents covers Chinese labor, 65 cents covers the cost of materials, and the remainder covers transportation and overhead, including profits earned in Hong Kong. The dolls sell for about $10 in the United States, of which Mattel earns at least $1, and the rest covers transportation, marketing, wholesaling and retailing in the U.S. The majority of value-added is therefore from U.S. activity. The dolls sell worldwide at the rate of two dolls every second, and this product alone accounted for $1.4 billion in sales for Mattel in 1995.[2]

The case of the Barbie Doll shows just how diverse and internationalized production processes have become.

Global Finance: The Tail Wagging the Dog?

The degree of globalization of production is impressive, but the increase in the volume of international financial flows is the most dramatic dimension of globalization. Finance has taken the lead in the world economy. In one sense, it is natural that international banking should rise as international trade grows. International trade often requires that companies borrow foreign currency to pay their bills or to protect profits earned in foreign money in terms of their domestic currency: The process, called *hedging,* is one of the largest sources of the international flow of currencies. Another cause for this explosion of financial flows is the rise of *speculation* in international finance. Speculative activity is simply the purchase of an asset in the expectation that its value will rise over time. As the cost of international financial transactions has fallen and information on foreign markets has become more available, investors have been more inclined to diversify their portfolios internationally, which has led to large dealings in foreign funds.

---

[2]Robert Feenstra, "Integration of Trade and Disintegration of Production in the Global Economy," *Journal of Economic Perspectives,* Vol. 12, Fall 1998, p. 7.

There is nothing inherently detrimental about speculation. In theory, it can lead to increased efficiency, channeling funds into high-return locations or assets. However, speculation can also be destabilizing if it sends asset prices soaring or tumbling to such a great extent that employment and production are severely affected, as it did in many developing countries in the 1990s.

At a more basic level, the liberalization of financial markets has encouraged a pattern of financial flows that is independent of the growth needs of specific countries. Financial investment aims at obtaining maximum returns on a portfolio, sometimes over a very short-run time period. If this indicates the purchase of $100 million of Mexican stocks one day and their sale 1 or 2 days later, the stability of the Mexican economy can be put at risk, as it was in 1994. Developing countries are especially vulnerable to these market fluctuations because of their heavy reliance on foreign capital for many basic industrialization needs.

CONSEQUENCES OF GLOBALIZATION

U.S. Trade Deficit and Foreign Debt

An important aspect of globalization is the expansion of markets. American firms today are selling their goods and services in markets including Southeast Asia, Eastern Europe, and China. For firms with near-monopoly power, such as the producers of Hollywood movies, foreign markets are now as important as the domestic market. However, many U.S. firms face stiff competition from abroad, such as steel, textiles, automobiles, and electronics. The overall decline in the U.S. trade position since the late 1970s is dramatic: From its position as a surplus country that was the backbone of the world financial system during the Golden Age, the United States has experienced a steady deterioration of its trade balance. As seen in Figure 12-2, the annual deficit on trade in goods and services—the surplus of imports over exports—rose to $160 billion in 1999. On goods trade alone, the deficit is even greater because the United States runs a surplus on trade in services, including financial, legal, and insurance industries. In certain sectors, such as steel, automobiles, textiles, and consumer electronics, the deterioration has been very rapid. In motor vehicles alone, a deficit of $17 billion in 1982 worsened to $104 billion by 1999.

The U.S. trade deficit is in part a reflection of the relative strength of the U.S. economy. Although the growth rate of the United States has been slow in the post–1973 era, it has still been more rapid than that of its major trading partners, especially since 1992. This has caused greater growth in Americans' demand for imports than in foreign demand for U.S. exports. In addition, the healthy and growing U.S. economy has attracted foreign capital, much of it to the stock market. This has meant a strong dollar, which in turn makes imports cheaper and exports less competitive in foreign markets. Traditionally a lender of capital to the world, the United States became a net debtor country in 1988 and by 1992 was the world's greatest debtor nation. Today, about one-quarter of the U.S. national debt of $5 billion is owned by foreigners.

The expanding U.S. trade deficit is also partly due to the rise of new sources of competition. As the world economy grew during the Golden Age, so did the competitive capacity of many countries. Germany's economic recovery brought back its highly sophisticated pharmaceuticals and machinery industries, among others, and that nation

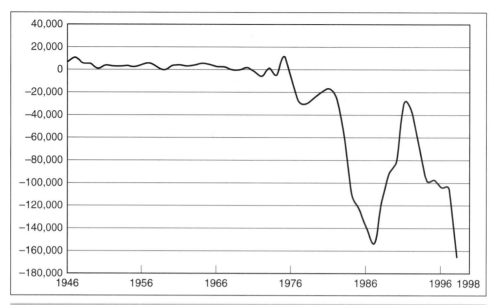

FIGURE 12-2 U.S. Balance of Trade in Goods and Services, 1946–1998 (in millions of dollars)

Source: Economic Report of the President (Washington, D.C.: Government Printing Office, 2000).

began to compete successfully with the United States. Japan's astonishing transformation from producer of simple consumer goods to powerhouse producer of cars and electronics became a major source of competition in these crucial sectors.

Another source of competition has been from low-wage countries. Some developing countries have become increasingly successful exporters of medium-technology goods, such as steel goods from Brazil, semiconductors from South Korea, and software from India. In sectors where high-tech technology was not necessary, countries with low wages found they could compete with the U.S. firms on the basis of price, the most important examples being the flood of textiles and apparel from Asia and footwear from South America. Today, the United States has its largest trade deficit not with Germany, or even Japan, but with China, and the trade deficit with Mexico has also risen sharply in the last few years. U.S. corporations have benefited enormously from this large pool of efficient, low-wage labor in developing countries. Through foreign investment or subcontracting with a foreign firm, U.S. companies purchase parts, services, and even final goods—look at the label of your Gap shirt—for sale in the U.S. market. These purchases count as U.S. imports and add to the U.S. trade deficit.

A Race to the Bottom?

It is useful to recall that the period we have been calling the *era of globalization* is the same span of years—roughly since the 1980s—that we earlier called the *silent depression,* with its unwelcome increase in inequality and its generally pessimistic tone. Is globalization the cause of this state of affairs? Is it the consequence?

Our answer is both. To begin with inequality, globalization contributes to much higher profits at the top and much greater pressures against wages at the bottom. Lower skill workers in the United States have seen their wages fall over the past 10 years. Surveys show that despite the signs of vigor in the U.S. economy, U.S. workers are insecure in their jobs and worried about their economic future. Slower economic growth in most other developed countries has led to even greater employment insecurity in those places. This insecurity is partly due to the heightened threat of job loss from the movement of production abroad. It is also due to cutbacks in the social safety net that have come as countries have sought to improve their international competitive condition. In Canada, for example, the liberalization of trade with the United States has had a noticeable effect in reducing the amount and duration of unemployment benefits toward lower U.S. levels. In Germany, the Volkswagen company recently threatened workers with a cutback in health benefits, arguing that their burden was resulting in a steady loss of international competitiveness. Although the company later retreated from its position, analysts of the German situation expect it to rise again. In Sweden, laws protecting labor unions have been weakened as employers have sought more global flexibility in their production decisions.

Diminished National Sovereignty

If the globalization of production and finance has brought considerable economic change, its political implications are perhaps even more momentous, as they put into question the legitimacy of that basic political unit, the nation-state.

National sovereignty is vulnerable when production can easily move from high-tax and heavily regulated locations to places where taxes and regulations are lower. Globalization thus favors the mobile factors of production over those factors—like labor and governments—that are unable to operate across national lines. As international markets become of equal or greater importance than domestic markets, and as firms increasingly integrate their operations across countries, the nationality of any particular firm becomes less important. The firm's interests do not coincide with those of any country, and the firm will seek to minimize its operations in those countries that impose the most burdensome regulations or taxes. Financial flows move in search of the highest rate of return and diversification. The production and investment needs of a particular country are largely irrelevant in the determination of these flows.

National governments' response to the pressures of globalization have been varied. In many respects, policies have encouraged globalization through trade and investment liberalization and the deregulation of financial markets. Many countries, especially developing ones, have embraced the logic of globalization and reduced the regulatory and tax burden on multinational corporations in the hope of attracting desperately needed foreign capital. Such changes are also aimed at keeping existing firms, foreign and domestic, in the country.

Does all this imply a fundamentally new relation between the private and public realms in the industrialized countries? Without a doubt, we are in an era of general government retrenchment these days, both at the microeconomic and macroeconomic levels. At the same time, there are a few ways in which the government's role is likely to expand in the near future. The first is the need to respond to the problems created by this new global economy. Workers thrown out of employment as the result of firms leaving the country must be aided, perhaps retrained, and ultimately reemployed. If the income inequality that is partly the result of globalization becomes a matter of serious political concern, it will very likely lead to a call for higher taxes at the top of the pyramid of incomes and stronger support systems at the bottom.

The second area for an enhancement of the public sector involves the role of international governing bodies. An example is the World Trade Organization (WTO), created in 1994 to promote the liberalization of trade. Recently—and highlighted by mass protests at the WTO meetings in Seattle—there have been efforts to expand the task of the WTO to promote the enforcement of international labor standards, such as the right of workers to organize unions and bargain collectively. Environmental standards could also be similarly enforced by an expanded WTO.

Because there is no precedent for effective worldwide governing bodies, the development of such institutions is more likely at the regional level. Many steps have already been taken in this direction. The European central bank, created by the Maastricht Treaty of 1997, manages monetary policy for 11 European countries. With the European Parliament and Court already having considerable power and likely to gain more, Western Europe is the most integrated region of the world.

So, too, NAFTA is in many respects a path-breaking treaty. It is the first free trade agreement among countries of very different levels of development: Per capita annual income in the United States is $22,000, compared with $3,000 in Mexico. NAFTA contains side agreements on labor and the environment, the first time a free trade agreement has been used to address the problem of harmonization of social standards that is inherent to the globalization process. The side agreements are modest, requiring each country to enforce its own labor and environmental regulations, and its enforcement mechanism is cumbersome; however, their inclusion in NAFTA may be a first step toward a global effort to impose certain minimum social standards in a world in which the need for regulation has become ever more pressing.

HOW GLOBAL IS GLOBALIZATION?

Finally, before we start claiming that the nation-state has completely lost its economic usefulness, we must take stock of the limits of the globalization process. Has globalization really been global—that is, has it involved all the countries of the world? There is no doubt that financial capital has moved into markets in Asia and Latin America that did not exist just 25 years ago. However, globalization mainly affects industrialized countries and a small group of developing countries. Much of the developing world, most notably the countries of sub-Saharan Africa and the dissolving Soviet system, have been left out of the process. In 1993, 37 percent of foreign direct investment in developing countries went to a single country: China. Almost all of the rest of investment in developing countries was in nine other countries—Singapore, Argentina, Malaysia, Mexico, Indonesia, Thailand, Hong Kong, Colombia, and Taiwan.

Not coincidentally, this list of recipients of foreign investment includes all the so-called newly industrialized countries. Taking a regional instead of national perspective on the world economy, we see that most economic flows take place within any of three regional blocks: Europe (the European Union), North America (NAFTA), and East

Asia. Trade within and among these regions accounts for about 75 percent of world trade and 94 percent of foreign direct investment. Studies show that transnational corporations are most likely to invest where there is economic growth and political stability.

Where does this leave the rest of the developing countries? Outside the loop of global investment and economic growth, these countries have languished over the past 25 years. The result is a divergence in the standard of living around the world, with some moving into the middle- and high-income group and others knowing only ever-worsening poverty, disorder, and hopelessness.

What we have, then, is not one world, but two. Moreover, the world in which we live, however linked by currents of financial transaction, trade, and investment, is less interconnected than may appear at first glance. Also, the existence of but three major trading and investment blocs opens the possibility for a degree of regional political and economic control that makes the future seem less overwhelming. NAFTA, for example, seems likely to expand into South America; the European Union is committed to both deeper integration and gradual expansion into Scandinavia and even Eastern and Central Europe; and the Asia-Pacific Economic Conference has recently announced its commitment to free trade by the year 2010.

Therefore, a possible scenario for the world economy is not further unification but deepening regionalization, in which nations become increasingly integrated with other nations within their region. This would likely increase the United States' own chances for lessening the adverse effects of globalization and maximizing its positive effects, as would be the case for all members of the region.

Is it inevitable that countries will be left out of the globalization process? Is integration with the global economy a necessity for a poor nation seeking to industrialize? It is to these challenging questions that we turn our attention in the next chapter.

Key Concepts and Key Words

Collapse of Bretton Woods
1. The collapse of the Bretton Woods agreement, which had made the U.S. dollar the key currency, signaled the end of an era of U.S. hegemony and the beginning of a new era of globalization.

Interconnected markets
2. Globalization spells a new era of increased capital mobility, whether as goods or money. An unprecedented increase takes place in international economic activity.

Transnationals
3. Transnational corporations now rise to central importance in all developed nations.

Financial flows
4. The purchase and sale of foreign monies becomes a major activity, with daily transactions of $1.3 trillion, more than the value of a year's trade in goods.

Technology and organization
5. Behind globalization lie technological improvements in transportation and communication, as well as in management skills. The Ford "world car" sets a new pattern.

Impact on national economies
6. Globalization leads to pressures against national economies from speculation, as in the case of Mexico. It also greatly intensified the pressures of competition.

Globalization adds to inequality
7. Globalization brings pressure against wages and very large profits. Thus it is one cause for the phenomenon of rising inequality. Its pressure against nations' ability to go against international currents also adds to the decline in the place and prestige of the public sector.

Limits on globalization
8. We do not know how far globalization will go, but there are signs that it may not extend beyond the developed world. Regional agreements may also provide safeguards against some of the less desirable features of the process.

Questions

1. How does a "fixed" exchange rate—say five U.S. dollars for one British pound—remove the risk in international trading that exists when the exchange rate fluctuates according to the supply and demand for dollars and pounds?

2. Could you notice the presence of growing globalization, even if you had never heard the word, from what you see in ads or in shops? Can you mention a few examples, say in automobiles, food, or clothing?

3. Can you explain why a concerted effort on the part of people who buy or sell foreign exchange can threaten the solidity of a whole nation's economy? If you were a Mexican businessperson who needed to import zippers from the United States to manufacture sportswear, which you then exported to Europe, can you explain why a collapsing peso would make business very difficult, or even impossible?

4. What do you see as the obstacle in reestablishing the kind of stable exchange rates that used to prevail under the pre–World War I Gold Standard, when all major countries declared the value of their currencies in terms of gold? Can you explain why England, which was then the hegemon of world trade, lost that position after World War I?

Thinking Back, Looking Ahead

FIRMS, STATES, AND MARKETS

We have emphasized in this chapter that one aspect of the globalization of economic life is the spread of markets into countries that had previously used central planning; into industries that had been controlled by capitalist governments; and, with the deregulation of international trade and finance, into the international arena. However, this characterization of globalization as the sweep of markets around the world misses an important feature of the world economy: the spread of firms. More generally, although economists often use the words *market system* and *capitalism* as synonyms, we must acknowledge that markets do not capture the totality of capitalism.

In our study of the history of capitalism, we have yet to discover a capitalist system that did not have both a private and public sector. That is, capitalism, since its inception, has required an active government in order for markets to function effectively. Adam Smith himself urged the need for effective government, not only to protect property rights and ensure fair competition but to build roads and educate the poor, as well. Thus, contrary to much popular belief, capitalism has always been seen as requiring effective public and private sectors.

However, the picture is still more complicated. Even the private sector is not best described as simply a market system. Firms are institutions for organizing production that is then bought and sold in markets, but firms themselves are quite distinct from markets; they serve a different function. Production takes place within firms, not markets. It is firms that establish markets, or extend the scope of existing ones.

As firms expand internationally, markets are transformed. Although globalization involves the expansion of markets across national borders, it also expands the role of firms, that is, nonmarket transactions. These nonmarket transactions range from trade within firms across national lines to joint ventures and other alliances among firms in different countries.

The intercorporate sharing of technological information is particularly common, with nearly 9,000 cases of interfirm technology agreements recorded between 1980 and 1996. Thus, globalization involves the expansion of both markets and nonmarket arrangements involving firms. When we look ahead to the long-term prospects for capitalism, we will see the importance of this distinction for issues involving the governance of the world economy.

CHAPTER

Why Some Nations Remain Poor

THE PROBLEM OF UNEVEN DEVELOPMENT

In the previous chapter, we noted that, contrary to its name, the process of globalization has not included everyone in the world. The globalization of economic life that has taken place over the past 20 years has also been a period of increased inequality, both within and across countries. Most of the world today toils under difficult working conditions and extremely low pay. Figure 13-1 shows just how much of the world's population lives at income levels that are but a fraction of those earned in the rich countries. Though high-income countries have an average annual per capita income near $25,000, the other five-sixths of the world population earns only a third as much. Over two-thirds of the world's population earns less than $5,000 per year.

How can we make sense of a twenty-first century world in which some nations have very high standards of living, while others seem hopelessly mired in poverty; in which some enjoy average life spans of 75 years and others only 55 years; in which some have armies of skilled workers, and others only mobs of untrained and often illiterate people?

A first answer to this important question must be obvious: Resources are unevenly distributed around the world. The inhabitants of some countries are literally born rich; others, poor. Thus, no one has to look for complex answers to the question of why there are no factories in Antarctica or the Sahara desert. There *are* factories in Iceland, which is pretty cold, if not quite subzero; there is a busy economy springing up in parts of Mexico that are pretty barren—although not quite Saharan—not to speak of parts of China that were regarded not many years ago as hopeless.

Can this situation change for the better, or will it inevitably get only worse? In this chapter, we are going to look at the uneven distribution of wealth and poverty around the world, asking how some countries have managed to improve their economic conditions, whereas others seem hopelessly consigned to economic stagnation. In the end, we will certainly not posses a formula for global economic betterment, but we may have a clearer understanding of what can be done within the foreseeable future.

COLONIALISM AND ITS LEGACY

Let us begin by looking backward, asking whether progress depends on the ability to overcome obstacles that may date back many centuries. In many parts of the world, it is clear that the roots of poverty lie in a history of neglect and oppression. This is especially true when we inquire how parts of sub-Saharan Africa or South Asia present such dismal profiles of poverty, ill health, and illiteracy. The answer is that these countries have emerged from longlasting submission to colonial supervision, such as that exercised by England over India or by France and Belgium over the nations of central Africa.

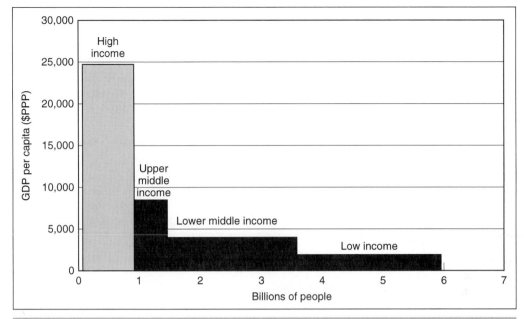

FIGURE 13-1   GDP Per Capita in the World, 1999

Source: World Development Report, Washington, D.C.: The World Bank, 2000.

That backward glance suggests a forward-looking possibility—namely, to throw off the past by political action and to strike out on one's own. This is, in fact, what India has done with a fair degree of success and what a central African nation like Uganda has been trying to do with much less good fortune, having first slid backward into a worse state of affairs and even today lacking the social, educational, and economic changes needed for a healthy and improving economy. These things seem clear: Social and political changes are necessary for lasting economic change; would-be workers have to know how to read; women must have access to a wide range of occupations; workers must have the right to vote.

Gaining such changes is by no means simple. Years ago, Korea was an impoverished and stagnant country, having emerged from a period of Japanese colonial rule followed by a tumultuous period of internal political conflict. In 1950, the country was involved in a war, with the United States supporting South Korea and the Russians and Chinese supporting North Korea. The war ended in 1953 and was followed by a military coup in 1961. The new regime was politically repressive, but nonetheless saw the political as well as economic gains that could arise from a modernization of production. The government began to give financial assistance to industry—but only if its productivity showed improvement or it achieved certain export targets. Slowly, through low-interest loans and other subsidies, the government set in place an industrial policy that wedded economic modernization with political self-strengthening.

The effects were dramatic. Within 25 years, South Korea was able to widen its industrial base sufficiently to export steel, computers, and even automobiles; its wage level had risen; and there had even been an increase in average educational attainment.

Thus, political change is among the more effective means of turning a nation around. However, it must not be forgotten that dictatorship can also be very effective in using the resources of its land to maintain its political leadership in luxury, while at the same time stripping a nation of its natural resources and its citizens of basic freedoms.

A few examples obviously cannot correct the vast problem of global backwardness in our time. Nonetheless, our glimpse seems to make two generalizations plausible. One is that intelligent political oversight is a necessary condition for ridding a nation of serious poverty. Second, it seems a near certainty that development will require poor nations to follow the route of industrialization. Korea, Mexico, and other countries have shown that it is possible, as did Japan before them. Before Japan, we have the classic era of industrialization of the eighteenth and nineteenth centuries in Western Europe and North America.

Industrialization is the key to economic development because it is the clearest path to higher labor productivity. Labor productivity is a measure of the amount of goods and services produced on average by an economy's working people. An abundance of natural resources can certainly bring a country substantial wealth—consider the gold of South Africa or the oil of Kuwait—but without industrialization this wealth will accumulate only as long as the resource lasts.

EARLY VERSUS LATE INDUSTRIALIZATION

Is the process of industrialization the same today as it was in the eighteenth and nineteenth centuries? Yes and no. In both eras, countries typically had only a few key industries—sometimes only one—that served as the original core of the industrialization process. Just as in England in the eighteenth century, textiles had served as a platform for the industrialization process for both Japan and South Korea. In both cases, the core industry serves to develop labor and management skills in manufacturing, in marketing, and in machine building. Once developed, these skills and technology are useful in the birth of other industries.

There is a second aspect in which the recent wave of industrialization is similar to its nineteenth-century predecessor. This is the role played by the government, which in both cases is consciously interventionist when it comes to foreign trade. In the recent wave, governments have subsidized and protected those firms and industries that they strategically viewed as important to the industrialization process. Japan's Ministry of International Trade and Industry (MITI), for example, became famous in the 1980s for its keen sense of competitive strategy and its effectiveness in promoting the skills and productivity of its firms.

In at least one fundamental way, though, the industrialization process today is different from that in Europe and North America 200 years ago. As we saw in chapter 5, the first phase of industrialization was propelled by invention and innovation: machinery, steam power, and mass production techniques that revolutionized production. The era of late industrialization is characterized more by imitation than innovation. It does not hinge on the invention of new machines or goods so much as on the ability to catch up technologically and to compete in niche markets with the world's leading producers.

Is Africa Different?

Many African nations have found themselves in a vicious circle of underdevelopment. Some countries lacked natural resources that might provide cash that could finance the beginnings of industry. These countries have been unable to afford decent education and health care and have not been able to develop their own industrial sectors. With their low productivity and considerable distance from the major world markets, most sub-Saharan African countries have been unable to attract foreign investment. Many countries that were fortunate to control natural resources [e.g., Nigeria, Congo (formerly Zaire), Uganda] or contain highly fertile soil (Zimbabwe, Ivory Coast, Ghana) have been subjected to repressive and corrupt governments that squandered the natural wealth, diverting it from use in the development of an industrial sector.

Because so much of sub-Saharan Africa has been left behind in the second wave of industrialization, the reader may be asking, "Is Africa different?" That is, are the countries of Africa incapable of breaking out of the vicious circle of underdevelopment? Most scholars of Africa say that the answer to this question is "no." Although the colonial legacy looms relatively large in many African countries and the political corruption of some autocrats (the examples of Idi Amin of Uganda and Mobutu of Zaire certainly stand out) has squandered unthinkable amounts of national wealth, there are reasons to think that African development has the same prospects as that in other regions. Once these countries attain the beginnings of industrial development, built on a minimal infrastructure of roads, telecommunications, schools, and health care, there is no reason to think they cannot follow a similar path to that in other successful new industrializers as they continue to demand democratic political change. There are signs of change and glimmers of hope. Uganda has moved quickly past the Idi Amin era to one of democracy and rapid economic growth. Mauritius has used its considerable wealth from mining to invest successfully in education and a number of industries that have had international success creating steady economic growth in that country.[1] South Africa has shown impressive gains in housing, electricity and water provision, and telecommunications since it ended its longstanding tradition of white rule, apartheid, form of government. There are few success stories and little doubt that substantial progress toward industrialization and improved living standards in much of sub-Saharan Africa remains far in the future.

The Politics of Economic Development

It is clear from even a cursory look at the problem that economic development hinges as crucially on politics as it does on economics. Governments that nurture economic development not only spur economic initiatives but also bring political stability. Developmentally-minded governments can promote industrialization with economic incentives and with direct involvement in building the infrastructure and improving the education system. Corrupt governments that siphon wealth from the country for the personal benefit of government officials invariably stall and may even reverse the process of industrialization. Even the issue of famine is a political one. Research by

---

[1]See Dani Rodrik, *Making Openness Work* (Washington: Oversears Development Council, 1999).

Nobel Prize winner Amartya Sen revealed the stunning fact that no democratic country has ever suffered a famine.[2] In the past few years, we have been reminded that political instability is, in turn, linked to ethnic or religious conflict. Thus, the prospects of economic development are tied not only to politics but to culture.

THE ROLE OF INTERNATIONAL ORGANIZATIONS

So far, we have focused on domestic solutions to the problem of underdevelopment, but there are also important international channels. In light of the globalization tendencies reviewed in chapter 12, it is not surprising that international organizations play an integral role in nations' development effort. The International Monetary Fund (IMF) and International Bank for Reconstruction and Development (World Bank) were formed in the aftermath of World War II as part of the Bretton Woods Agreement in 1944 among the allied countries that emerged victorious from the war. They have since become the key international institutions molding the process of economic development.

The IMF was created to provide financing to countries in need of short-term loans to pay off foreign debts. The World Bank was to provide grants and long-term loans to support major infrastructure rebuilding projects in war-torn Europe. In many respects, these institutions were a success in helping the rebuilding of Europe, which was able not only to rebuild but to attain some of the highest income levels in the world and, more recently, build a powerful economic and monetary union.

With the European reconstruction task largely accomplished, the IMF and World Bank began to take on the financial and economic problems of the underdeveloped countries. The role of the IMF is to provide short-term loans to countries that are temporarily unable to pay their foreign debts. The World Bank has continued to devote most of its resources to development projects, but it also provides help to countries with excessive buildup of foreign debt.

After 40 years of action in the developing world, it is fair to say they have been much less successful in this task than they were in the earlier one. Not surprisingly, the obstacles have been greater: The European countries generally had skilled people and considerable infrastructure still intact; the developing world was in many cases starting from scratch. Moreover, the fixed exchange rate system was replaced by a flexible exchange rate system, allowing large and detrimental currency movements that no regulatory body could possibly reverse.

In 1994, the IMF and World Bank were joined by a third international organization, this time to regulate foreign trade. The World Trade Organization (WTO) was established to administer the most important multilateral treaty regulating international trade. This was known as the General Agreement on Trade and Tariffs (GATT), an agreement signed by 141 countries after many years of negotiation. The agreement calls for the reduction of tariffs on most goods, including textiles, apparel, and agricultural products, and the regulation of types of trade, such as in services or intellectual property (music, movies, and other things that merit patent protection) that had previously been unregulated. Unlike its precursors, the WTO has the ability to impose a penalty on a country if it finds merit in a complaint against it made by other countries.

---

[2]Amartya Sen, *Poverty and Famines: An Essay on Entitlement and Deprivation* (Oxford: Clarendon Press, 1981).

NEOLIBERALISM: OPPORTUNITIES AND CHALLENGES

The "market friendly" approach to economic development promoted by the IMF, World Bank, and WTO—sometimes referred to as *neoliberalism*—has created enormous opportunities for many countries. Pakistan's success in clothing production and exports creates income and jobs for that country that can serve as the basis for a program of industrial diversification. China's ability to attract billions of dollars of foreign investment each year will bring in new technology, new management skills, and stronger connections to foreign markets. Hungary's relatively skilled labor force and proximity to the rich Western European market has made it a competitive producer of a variety of middle-technology goods.

However, neoliberal policies have also been known to backfire by lowering real wages, increasing nations' vulnerability to financial crisis, and raising social tensions because of the increased economic vulnerability and the shrinking social safety net. The financial instability resulting from the deregulation of international capital markets has led to a widespread questioning of the neoliberal policies of the 1980s and 1990s. Mexico suffered a crisis in 1994 when investors fled en masse from that country, creating a fall in the value of the Mexican peso that sent the economy into a prolonged recession. A similar financial crisis occurred in East Asia in 1997, beginning in Thailand and then spreading to South Korea, Asia, Russia, Uruguay, and others. Brazil and Argentina were able to avoid a collapse—but just barely—by taking restrictive measures that slowed the economies. As a result of the inability of the IMF and World Bank to avoid these crises, many governments and economists are now calling for a major reform of the World Bank and IMF. A variety of proposals are being debated, but most of them share the ideas of regulating banks and other financial institutions to reduce their risk of collapse and to reduce their involvement in large, short-term international capital movements.[3]

Whatever regulatory regime emerges from the current debates over international financial reform, tensions between developed and developing countries would no doubt be eased by more generous aid to the developing world. As is evident in Table 13-1, the largest countries are among the smallest donors in terms of aid as a share of national GDP, with the United States offering only 0.1 percent of its gross domestic product as development assistance. Nordic countries like Denmark and Norway give 10 times that amount (as a share of gross domestic product).

PROSPECTS FOR THE FUTURE

Why do some nations remain poor? The answer, of course, is that it depends on the country. Some countries are plagued by corrupt, antidevelopmental governments. Some are trapped with such limited resources for education, health, and infrastructure that even a well-intentioned government cannot break the vicious cycle of low productivity, poverty, and slow growth. To this sobering list we must add the pressures of the global economy. As we have seen, the increased openness of world markets creates new

---

[3]For one set of proposals, see John Eatwell and Lance Taylor, *Global Finance at Risk* (New York: New Press, 2000).

TABLE 13-1 Official Development Assistance from Selected Countries (% of GDP)		
Major Industrialized Countries	*1987–1988*	*1998*
Canada	0.5	0.3
France	0.6	0.4
Germany	0.4	0.3
Italy	0.4	0.2
Japan	0.3	0.3
United Kingdom	0.3	0.3
United States	0.2	0.1
Nordic Countries		
Denmark	0.9	1.0
Netherlands	1.0	0.8
Norway	1.1	0.9
Sweden	0.9	0.7

Source: Human Development Report 2000, New York: United Nations.

opportunities for countries at the same time that it creates hurdles and traps. Some countries, especially in sub-Saharan Africa, have simply been left out of the process, unable to attract foreign capital and so inefficient that they cannot compete for even a low-skill niche of the world market. Other countries—Haiti or other Caribbean countries, for example—find themselves participating in the global production process but are stuck in the role of producing low-skill, low-wage products with little chance for moving into more skill-intensive sectors. Others have found that as many nations gain the know-how and capacity to produce certain goods—steel, for example—there is simply not enough demand in the world to absorb the available supply.

Despite these obstacles, a number of nations have slowly moved up the ladder of income, technology, education, and health care that is required if development is to be sustainable. Although that has often come with political democratization, it has also required significant state involvement in the economy, along with an ability to capture gains from greater openness and market competition. It is a delicate path, but one that countries as varied as Korea, Mexico, Hungary, the Dominican Republic, and Uganda have each followed with some success.

Overcoming Tensions Between North and South

The notion of a fully unified global market conjures up an image of a harmonious and healthy competitive economic environment. In reality, globalization has created some areas of heightened tension between the developed countries (the "North") and the developing countries (the "South"). Much of this tension results from the employment effects of foreign trade. As the developed countries open up their markets to imports from low-wage, developing countries, their own, more highly paid workers are thrown out of work. American textile and apparel companies and textile workers' unions, for example, complain that opening trade to low-wage developing countries such as Pakistan or China will lead to the destruction of the domestic industry and the jobs it supports. Developing-country governments, such as India, Pakistan, Thailand, and others, complain that their prospects for development are constricted by developed countries' protection of their markets.

Both sides are right, and how these tensions get resolved in the future will be an important factor in the making of future economic society. One thing is sure: In a growing economy, the effects of economic change such as the employment effects of rising imports are often not even noticed. Because the world economy has grown more slowly since the end of the Golden Age, the tensions created by market liberalization have had more sting. If countries cannot find ways to raise the rate of economic growth to levels enjoyed during the Golden Age, then other solutions will have to be found to ease the social tensions created by globalization. Although there are no simple answers, we will try to describe the range of possibilities as we confront the challenges facing world capitalism in the next and final chapter.

Key Words and Concepts

Uneven development
1. Historically, the world economy has developed at very different rates in different regions and countries, leaving today an enormous gap between high-income industrialized countries who comprise less than 20 percent of the world's population, and the developing countries, who contain most of the world's population.

Late industrialization
2. The wave of industrialization in East Asia since the 1960s, beginning with Japan and then South Korea, Taiwan, and Hong Kong, differed in some respects from European industrialization of the eighteenth and nineteenth centuries. Late industrialization has relied more heavily on imitation of existing technologies and products than on grand innovations like those that spurred the first industrial revolution.

Developmental states
3. Political factors are an important element of economic development. Developmental states promote domestic industry and public investment in human capital and infrastructure. Predatory states are those that appropriate the wealth of the nation for the benefit of a few political elites. Many states are best described as intermediate cases, that is, neither completely developmental nor fully predatory.

Bretton Woods Institution
4. The International Monetary Fund (IMF) and the World Bank, which were created at the Bretton Woods conference in 1944, are now the two most prominent international organizations for economic development. The IMF's role is to provide short-term loans to help countries facing a crisis in their balance of payments. The World Bank provides loans for large-scale development projects. The World Trade Organization (WTO) was created in 1994 to administer regulations on world trade.

Neoliberalism
5. All three international organizations just mentioned, the IMF, World Bank, and WTO, tend to promote deregulation and the liberalization of markets in international trade and finance. This policy stance, combined with support for fiscal austerity, has been characterized as neoliberalism. The policy has been contentious because it has a very mixed record at best in moving countries out of macroeconomic crisis and onto

the path of rapid economic development. Protests at the annual meetings of the international organizations have focused on the social costs (to workers, to the environment) of neoliberalism.

Questions

1. Is it in the interest of high-income countries to promote the development of poor countries? Why?
2. What are the reasons for the poor economic performance of most countries in sub-Saharan Africa?
3. The maquiladoras are the (mainly foreign-owned) factories located in Mexico on the border with the United States. Why do you think the maquiladora sector has expanded in the last 10 years? Do you think the maquiladoras are a positive factor in Mexican economic development?
4. Should governments seeking to develop domestic industry protect such industries with tariffs and regulations, or should they subject them to foreign competition?
5. There is currently a worldwide campaign to reduce the foreign debt of the least-developed countries. Discuss the economic benefits of debt relief for these countries.
6. In his well-known hypothesis about income distribution and economic development, economist Simon Kuznets argued in the 1950s that developing countries must first suffer an increase in inequality as they grow. Only as economic development proceeds, Kuznets argued, will inequality begin to decline. What do you think is the logic behind Kuznets's theory? Recent research shows that the Kuznets relation no longer holds. Why do you think this is?
7. Why is U.S. aid to developing countries so low (as a percentage of GDP) compared to most other industrialized countries?

Thinking Back, Looking Ahead

THE POLITICS OF ECONOMIC HISTORY

We have described the East Asian experience in more detail than we might otherwise because it poses a fascinating problem for economic historians and students of economic development. The causes of the Asian miracle have been debated by economists for over a decade.

There is now fairly broad agreement that the activist and relatively autonomous role of the state, the relative weakness of the land-owning classes, the structure of the financial system, the international perspective, the emphasis on educational attainment, and the resilience of the family structure in the face of economic change were all important in creating an industrial society. The focus of the debate over how to explain the Asian miracle was fundamentally about the nature of market society and the role of the state in relation to markets.

Did active state intervention nurture industrialization, or did industrialization occur in spite of this intentional effort at market distortion? Most analysts gave credit to Asian industrial policy, but the intensity of the debate is important. For one, it showed the inevitably political dimension of economics. For another, it showed the importance and contentiousness of economic history. Who gets to tell the story matters not just for how the story is told but for what lessons we learn from its telling. After all, at issue in the debate over the causes of the Asian miracle is not just an arcane academic debating point but an important lesson for economic policy makers—can the Asian miracle be replicated in other parts of the world? This is one of the many challenging questions we will address in the final chapter.

CHAPTER

14

Problems and Possibilities

What we want to know, of course, is what the future will bring. However, even as we ask the question we recognize that it has no dependable answer. If we were so incautious as to spend this chapter predicting the outcome of the trend to inequality, or the availability of jobs, or the place of the United States in the world economy 10 years hence, no sensible reader would put much credence into what we wrote. How, then, to deal with the pressing questions to which we all want answers? Our reply is that we must make use of the past to think more clearly about the future. We start with what may seem like an odd question: How has the past seen the future?

TRADITION-RUN SOCIETIES

We begin by turning to the very distant past—the hunting and gathering societies that were the only mode of social organization for the first 99 percent of human life on earth. How did these societies perceive the future?

Such a question seems at first impossible to answer. When we reflect on what we know, or can reasonably reconstruct about these tribal bands, it is not so impossible as it seems. In fact, we can make a generalization about primitive societies that enables us to reconstruct with a high degree of likelihood how they actually perceived the future: It would be a continuation of their pasts.

How can we make such a generalization? One powerful reason is that primitive societies enjoyed a generally quite successful, but limited, relation with nature, so that there was no means to alter their material well-being. Likewise, our distant forebears had a simple but adequate political life, in which decisions such as whether to move the group's hunting grounds were made in general discussions led by village elders—which did not prevent individual persons from going off on their own if they wished. Therefore, there was no motivation to alter the political process. Finally, hunting and gathering bands had a strong sense of age-old tradition that spelled out clearly the obligations that members of the society owed one another, especially as regarding kinfolk. So, what was there to change?

All these generalizations point to a single conclusion. To our distant ancestors, the future was not a destination to which men and women looked with anxiety, but with a certain assurance. What would the future be like? It would be like the past. How could it be otherwise?

COMMAND SOCIETIES

We recall that societies run by tradition gave way to societies run by command in the fifth and fourth millennia along the rivers of the Nile, the Tigris and Euphrates, the Yangtze, and the Ganges. Settled agriculture and the first metalworking technology made possible social structures quite different from those of the very distant past, not only in their ability to build great pyramids of stone, but equally remarkable pyramids of social architecture. At the base of these social pyramids peasant farmers toiled under the supervision of bailiffs and seneschals—there were no such overseers in hunting and gathering bands—to support permanent armed forces; above them were retinues of priests and functionaries, and finally the all-powerful pharaohs, kings, and emperors.

Thus, a kind of society emerges in the greatest imaginable contrast to that which preceded it. Did it bring with it a new vision of the future? Strangely, it did not. To be sure, at their summits the rulers of the new societies entertained ambitions that surpassed anything to be found in the preceding tens of thousands of years. The new rulers envisaged changing the world in a manner unthinkable prior to the era of armies that could traverse continents and workforces capable of building structures that even today instill a sense of awe.

However, if we look anywhere but at the summit we get quite another sense of the world to come. Kings and emperors now cast long shadows into the future, but so far as everyone else in these societies was concerned, what difference did that make? There would be good kings and bad kings, victorious campaigns and disasters, just as there had always been. The weather would favor crops in one year and blight them in another. Thus, for the vast majority of its members, the future of command societies, like that of societies ruled by tradition, was a projection of the present into the void ahead. As the great political writer Nicolo Machievelli wrote in the fifteenth century: "Whoever wishes to foresee the future must consult the past, for human events ever resemble those of preceding times."[1]

CAPITALISM

When did this passive view of the future change? Here we all know the answer: It changed with the advent of modern economic society itself—that is, with the appearance of the capitalist world, whose history has been our main focus of inquiry. Only in the era of capitalism is the future perceived as one of limitless possibilities, growth, accumulation, expansion, and transformation.

Perhaps we can also see now why a study of the past can illumine the shape of things to come. The history of capitalism reflects three attributes that existed in none of its predecessors. The first of these is the pervasive drive for capital accumulation that endows capitalist economies with their characteristic vital energy, expressed in a ceaseless search for new technologies and markets. This was the attribute that gave us the Industrial Revolution in the past and that is giving us the computer revolution in the present; the age of imperialism in the past and of globalization in the present.

A second attribute of capitalism that sets it apart with respect to its movement into the future is the network of competitive markets that provides its mechanism of internal coordination. There is nothing like the freedom of choice and the discipline of competition among buyers and sellers in earlier social orders; much like the drive for capital, the market network supplies this social order with a nervous vitality and a constant effort to innovate that has no counterpart in earlier societies.

---

[1]Nicolo Machiavelli, *The Prince and Other Discourses Book Three,* chap. 43 (New York: Carlton House, n.d.), p. 530.

Third, and less immediately familiar, is another aspect that sets capitalism apart from its predecessors and again orients it to the future in a new way. This is its division into two realms or sectors: a well-defined government, whose right of entry into economic affairs is strictly defined, and a much larger surrounding private economy, whose governmental prerogatives are likewise carefully limited. Accustomed as we are to complaining about "too much government meddling" in the economy or "too much business influence" on the government, we forget that no government—state, local, or federal—can set up a profit-making enterprise to compete with business unless it has explicit authorization to do so and that no business, no matter how much it might be tempted, can put a trouble-making employee into jail.

In a word, the coexistence of a private sector charged with carrying out the main productive effort of society and a public sector charged with guiding and protecting this basic thrust provides a social structure capable of shaping the economic future to a far greater degree than anything preceding it. To say as much assuredly does not mean that this capability will be wisely used, or that it may not create baffling new problems along with would-be solutions. Nonetheless, a capability exists that did not in the past.

We will have a chance to see all that in the pages to come. However, it is well that we begin this final chapter with an awareness of the difference between the way the future looks to us and the way it appeared to ages past.

ANALYZING THE FUTURE

Let us now turn to the question we are all eager to face: What can be said about the array of problems we surveyed in chapters 10 through 13? Here we begin by making a crucial distinction between two ways of looking into the kind of future peculiar to the structure and dynamics of capitalism.

We call the two *prediction* and *analysis*. The first concerns itself mainly with outcomes; the second, with processes. We encounter predictions every day, outside economic life as well as within it. The racetrack tout who tells you that Highway Robber is a sure thing in the third is predicting, as is the financial columnist who says that the Dow Jones is due for a spectacular rise by the year's end. Analyses may or may not play a role in predictions: The tout may base his tip on the genealogy of Highway Robber and the Dow Jones predictor on a raft of data before him. In general, however, we ought to note that analysis plays a smaller role in noneconomic predictions than in economic ones, not only because there is usually a much larger amount of statistical information about economic events than noneconomic ones, but also because economic life, as we know well by now, has a core of behavioral tendencies like supply and demand that give us a generalized way of understanding how economies work. This is not true of horse races or politics or international affairs, in which analysis plays a much smaller role.

The distinction between prediction and analysis plays a decisive role in this chapter. We will not make predictions to the effect that inflation or unemployment or inequality will be better or worse one, two, or 10 years hence by such and such an amount. We will not because we cannot, for two reasons: First, there is no way of predicting outcomes into which so many variables enter—international as well as national, political as well as economic; second, and even more fundamental, the uncertainty of the future means not just that all predictions are risky, but that their outcomes simply cannot be known.

In light of this unknowability of the future, our purpose will not be to predict, but to make as clear as we can the economic forces underlying the trends in which we are interested. This analysis may point in one direction or another, as we demonstrate, but pointing is by no means the same thing as predicting. Indeed, when pointing indicates a direction in which events have not moved, it opens an interesting and important question: Was the direction of the compass wrong because elements have intervened, or because our own analysis was faulty? Discussing why our analysis was off the mark may teach our readers more economics and more economic history than any amount of preaching we could do!

THREE MAJOR ISSUES

1. Unemployment and Stagnant Earnings

Unemployment, we remember, has been a persistent problem in the United States from the mid-1970s on. In 1983, unemployment rose to 7.3 percent of the labor force, thereafter gradually falling to 5.3 percent in 1989; in 1992, it rose again to 7.5 percent, falling by the late 1990s to just over 4 percent. These are not devastating numbers on the face of it, but the face may not be the reality. As we have seen, if we add in discouraged workers, involuntary part-timers, and members of the workforce not picked up in the statistical surveys, the total number may easily be twice as large as that—still not comparable to the near 25 percent of the Great Depression, but certainly a large enough figure to give us pause. In addition, the unemployment rate for African-Americans continues to hover around 11 percent. Corporate downsizing has led to the loss of relatively high-paying jobs, and the new jobs being created are low-paying entry-level positions. As a result, families increasingly need more than one wage earner in order to make ends meet. The average family income actually fell by more than $2,000 from 1989 to 1994. This was the first drop over any 5-year period since World War II. Thus, in spite of the relatively long period of economic growth, Americans feel insecure about their jobs and income. Pundits have referred to this period as one of "jobless recovery." A better description might be a stagnant wage recovery. The focus of macroeconomic policy may now have to shift from growth, pure and simple, to a concern with wages, especially those of low-wage workers.

What is the cause of this disturbing state of affairs? Here we must distinguish between two analytical directions of inquiry. The first begins from the well-established connections between the level of unemployment and the volume of output. In the days of the all-out war effort, unemployment fell to less than 2 percent of the labor force—probably as low as it can fall in a free society in which some workers will always be leaving their jobs voluntarily, perhaps to search for a better job. Thereafter, during the immediate postwar years when Americans went on a great spending spree, joblessness hovered around 3 percent, rising to about 5 percent as the postwar boom gradually wound down. As we know, this 33-year (1940–1973) period ended with the first oil shock. Therefore, our analysis must first inquire into what can be said about the likelihood of a return to the employment-generating days of the Golden Age. Macro analysis tells us that this will require a large and sustained increase in investment spending. Moreover, we can make a further analytical statement: Such a stimulus must come either from a spontaneous private enterprise boom or from a deliberate increase of public spending—another Golden Age period or another New Deal. Analysis cannot give us likelihoods for either; it *can* make us aware of the profound differences between the 1950s, which filled the needs of a goods-starved country, and today; or of the change in political climate between the days of Franklin Roosevelt and Lyndon Johnson, and those of Ronald Reagan and Bill Clinton.

However, there is also a second analytical consideration. It springs from the fact that the level of employment is not entirely determined by the level of national expenditure. As we have seen, there are also factors such as changes in technology or in the structure of business enterprise that give rise to downsizing and overseas outsourcing. Here our task is to see what analysis can be ventured with respect to these micro considerations.

Let us begin by considering the prospects for a nonwartime boom that could bring back high-employment days. Much as we would like to, we cannot predict—and certainly cannot analyze—whether some astonishing new invention will appear tomorrow, opening up possibilities for a return to full employment. In fact, the U.S. economy has grown quite steadily from 1991 to the late 1990s, but as we have seen, this rosy statistic veils some disturbing facts.

Must we, therefore, resign ourselves to very modest expectations for employment and wage growth, not only here, but throughout the highly developed world? That does indeed seem the most likely prospect—unless we can design new modes of spurring demand, raising productivity, and holding back any inflation-producing consequences of sustained high employment.

Stakeholding—A Way Out?

Is there such a method? Perhaps. In some countries abroad—for example, Germany, the Scandinavian trio, Holland, Austria—a relationship called "stakeholding" has emerged between workers and employers. *Stakeholding* means that a new form of contract between labor and management has given labor the right to a stake in the job, in exchange for labor's agreement to allow management to restrain wage increases when necessary to maintain a competitive place in their industry.

Some form of stakeholding might indeed form the basis for a long-term period of high employment that would avoid self-destructive inflationary wage pressures. Is it a realistic possibility for the United States? On the basis of the long history of antagonistic labor-management relations in this country, ordinarily we would answer no. But times change, and we may change with them. If stakeholding becomes a widespread relationship in Europe, that would put great pressure on the United States to do the same. It is not impossible that the way toward a noninflationary boom may yet be cleared. Do we need to add that one cannot predict the likelihood of such far-reaching institutional changes? Nonetheless, the idea seems sufficiently promising to be put on the agenda for the future. As we go along we shall find there are other possibilities to be added to it.

2. Inequality

So we can describe with some analytical clarity the preconditions for high employment and earnings growth. Matters are not so simple when we turn to the next of the major problems that confront us: the distressing, even alarming redistribution toward families in the upper 10, even 1 percent. Here, there are macroeconomic and microeconomic considerations. From the macro perspective, the slowdown in productivity growth and investment that has characterized the post–Golden Age remains one source of growing inequality. A rising tide may raise all ships—as it did in the Golden Age—but rough waters pull down the weak. As we saw in chapter 12, growing inequality is occurring in many developing countries, as the relative earnings of those without education or training has fallen. Many economists have argued that the response to this situation is to increase the skills of labor everywhere.

Then we must consider the role of technological change. Computerization certainly seems to cut with a two-edged sword, making obsolete certain kinds of formerly well-paid occupations on the assembly line, while opening up service occupations, some very poorly paid, others very well paid. Because computerization raises the skill requirement for employees, it militates against the poorly educated, who are, generally speaking, low earners. Given the likelihood that there will be an increasing degree of computer technology throughout tomorrow's economy, income distribution is likely to worsen. In summary, our reading of this complex picture inclines us to doubt that existing levels of income distribution are likely to improve, although we hasten to add that this does not have the degree of analytical clarity that underpins our argument for dealing with unemployment.

There is, however, another extremely important element in the trend toward inequality. It is the remarkable widening between the pay of top-ranking CEOs and the median wage of their employees. Here, even more than in considering the impact of technology, it is difficult to find an analytical explanation than can guide our expectations of future developments. Social norms and institutions change over time for political and cultural as well as purely economic reasons.

Consider two facts in this regard. In chapter 10, we note that the ratio between top and median pay had increased from 30 to 1 in the 1960s to more than 200 to 1 in the 1990s. Now let us add a second consideration: It is that the ratio between American top CEO remuneration and that of their average workforce is many times greater than in any other capitalist nation. It is roughly 20 to 1 in Germany and 10 to 1 in Japan, and we might also note that the foreign corporate top bureaucracy burden is also significantly smaller than our own.

Is there an explanation for this disproportionately large bureaucratic load that would throw some light into the future? One explanation again draws on the unusually antagonistic relations between management and labor in the United States compared with virtually all European nations. This leads American corporations to feel a need for much heavier supervisory staffs than are needed in companies where a closer understanding exists between the management and the workforce.[2]

To be sure, this only raises the deeper question as to why U.S. corporations have not developed the stakeholding and other cooperative institutions that have proved useful elsewhere. The answer no doubt lies in the very different cultural traditions of the United States and Europe, but this gives us no very clear basis to project what lies ahead; after all, the United States was just as antilabor in the 1930s as it may be today, but that did not prevent the emergence of the New Deal, which set the standard for Europe. As a result, once again we cannot assert with any high degree of probability that the necessary changes in corporate attitude will take place. All that we will risk is to

---

[2]See David Gordon, *Fat and Mean* (New York: The Free Press), chap. 3.

assert that in the absence of a change in corporate attitudes there is little reason to expect a changing shape of income distribution.

A New Corporate Attitude?

Is such a change a realistic possibility? A few firms in the United States have, quite on their own, begun to experiment with changed wage contracts, seeking to increase worker–management mutual trust and thereby to break the top-heavy payrolls that ultimately undermine, rather than increase, corporate efficiency and profitability.

We might listen to the testimony of Francis Fukuyama, a much-respected conservative critic, who tells of an interesting experiment carried out by Nucor Corporation, a steel firm in the Midwest:

> The recession of 1983–1984 . . . hit the Nucor Corporation very hard. Nucor had just entered the steel-making business. Its mills were operated by nonunionized workers, many of them former farmers. To deal with the drop of revenues, Nucor put its employees—from the CEO to the lowest maintenance worker—on a two- or three-day workweek, with a corresponding cut in pay. No workers were fired, however, and when the economy and the company recovered, it enjoyed a tremendous esprit de corps that contributed to its becoming a major force in the American steel industry.[3]

It should be noted that Nucor was ranked 379th on the *Fortune* list of the largest 500 industrial corporations in 1996. Despite its rapid rise, it continues its policy of treating all employees alike, from lowest to highest: All earn bonuses that are distributed every week, and workers receive a steady 10 percent of the company's pretax profits. Indeed, Nucor officials cite this deliberately antibureaucratic attitude as the reason for superior efficiency.

A few other companies, including some with powerful labor unions, have also experimented successfully with a much higher degree of cooperative management. The United Auto Workers collaborates with Toyota and General Motors in an experimental plant in Freemont, California; in 1991, Magma Copper signed what *Fortune* magazine called a "revolutionary labor agreement" with the steelworkers' union to institute participatory and cooperative labor–management relations.

How well these few and still new ventures will fare, we cannot foretell. They do at least suggest that it may be profitable, as well as possible, to institute agreements that would help redress the income distribution problem.

3. Globalization

We move now to the third, and perhaps most difficult, of the challenges before us. What historical perspective can we apply to the increasing involvement of the United States—and all other advanced capitalisms—in a world economy? Are there lessons from the past that may illumine the future?

In chapter 12, we define globalization as the increasing interconnectedness of markets in different countries and focus especially on the international mobility of capital. Now our task is to step back and consider the globalization phenomenon from our

---

[3]Francis Fukuyama, *Trust* (New York: The Free Press, 1995), p. 7–8.

broad lens of the making of economic society. From this perspective, the power of globalization is most clearly reflected in the fact that capitalism is now the reigning economic system in a larger portion of the world than ever in history.

The most important cause of this state of affairs is the collapse of the Soviet Union and the fall of communism in all of Eastern Europe. Many developing countries that pursued a socialist strategy in the 1960s and 1970s—for example, Tanzania, Jamaica, and Nicaragua—have now turned to a market orientation. Even in countries that were nominally socialist, there has been a massive move to privatize major industries—that is, to sell government-run companies to the private sector. A large number of countries have, either willingly or under international pressure, removed subsidies and price supports in their domestic economy and opened the economies to foreign trade and investment. According to one study, 16 developing countries turned to considerably more freemarket trade and exchange rate policies since 1990, and 18 countries did so in the 1980s. These policy shifts have been strongly encouraged by the World Bank and International Monetary Fund, which will often make loans only if a country agrees to implement these free-market policies. In total, 61 countries have accepted the World Bank/IMF conditions in return for long-term low interest loans. The required reforms were mainly in trade and sectoral policies, and especially the liberalization of agriculture and finance.[4]

What does this transformation imply for the future of economic society? If we are to assess the possible future of (global) capitalism, we should first consider the fate of an economic society very different from our own—a social order we call *socialism.*

SOCIALISM

Is there, in fact, a reason to look into the future of socialism? It must be apparent that the answer depends on what we mean by the word. The Russian experience, discussed in chapter 11, warns that highly centralized, rigidly bureaucratic economic systems develop a kind of sclerosis that may be fatal. Indeed, the wonder is that for so long this inflexible, inefficient, and extremely repressive system seemed to many to hold the key to economic growth!

China Tries Another Route

That is not, however, to declare that other kinds of "socialisms" may not play an important role during the twenty-first century, especially in the less-developed parts of the world. Here the example of China is important. The Chinese revolution broke out in 1947 under the leadership of Mao Tse Tung, who for many years pursued a "socialism" that much resembled that of the Soviets, combining dictatorial leadership and repression with a program of centralized planning much like the Soviets. By the 1970s, it was already apparent that the Chinese economy, although awakened from its age-old torpor, was in danger of falling into the rigidity that was soon to undo the Soviet revolution. Little by little, a new, very un–Soviet-like policy took the place of the old—a policy

---

[4]Dani Rodrik, "The Rush to Free Trade in the Developing World: Why So Late? Why Now? Will It Last?" in *Voting for Reform,* S. Haggard and S. Webb, eds. (New York: Oxford University Press, 1994).

of continuing political centralization combined with highly permissive, capitalist-like encouragement to private enterprise, both domestic and foreign. China today is thus a curious mixture of political piety and of laissez-faire heresy. The result has been a burst of expansion in its main cities that has made its urban China perhaps the fastest growing economy area on earth, while rural China remains under a degree of control that would be impossible under any kind of democratic capitalism.

Will the Chinese example succeed in the long run? Will it find followers in the stagnant backwaters of Africa, South Asia, or elsewhere? None of that can be foretold with any degree of certainty. But it seems possible that some form of "socialism" along these lines, combining a considerable toleration—even encouragement—of private economic activity with a strictly disciplined and nondemocratic political core may play a considerable role in the modernization of large areas of the underdeveloped world during the twenty-first century. Oddly enough, this raises the prospect of an expanding presence of "socialism" in the poorer regions of the world, along with an expanding presence of a world economy that begins to tie these areas into those of the affluent West.

Western Socialism

We have frequently put quotation marks around the word *socialism* when we have spoken of its possible appearance in the poorer portions of the globe. In its origins, socialism has always been a Western ideal—certainly Marx, its great advocate, saw socialism not as a means of modernizing a backward land but as a guide to the evolution of the most advanced countries beyond capitalism into something else. Marx himself is none too clear a guide as to what lay beyond capitalism: If we read the *Communist Manifesto,* we find a program that is much more widely removed from Soviet realities than from, say, New Deal aspirations.

Indeed, non-Soviet, democratic socialism in the West has always been more focused on political and social democracy than in wholesale economic restructuring. Socialism did indeed advocate the end of the capitalist drive for accumulation, but it was never opposed to markets or to modest holdings of private property, and certainly not to representative democratic processes. Planning—the great goal of economic socialism in the backward areas—was never at the heart of the Western conception, so much as the full participation of workers in decision making, the breakdown of the privileges of ownership, and the general diminution of the importance of the economic side of life to make way for its social, political, and aesthetic dimensions.

Nothing like such a social order has ever appeared in Western civilization, but the appeal of its humanistic vision in life has inspired many. To others, the word *socialism* conjures up images very different from these hopes: intrusive governments, swollen bureaucracies, and the subordination of private achievement to the levering influence of public standards. It is not our task to declare which of these views is the more correct. No doubt a polarized view on socialism will remain a part of Western political life for a considerable period. We raise the issue only to clear the way for our undertaking—to complete our inquiry into capitalism. The outlook for socialism hovers in the background, not the foreground, of the making of the economic society that we know first-hand, but it cannot be lost to sight in trying to estimate, as historians, the prospects for that society.

THE OUTLOOK FOR CAPITALISM

Where to begin? Best, we think, by reflecting one last time on the complex tripartite structure that gives capitalism its historical uniqueness. Rather than trying to talk about "capitalism" as a whole, let us consider the future of a system motivated by the drive to amass capital; knit together and internally disciplined by a market network; and uniquely characterized by a division of power between two realms, one public, one private. These three distinctive attributes may enable us to think more clearly about the shape of things to come than if we tried to consider "capitalism" as a single entity.

The Drive to Accumulate

What is the long-term prospect for the drive that endows capitalism with its life force? Economists have long seen that drive as the Achilles' heel of the system. Even Adam Smith believed that after a time a Society of Perfect Liberty, as he called nascent capitalism, would create all the goods for which there was any need—after which the system would descend to a kind of stagnation at a low level of subsistence![5]

Later economists placed their faith in the inventive capacities of an Industrial Revolution that had not yet appeared in Smith's day. Nonetheless, virtually all the great economists saw the system ultimately coming to an end because of an inability to continue indefinitely to find new profitable areas for investment. Marx envisaged ever more self-destructive crises that would eventually create the political conditions for an overthrow of the system in favor of socialism. John Stuart Mill foresaw a less violent transformation, as workers bought out their employer's interests and thereafter ran a kind of competitive, market-coordinated "socialistic" capitalism, in some ways like the Sweden of the 1950s and 1960s. Keynes entertained a more conservative outlook, believing that slumps could be kept within bounds by appropriate increases in government expenditure—indeed, for all his reputation as radical reformer, save for a more or less permanently larger core of public investment, he foresaw a future not unlike the past. More conservative economists have looked more to the "supply side" for answers to slow long-run economic growth, urging tax cuts and investment subsidies, but to date these policies have had only a very limited impact in practice.

Ecological Overload

We now turn the discussion in a different direction. The outlook for capitalism in the future is far from resolved in our time, as we have seen with regard to the uncertain consequences of automation and globalization. In one vital regard, the long-run prospects for expansion have changed. The key question today is no longer so crucially tied to the *availability* of profitable investment as with the *consequences* of its indefinite continuation.

Here the most formidable barrier appears to be ecological overload—spilling into the atmosphere, the water, and the earth more noxious by-products of production than the environment can absorb. Chief among these by-products is the heat generated by the great majority of production processes—a great blanket of energy that rises into the atmosphere, creating an effect called "global warming."

---

[5]Adam Smith, *The Wealth of Nations* (New York: Modern Library, 1972), chap. 9, p. 96.

Summing the problem, historian-economist Paul Kennedy has written:

> The scientific consensus is that average global temperatures are between 0.3 and 0.7 [degrees] warmer than they were a century ago. This is a modest rise, but the real concern is the rising pace of temperature increase in the twenty-first century, especially as world population and industrial activity grow. Most scientists in the field hold that there would be serious consequences, [including] rises in the sea level, depleted agriculture, reduced water flows, increased health hazards, more turbulent weather. All suggest that both developed and developing countries have good reason to worry about global warming.[6]

This serious long-term threat derives its energies from the constant enlargement of the scale of production that is the life force of capitalism. If pollution must be greatly curbed within the lifetime of the next two or three generations, as increasingly seems to be the case, how will that affect the self-regenerating capabilities of our social order? Meanwhile, what will happen to standards of living in the poorer parts of the world? Would horrendous poverty in, say, Africa, lead the rich nations to allow the poorer ones to go on polluting for a while to bring their living standards up, while voluntarily reducing their own dangerous outputs? Whatever the arrangements by which pollution is curbed, who will police so vast and so vital an undertaking?

Only one persuasive conclusion emerges from this difficult prospect: The future contains an ecological challenge whose dimensions are just beginning to enter our awareness. The challenge arises not only in the fact that capitalist economic momentum itself lies at the core of this prospective danger, but in the unmistakable conclusion that only the political will of the advanced—that is, the capitalist—world can ultimately determine the extent of its damage. Fortunately, there is a period of grace before us: The challenge is to make it a time of investigation, resolution, and thoughtful change.

The Tightening Market Web

The second identifying attribute of capitalism lies in its market network. By and large, economists have always seen the market as a source of great strength and flexibility for the system, and many would assert that the system itself will endure only as long as self-motivated competitive interplay continues to be its most prominent feature.

This does indeed seem a safe generalization, but there is nonetheless an aspect of markets that demands our attention in this long look into the trajectory of our order. It is that all markets, without exception, serve two purposes, only one of which falls under the scrutiny of economists. That self-evident aspect is Adam Smith's celebrated depiction of markets as an "invisible hand" that resolves otherwise difficult problems of coordinating production and distribution.

However, markets have another, less celebrated side. It is that they all create externalities, that is, side-effects that emerge from the relatively unsupervised interaction of buyers and sellers. Some of these, like the heat and smoke from factories, fall into the category of the environmental disturbances we have just examined. However, there are other externalities that may not disturb the environment but may seriously disturb society. These relate to questions of equality and justice and thus concern the level of social morality.

---

[6]Paul Kennedy, *Preparing for the Twenty-First Century* (New York: Random House, 1993), pp. 105, 111.

These are not new issues, of course. Consider the writing of St. Thomas Aquinas, the great sage of the thirteenth century, who asks in his *Summa Theologica* whether some-one may lawfully sell an object for more than it is worth.[7] The question takes us utterly by surprise. What does it mean, to "sell an article for more than it is worth"? Is it not worth whatever the buyer will pay for it? Not so, says Aquinas. He quotes Matthew (7:12): "All things whatsoever you would that men should do to you, do you also to them." No one, says Aquinas, wants to be offered something for more than it is worth. Hence, to do the same is to commit sin.

The pronouncement leaves us nonplussed. Why? Because one of the functions of markets is to allow us to forget the moral promptings that guide us in nonmarket relationships, such as our relations with friends. To no small extent, markets gain their efficiency precisely because they direct our attention away from such troubling considerations.

Is this a finding with serious consequences for the longevity of our system? Let us consider it from the perspective of truth-telling. One of the attributes of markets is that sellers go to great lengths to convince buyers of the desirability of their wares. In old-fashioned markets, this was called "puffery"; in modern-day capitalism, it is the stuff of advertising. Let us now look at advertising as a multimillion television screen phenom-enon in which children, youngsters, and grownups alike witness men and women en-thusing over brands of hair shampoo, aspirins, and automobiles, *every one of them paid for his or her carefully scripted enthusiasms.* Does not this behavior convey a moral mes-sage? That is, does it not show that grownups, posing as "real" people, may say with feigned conviction things in which they likely have no belief whatsoever? We leave that to our readers to decide. Our point is simply that markets must be recognized for what they are—economically effective but often morally dubious means of motivating our economic behavior. This may be a very difficult problem to bring under control, but it strikes us as one that must eventually be faced if our system is to develop the moral in-telligence it will need to move safely through the new century.

The Two Sectors

This leads logically to the last key feature of capitalist society: its division of power and authority into a government and a private sector—unique to capitalism, and from early on a source of contention, disagreement, and trouble. Perhaps because there has been such division over this issue, we fail to realize it is one of the central sources of strength for capitalism—a remarkable solution to a problem that has defined satisfactory reso-lution in other systems.

There seems little doubt that the importance of this unique bifurcation of authority will increase over the coming decades. If we are to avoid the disasters of ecological overload, where else can we look except to the public sector? If we are to find ways of matching the attractions of economic globalization with defenses against its accompany-ing dangers, where can we turn other than to political constraint and guidance? What is needed here is not an elevation of the public sector over the private, save in extreme cases, such as war and conceivably the prevention of ecological disaster. What is needed

---

[7]From A. E. Monroe, *Early Economic Thought* (Boston: Harvard University Press, 1930), p. 53.

is the long-overdue recognition of the parity of the public interest with the private. Therefore, we tend to think of private borrowing and investing as inherently good, and call it "investment"; we see public borrowing and spending as bad, and call it "deficit spending" even if it is used to build public investment goods like roads and bridges and schools. Of course, private investment can be foolish and public investment wise, and vice versa. Our task is to learn that both sectors must operate efficiently and to wise ends, if our system is to work well; that realization requires a new look at the two-sector problem, seeing both sectors through glasses ground with the same prescription.

A Spectrum of Capitalisms

We are acutely conscious that our analytical perspective into the future may not at all be that of our readers. However, we hope that our tone of voice has made it clear that we are putting forth personal views, not incontestible truths. The whole purpose of this inescapable risky and error-prone attempt to think about the future has been made to encourage similarly risky and error-prone thinking on the part of our readers—not because that will give them a grasp in the Truth, but because it will serve as an exercise that we hope will become a habit.

One last generalization, and we are done. Taking the measure of modern economic society as we see it, one generalization seems impossible to escape. Capitalism will almost certainly be the predominant mode of economic organization, at least in the advanced countries, during the twenty-first century, and indeed, perhaps during the next. But the word *capitalism,* as we now understand it, is flexible enough to encompass a range of societies. All will be driven by the need to amass capital, all will be coordinated by a market framework, all will have two sectors. But despite these deep and all-important common features, they will still differ considerably from one another. Some will be geared to high profit margins, some able to work satisfactorily on much lower ones. Some will have top-heavy managerial bureaucracies, some will not. Some may have head-to-head labor–management relationships; others may have worked out very satisfactory stakeholder arrangements. Some will be more democratic than others, some more moral, some more environmentally conscious; some will have worked out arrangements for amicable and mutually coordinated public–private sectoral relations, some will not.

If there is one objective that we hope our readers will carry away with them it is the usefulness of thinking of the future of capitalism as a social order that, for all its specific institutional structure, has room for a spectrum of possibilities. Moreover, we hope that readers will use that awareness to help make our place in that spectrum at the leading edge of the procession.

Key Concepts and Key Words

This is not a chapter that lends itself to the kinds of summaries and questions that we hope have helped to clarify previous chapters. This is not a chapter to "learn" but to ponder. We hope reading it will make you as thoughtful as writing it has made us.

Thinking Back, Looking Ahead

ECONOMICS AS CAPITALISM'S EXPLANATION SYSTEM

We'd like to step back from our inquiry into the making of economic society and return to a question we posed very early in the book: What is economics? That question can be answered by thinking about the chapter you've just read, in which we assessed the long-term prospects for capitalism and socialism. This was necessarily a speculative task, and no doubt many of our claims will be proven false over time. However, the ease with which we write the words *no doubt* relates directly to the question asked. Is economics a science of prediction? This is the view held by many economists, although prediction often refers less to the future than to the hypothesized outcome from a theoretical model. In this view, the best economic theory is that which best predicts the outcome. An alternative view is that economics is not primarily for prediction but for explanation, that is, to give a rich description of our economic experience.

These two views of economics are not mutually exclusive. Both insist that theory be logical and parsimonious. However, there is an important distinction: In the view of economics as theory for prediction, greater abstraction is viewed as a strength. In our understanding of economics as an explanation system, abstraction is much less important than capturing the details of institutions and behavior that give meaning to economic life.

Name Index

Subject Index